FREE AT LAST

FREE
AT LAST

*What Really Happened
When Civil Rights
Came to Southern Politics*

MARGARET EDDS

ADLER & ADLER

Published in the United States in 1987 by
Adler & Adler, Publishers, Inc.
4550 Montgomery Avenue
Bethesda, Maryland 20814

Library of Congress Cataloging-in-Publication Data

Edds, Margaret, 1947-
    Free at last.

    Bibliography: p.
    Includes index.
    1. Afro-Americans—Southern States—Politics and
government. 2. Afro-Americans—Civil rights—Southern
States. 3. Southern States—Politics and government—
1951-   . 4. Southern States—Race relations.
I. Title.
E185.92.E34 1987   975'.00496073   86-28682
ISBN 0-917561-37-6

Printed in the United States of America
First Edition

*To Bob, for his faith, and to the
Tom McCains and David Jordans of
the American South, for theirs.*

————————

"Do not let a single nigger register and vote.
If you let a few register and vote this year,
next year there will be twice as many,
and the next thing you know
the whole thing will be out of hand."

Theodore G. Bilbo, U.S. Senator, Mississippi
1946 reelection campaign

CONTENTS

INTRODUCTION

This book began to take form in a Richmond public school athletic center named for one of the Confederate capital's latter-day heroes, Arthur Ashe, Jr. The year —1985—marked the twentieth anniversary of the passage of the Voting Rights Act, hailed by many as the seminal congressional act of the civil rights era. I had just been granted a fellowship from the Alicia Patterson Foundation and a year's leave from my job as a reporter for the *Virginian-Pilot/Ledger-Star* newspapers to consider whether the law had fulfilled its promise. Coincidentally, I began the project on January 15, Martin Luther King, Jr.'s birthday, and my first step was to attend a citywide commemoration of that anniversary at the Ashe Center. The event was one of many over the next months that would signal both progress and stagnation in race relations in the South. As a youth, Ashe was denied access to city tennis courts because of color, and the fact that several hundred Richmonders were now gathered in an arena bearing his name was in itself remarkable. The fact that virtually every face in the room was black was striking as well. The nation was then moving toward making King's birthday a national holiday, but Richmond whites were clearly not compelled enough by the significance of his life to join in celebration.

The speaker that day was John Lewis, a man who demonstrates as eloquently as any southerner the transition in regional black politics from 1965 to 1985. Twenty years earlier, Lewis had marched at the front of a column of mostly black men and women as they crossed the Edmund Pettus Bridge in Selma, Alabama, and strode headlong into a storm of officially sanctioned violence. Lewis' skull was bashed by a club-wielding Alabama state trooper, and his sacrifice helped set in motion passage of the Voting Rights Act a few months later. By 1985, Lewis was an Atlanta city councilman and part of a neighborhood voting coalition that included as many whites as blacks. A year later, he would be elevated to Congress by a biracial coalition. Lewis, who combines a perpetual slight scowl with a gentle manner, spoke on King's birthday of a nonviolent revolution that had swept the South. All across the region, he said, there were black voters and black elected officials. When the Selma marchers passed through remote, moss-draped Lowndes County in 1965, for instance, there was hardly a black voter, despite a population some 80 percent black. By 1985, Lowndes County had a black sheriff, a majority-black county commission and a majority-black school board. "There are some people who will say in 1985 that we haven't made any progress," said Lewis. "But as one who grew up in rural Alabama, I have seen a nonviolent revolution take place in the last twenty years."

A few weeks later, I sat in the tidy kitchen of Alma Barlow's three-room apartment in a Richmond public housing project and heard a different story. A large, commanding woman, Barlow is the president of the Richmond Tenants Organization. The group was born of her frustration when on a freezing day in 1977, the city-run housing authority responded to the energy crisis by turning down the heat. Over a cup of steaming coffee, Barlow spoke of her disappointment that political success by blacks had not bred greater change. On the day eight years earlier when blacks took over the Richmond City Council, "I felt it was one of the greatest things that had ever happened," she said. "I thought we'd get more police protection, better maintenance of the streets, better lighted areas. I felt God himself had come down. It didn't quite work out that way. For us, over here, it really didn't seem any different." She paused, resting her elbows on the lacy tablecloth, and then continued. "Either they haven't lived up to expectations or we expected too much. . . . What in the world good is it to have black elected officials if you have to go and fight for everything?"

During the next months, I would travel thousands of miles and interview several hundred people searching for answers to Barlow's question and others. In north Atlanta mansions and Mississippi Delta shanties, in big-city mayors' offices and dusty country stores, on college campuses and at civic league meetings, the queries were the same. Had the South, once smothered and defined by racial injustice, overcome? Had black southerners been truly integrated into a political world from which they were once barred? And, in terms of how people live, had their advances mattered? My focus would be the seven states originally covered by the Voting Rights Act—Alabama, Georgia, Mississippi, Louisiana, North Carolina, South Carolina, and Virginia. My guides would be dozens of elected officials, civil rights leaders, political scientists, and ordinary men and women, black and white. I would visit metropolises like Atlanta and Birmingham where, in startling evolution from the South of 1965, blacks sat in the mayors' offices, on city councils, and in at least some corporate boardrooms. The path would lead to isolated Black Belt counties, where a decade and a half of black political control had freed spirits but brought little in the way of economic and educational gain. The itinerary included Edgefield County, South Carolina, the home of Senator Strom Thurmond, a one-time segregationist. There, in a locality 50 percent black, a ten-year court battle had just ended with election of the century's first black county officials. Whites—in a pattern played out time and again since 1965 across the rural South—warily awaited the transition. The road led also to Greene County, Alabama, which in 1969 made history as the second county in the South to be run by black officials. Fifteen years later, in 1984, Greene County again was in the forefront of change. This time, a group of young black activists, ignoring the taunts of other blacks, joined with whites to oust civil-rights-era leaders whom they accused of failing to improve county fortunes. And the route wound back through time to spots like Sunflower County, Mississippi, where most residents were black, but politics—as surely as two decades earlier—was run by whites.

The conclusions prompted by that journey are based primarily on the words and impressions of men and women who have lived through what Lewis called a peaceful revolution. A few quotations are taken from newspaper clippings or magazine articles, but most are the products of personal interviews ranging up to several hours in length. Portions of several chapters appeared first in *The APF Reporter,* a publication of the Alicia Patterson Foundation. Because local politics is continually in flux, certain material may already have been overtaken by events. Officials may have been voted out of office; court rulings may have altered election procedures. However, the sites portrayed here were chosen less for specific detail than because they reflected some larger truth about southern black politics. Those lessons remain.

Not all of those with whom I spoke agree on the merit of the change that has occurred, and debate is particularly sharp when it involves the Voting Rights Act. This book is not intended to be a definitive study of that law and its evolution. While some of the hundreds of court cases and electoral changes prompted by the act will be discussed, many others will not. However, any progress is so intricately tied to the act that an understanding of it is essential to explaining the changes that have occurred.

Those southerners with whom I spoke were almost unfailingly courteous, even when they suspected my motives. On a cool March night in Eutaw, Alabama, I listened as Wendell Paris, a black Sumter County school board member, gave an inflamed speech to an all-black audience that focused on the general untrustworthiness of whites. Later, however, over a fried chicken supper, Paris put aside the racial hostility and his demeanor was more friendly. Across the racial spectrum, members of the all-white county commission in Mississippi's Sunflower County at first responded warily to my questions during a recess in a local budget hearing. But they, too, soon replaced coolness with civility, even as they continued to protest that their county had been unduly criticized for years.

My appreciation extends to them and to many others. Guy Friddell, Staige Blackford, Larry Sabato, Cathy Trost, Bill McAllister, and Bill Connolly all provided encouragement when it was needed. Jim Raper and Sandy Rowe were generous in their support. Amy Pastan's careful editing much improved the text. Pat Wright contributed research to the Richmond chapter. Evelyn Best gave me the freedom to work in peace. As always, my greatest debt is to my family, especially Bob, Thomas, Rachel, and Elliot, whose support makes all things possible, and to Bob's and my children, Sharon, Kate, and Adam, who make all things worthwhile.

1. PROLOGUE: DAVID JORDAN
A Personal Odyssey

IT WAS THE SUMMER of 1955, and for David Jordan, a time of sharpened senses and the sweetly invigorating moments of youth. He was twenty years old, just graduated from Greenwood's colored high school, primed to start college at Mississippi Valley State University, high spirited, alive. That day, David, his brother, and two buddies caught the feature at the downtown movie house —a replay of *Duel in the Sun,* with Gregory Peck, Joseph Cotton, Jennifer Jones—and then strolled home. They were four young men wiling away a sticky, hot August afternoon in quiet oblivion in the eastern Delta.

Outside Century Funeral Home on Walthall Street, an ambulance was parked and a crowd had begun to gather. As he passed, Jordan saw tight, drawn faces and heard muted whispers. "The boy from Chicago," someone was saying. "Tallahatchie River . . . Emmett Till." The friends walked further, and as radio reports drifted from unscreened doorways and windows, they sensed what had happened. A body had been found in the Tallahatchie River. It appeared to be that of Emmett Till, a fourteen-year-old black boy down from Chicago to visit relatives on a farm near Greenwood. The past Saturday evening, Jordan already knew, some white men had burst into the house where Till was staying, searched the beds using flashlights, and dragged the boy into the dark of a Mississippi night. The older folk were speculating that Till had been lynched. They were wrong. He had just been found dead in the river with the fan of a cotton gin hooked with barbed wire to his neck. It was his penalty for having whistled at a white girl. The breezy camaraderie of the day had evaporated. Jordan felt only a churning in the hollow of his stomach.

Some years earlier, when Jordan was thirteen years old, he had taken a job at Malouf's Store down on Highway 49, about four miles outside Greenwood toward Jackson. It was a variety market, selling gasoline and light groceries, as well as illegal bottled whiskey for those who knew how to ask. One day, two white men drove up and sat in their automobile. Jordan walked over to take their order. Spitting the words out an opened window, one of them asked, "Aren't you that smart son of a bitch?" Jordan, who left his plantation shanty home at 5:30 A.M. each weekday to walk the four miles to a segregated school in Greenwood, did not know what to say. He was afraid to retreat, afraid to move. He was silent. One of the men got out of the car and walked toward him. Slowly, methodically, the man struck the boy. Jordan was not injured, but his pride was crushed. Years after the hurt was gone, he would remember the faces of those who had watched his humiliation.

At 2:00 A.M. on a Sunday morning in 1962, Jordan heard frantic knocking at the door of the bungalow on Avenue H in Greenwood where he lived with his wife, Chris, and their three small children. He peered into the night, and saw three men—Sam Block, Willie Peacock, and Lawrence Guyot—who were in Greenwood with the Student Non-Violent Coordinating Committee (SNCC). The trio and others had come to this leafy and drowsy town to set up a voter registration project that was the first major SNCC foray into a hostile Delta. Blacks in LeFlore County, Greenwood's home, far outnumbered whites, yet there was hardly a black voter to be found. That night, some arms-brandishing whites had burst into SNCC headquarters a few hundred yards away on Avenue I, and Block and the rest had escaped through a window. They knew Jordan as a friend of the movement, even though his teaching job compelled him to remain behind-the-scenes. They slipped into the house and hid there until Robert Moses, SNCC's charismatic Mississippi leader, arrived to spirit them away. Once again, Jordan was gripped with fury at the degrading way in which black southerners lived.

The episode moved him a step closer to the day when he would become the swirling eddy at the core of black activism in Greenwood, relentlessly pushing, prodding, filing lawsuit after lawsuit *(Jordan v. State of Mississippi, Jordan v. City of Greenwood, Jordan v. LeFlore County, Jordan v. LeFlore County Election Commissioners)*, ignoring those who called him arrogant and a black racist, focusing single-mindedly on the day when black men and women would go to the polls and elect candidates who shared their suffering and their dreams.

In 1965, Jordan reactivated the Greenwood Voters League and became its president. Quietly at first, then more openly, and at last with a vengeance, the league began to register black voters, challenge election discrepancies, and endorse candidates for local office. Along the way, Jordan would pay a price for his failure to conform. He held a master's degree in chemistry from the University of Wyoming, earned out-of-state because the University of Mississippi would not accept his undergraduate degree from the nonaccredited, all-black Mississippi Valley State. But, even in a town where advanced science degrees were rare, he would be turned down for teaching posts at the high school. He would never move beyond his job at W. C. Williams Junior High. The superintendent was willing to promote him, Jordan was told, but the high school principal feared he would be a "negative influence." When white parents filed charges against him over a paddling incident, Jordan was convinced that the real motivation was intimidation. The charges were thrown out of court.

In June 1979, in a climactic episode, Jordan was fired by the school board for his public criticism of the superintendent and for something called "failure to follow school policies on leave days and grievances." The previous fall, when Mayor Charles Evers of Fayette was running for the U.S. Senate, Jordan had asked for a day off to work the polls. When he was turned down, Jordan called a press conference and on local television railed that his constitutional rights were being denied. The refusal, he said, was racially motivated. When election day came, Jordan did not show up at school; he was electioneering. A few weeks later, in a quote that hit the local newspapers with hurricane force, Jordan told the Voters League: "The superintendent has gone too far. We'll either have to discipline him or put him back on one of those long midnight trains to Georgia." The combination was enough to cost Jordan his job. Unrepentant after the firing, he hired lawyers and went to court. There were rallies and prayer services on his behalf, and when a U.S. District Court judge reviewed the evidence, he decided that Jordan's constitutional rights had indeed been violated. The judge ordered him rehired. The school board appealed, and the Fifth Circuit Court of Appeals ruled in Jordan's favor as well.

Five years later, in another court decision, Jordan won an even greater victory. This time, the ruling brought him to the apogee of his long drive toward equality. The legal case was styled *Jordan v. Greenwood,* and it was filed in 1977. The goal was straightforward. Since 1914, Greenwood had been governed by a three-member commission elected at-large by city voters. The city was 52 percent black; no black person had ever been elected to the commission. Jordan and others sought a change to district elections. Black residents would almost certainly be a substantial majority in some of those districts, and black candidates could perhaps be elected.

Jordan's ticket was the Voting Rights Act, which forbids racially discriminatory election practices. For seven years, the case would be in and out of various courts, but in 1984 a final decision was reached. The findings read like an indictment of a dual system of life. No black candidate had ever received more than 2.3 percent of the votes in North Greenwood, the whitest of the city's three precincts, the court found. Most often, black candidates got 1 percent of the vote there. Bloc voting, an expert testified, surpassed that found in even highly polarized communities. Of fifteen boards and commissions filled by the city council, six had never had a black member. Only thirteen of the sixty-two board members appointed by the council were black. Those slights occurred in a city where blacks were substantially disadvantaged compared to whites in education, income, living conditions, and health. Forty-six percent of Greenwood's black families, compared to 7 percent of its whites lived in poverty. Eleven percent of blacks and 1 percent of whites had no bathroom. Forty-seven percent of blacks and 6 percent of whites had no car or truck. Thirty-four children under the age of one died in Greenwood between 1978 and 1980; twenty-eight of them were black. And so on. His conclusion, said U.S. District Court Judge William C. Keady of Greenville, was this: "It is inescapably clear that the black voters of Greenwood have less opportunity than whites to participate in the political process and to elect representatives of their choice." Keady ordered district elections.

On June 4, 1985, thirty years after Emmett Till met a watery grave and twenty years after the Voting Rights Act became law, Greenwood elected its first black aldermen since Reconstruction under the new plan. One of them was David Jordan.

A month later, on a warm July evening, Jordan drove his oversized Chrysler with the "Believe in Greenwood" bumper sticker through a black neighborhood on the east side of town. He threw up his hand in greeting to a cluster of women chatting over a front yard flower bed and to a pair of schoolboys racing by on bicycles. Jordan pulled to a stop before a trim ranch house with chocolate shingles and hurried in to catch the evening news. He expected to be featured in a segment filmed at the city council meeting earlier in the day, and he was anxious to hear the report. A tall man with wire-rimmed glasses and a retreating hair line, Jordan dangled a leg over the arm of an Early American rocker and reflected on black progress as he waited. Life was good for him now. He and Chris drew teachers' salaries. Two of their boys were in medical school. His position in Greenwood politics seemed secure. "We could easily become complacent," he said. "We could say, 'Forget it,' " to others who ask for help.

But Jordan believed there were still battles to win. The very statistics on living conditions cited in *Jordan v. Greenwood* proved his case. Down the road in Sunflower County and elsewhere in the Delta, black majorities had still not elected black candidates to office. Across the South, even when blacks were elected, they had sometimes proven themselves inadequate or powerless to produce hoped for change. And so, the fire inside him raged on. "Everybody says, 'You're free now.' So they say, 'Catch up.' We can't do that overnight," he said. "When we lose elections due to all these circumstances, people say, 'Well, they didn't care.' That's the baldest lie that's ever been told."

2. SELMA
The Beginning

IN THE EARLY DAYS, the civil rights movement found its soul in the churches of the region. There was Atlanta's Ebenezer Baptist, Sixteenth Street Baptist in Birmingham, Dexter Avenue Baptist over in Montgomery, and dozens of Mount Shilohs, Gethsemanes, and Calvarys dotting the landscape from the red clay fields of Georgia to the lush and sultry Mississippi Delta. In ghetto sanctuaries and corn field chapels, black ministers preached awesome truths, and people listened. "If God be for me," the preachers asked, "who can be against me?" Who indeed? "Though I walk through the valley of the shadow of death, I will fear no evil," they said, and humble men and women without education or birthright, without land and with only a few dollars in their pockets, found courage and purpose and a power beyond all reason. "Wherever two or three are gathered together in My name, there am I," the ministers intoned. And so, the people linked arms, two by two, in Rich's Department Store and F. W. Woolworth's, and then by the bus load down through Anniston and Montgomery into the heartland of southern darkness, and at last by the thousands in Selma and Washington and beyond.

So it was that on March 7, 1965, when about five hundred marchers set out to walk the fifty-eight miles from Selma to Montgomery, Alabama, they began with prayer and song at Brown Chapel African Episcopal Methodist Church. Nestled in the midst of a black housing project a leisurely walk from downtown Selma, the church is a sturdy, fortresslike structure. Its red brick, twin steeples are separated by a circular glass window and a small balcony that is an ideal pulpit for stirring a crowd in the church-yard below. In the winter of 1965, Brown Chapel was a command post, a rallying point, a refuge for hundreds of blacks who had followed Dr. Martin Luther King, Jr., to this Old South cotton town on the banks of the Alabama River. What they sought was nothing less than a turning point in the southern movement, a voting rights campaign so dramatic that it would compel the nation to act. In a sheriff named Jim Clark, in tear gas and bull-whips, in a breezy March day that would live in infamy as "Bloody Sunday," they found what they were seeking.

That day, walking arm in arm, the marchers set off from Brown Chapel. Six blocks later, they mounted the gently sloping crest of the Edmund Pettus Bridge, separating Selma from Dallas County, and saw spread below them a mosaic of blue hard hats, stamping horses, state highway patrol cars, and curious white onlookers. Dallas County sheriff's deputies and Alabama state troopers standing three-deep blocked the way up Route 80. A voice amplified by a bullhorn sounded loud and ominous: "I'm Major John Cloud. This is an unlawful march. You will not be allowed to continue. I'll give you three minutes to go back to your church." In less than half the allotted time, Cloud sounded the order, "Troopers advance!"[1] With night sticks and bullwhips, on horseback, and using tear gas, the troopers charged. There was wailing and shouts of pain as men and women fell to their knees, and a battered throng limped and ran and stumbled its way back to the bosom of Brown Chapel.

A nation that fancied itself a beacon of morality in a troubled world could not ignore the sight of Selma. News film of elderly men and women clutching bleeding skulls, of police officers raising bullwhips against individuals seeking elemental rights, of dazed marchers frantically dragging away their wounded was more than the American conscience could stand. And so in Washington, the gears of power were set in motion at last, and they began to turn, faster and faster, with an unrelenting synchrony. On March 11, President Lyndon Johnson went on national television to an-nounce that he was submitting to Congress legislation that would clear the way for blacks to exercise their constitutional right to vote. In one of the most moving speeches of his presidency, Johnson proclaimed: "At times, history and fate meet in a single place to shape a turning point in man's unending search for freedom. So it was at Lexington and Concord. So it was a century ago at Appamattox. So it was last week in Selma, Alabama."

Four months later, on August 6, 1965, Johnson signed into law the Voting Rights Act. The final version banned literacy tests as a prerequisite for voting. It provided for federal examiners to register voters in certain southern states and for federal observers to monitor elections there. And it required all or part of seven states—Alabama, Georgia, Louisiana, Mississippi, North Carolina, South Carolina, and Virginia—to have every change in local or state election laws approved by the U.S. Justice Department or federal courts in Washington, D.C.

Johnson's pledges were euphoric that day as he sat in the gilded splendor of the President's Room at the Capitol, surrounded by the elder statesmen of the Congress and the civil rights movement. The last shackles of slavery had just been removed, he vowed. There would be no stopping black Americans now. The world was theirs. Godspeed. All this was to flow from the simplest, the least costly, the most basic of American rights, the privilege Johnson had just delivered into the hands of southern blacks—the right to vote.

Two decades later, on a balmy March day in 1985, the generals and foot soldiers of America's "Second Revolution" returned to Selma. There, at the scene of their greatest triumph, black southerners paused to reflect on all that had been accomplished and all that remained to be done. They would again march from Selma to Montgomery, as they had in 1965 two weeks after "Bloody Sunday." This time, their challenge to a nation no longer preoccupied with racial progress was to take stock. In twenty years, the American South had undergone radical change. From a sleepy, backwater region, primarily rural and dependent on agriculture for its survival, a new South had emerged. Its people, as a whole, were more prosperous, better educated, more urban, and, yes, less distinguishable from other Americans than at any time in the nation's history. But what of black southerners, a group long forced to languish not years, but generations behind? Were they part of the transformation? Had the desperately sought right to vote changed their lives? Was it the magic key to full citizenship, to social and economic gain? In short, was Johnson's promise two decades earlier a prophetic omen or a political promise turned sour?

By the mid-1980s, evidence lay everywhere of a more tolerant and open South, where young black dissidents of the 1960s—men and women who marched, shed blood, saw friends killed—moved with extraordinary ease through the mainstream of political life. In 1965, there were three hundred black elected officials in the nation. By 1985, there were more than twenty-three hundred in the seven states first covered by the Voting Rights Act alone.[2] Sixty percent of the increase in black officials nationwide had come in the South. The southern figure included mayors in Atlanta, New Orleans, Birmingham, Richmond, Charlotte, and dozens of smaller cities and towns. Before the year was out, state senator Doug Wilder would be elected lieutenant governor of Virginia, breaking the twentieth-century jinx on electing black candidates for southern executive office. Among King's lieutenants, Andrew Young, the dispassionate intellectual, was mayor of Atlanta. John Lewis, the stoic warrior, was an Atlanta city councilman, soon to be elected to Congress. Hosea Williams, the firebrand young radical who marched beside Lewis on "Bloody Sunday," had served in the Georgia legislature and would win an Atlanta council seat in the fall of 1985. Elsewhere, Reuben Anderson, who integrated the Ole Miss law school in 1967, had just been appointed to the Mississippi Supreme Court. Harvey Gantt, who integrated Clemson University, was mayor in Charlotte, North Carolina. Charles Sherrod, a prominent black organizer in the 1960s, sat on the city council in Albany, Georgia. John Hulett, who helped found the Black Panther Party, was sheriff of Lowndes County, Alabama. Chris McNair, whose daughter died in the Sixteenth Street Baptist Church bombing in Birmingham in 1963, was a member of the Alabama legislature. And there were other individuals, less prominent, little known outside their own communities, but with stories no less rich—men like David Jordan of Greenwood, Mississippi, or Tom McCain of Edgefield, South Carolina, ordinary, middle-class people made extraordinary by their persistence and courage in battling for a share of the American dream. McCain, who over a decade and a half had challenged everything from the fight song at Strom Thurmond High School ("Dixie") to the county's at-large elections, had just been named Edgefield County administrator. On and on, across the South, individuals once barred from the political process voted on zoning ordinances, set tax policy, and scrambled to attract industry and jobs.

Such showy successes masked another, harsher reality, however. Those who in 1965 jubilantly celebrated passage of the Voting Rights Act, predicting immediate and dramatic change, underestimated the ingenuity and persistence of their foes. Achieving political equality, they were to find, was not nearly so simple as pulling the lever of a voting machine. And producing a socially and economically integrated society was yet more awesome a task. The experiences of the two decades between 1965 and 1985 confirmed what blacks already knew—that some whites would go to great lengths to prevent blacks from attaining political power and that many others would at least try to retain power for themselves. Despite progress, white insensitivity to black aspirations remained.

A telling example arose in Alabama's Dallas County in the spring of 1985. Dallas County is a pastoral expanse of farm and timberland linked to Selma by the Alabama River. The county's population is about 55 percent black, but two decades after the Selma-to-Montgomery marchers passed through the county, no black person still had held a county office since Reconstruction. That was to have changed in 1985. Jackie Walker, a young black woman, had been elected tax collector the previous fall. Her election climaxed a community-wide push by black leaders. But Walker was killed in an automobile crash on an icy highway before she could take office. At first, blacks were hopeful that the all-white county commission would appoint Walker's husband— or some other black person— to the post. Filling a vacancy with the spouse of a dead official is traditional in rural Alabama, blacks argued. And besides, they added, Walker's election had been a victory for all Dallas County blacks, a breakthrough that should not be so capriciously erased. A major campaign was mounted toward installation of a black successor. In the end, blacks were able to muster one vote for their cause. The all-white county commission voted four to one to name Tommy Powell, the white man whom Walker had defeated, to the post.

Nor in 1985 was Dallas County the only southern site where the political power of blacks did not reflect their numerical strength. Blacks were 26 percent of the population in the seven states, but by the most optimistic projections, they held no more than 8 to 10 percent of the elective offices.[3] Perhaps the most graphic reminder of the bonds still shackling blacks politically lay in the eighty-two counties in Alabama, Georgia, Louisiana, Mississippi, North Carolina, South Carolina, and Virginia where blacks equaled or outnumbered whites. In sixty-one of those counties in 1985, whites still ran local government. Among the sixty-one, there were twenty-three majority-black counties with only one black county commissioner. And in fifteen others—Dallas and Marengo counties in Alabama; Calhoun, Macon, Randolph, Stewart, Taliafero, Washington, and Webster counties in Georgia; Jefferson Davis, Kemper, Sunflower, Tallahatchie, and Washington counties in Mississippi; and Gates County, North Carolina—the boards were lily white.[4] Moreover, despite dramatic gains in numbers of black officials, most of the offices held by blacks were lower-level, county, and municipal jobs. Until Wilder, there were only three statewide black elected officials in the seven states. The three were judges, sitting on courts dominated by whites, and each had initially been appointed by a white governor to fill a vacancy. Not until 1987 would two blacks be added to the congressional delegations from the seven states. Both—Atlanta's John Lewis and Mississippi's Mike Espy—were from majority-black districts. Tokenism, it seemed, was acceptable. But the most prestigious offices were still reserved for whites.

In other ways as well, progress was clouded. By 1985, the most odious forms of discrimination were gone. Literacy tests, violence, and most overt economic pressure had disappeared. Two decades earlier, black sharecroppers who tried to register were greeted with questions ranging from "How many bubbles are in a bar of soap?" to "How many associate justices are on the Supreme Court?"[5] Those who dared to vote were threatened with eviction or worse. In several settings blacks were killed during the 1950s for voter registration activity.

The change by the 1980s was reflected in improved registration statistics. In the seven states first covered by the Voting Rights Act, the percentage of eligible blacks registered was up from 31 percent in 1965 to 66 percent in 1984.[6] Mississippi, which trailed the nation with an abysmal 7 percent black registration in 1965, was first with 86 percent of its black voting-age population registered. In three states, Louisiana, Mississippi, and South Carolina, a higher percentage of eligible blacks than eligible whites was registered. Meanwhile, the gap in black and white voting had narrowed dramatically also.[7]

Yet electoral discrimination against blacks had not disappeared. Numerous techniques more subtle than literacy tests or poll taxes—among them, annexations, at-large voting, and gerrymandering—could be and were used by whites to control political systems. Between 1965 and 1985, the Justice Department acting under the Voting Rights Act blocked over one thousand election law changes in the seven states, arguing that they were discriminatory. Most often, the objectionable changes did not directly hamper the ability of blacks to cast a ballot. Instead, they diluted the importance of those black ballots that were cast. By 1985, such practices had not ended. That year, ninety-nine objections were lodged in South Carolina, thirty in North Carolina, six in Mississippi, four in Georgia, and three in Alabama.[8] For instance, in Griffin, Georgia, just south of Atlanta, Justice Department officials protested that a proposed redistricting in a city 42 percent black created only one district, out of five, in which blacks had a reasonable shot at electing a city commissioner of their choice. In Yazoo City, Mississippi, a site of racial turmoil in earlier decades, federal officials blocked a supervisor redistricting plan which, they said, unnecessarily split up black voters, limiting their election hopes. In Greensboro, Alabama, northwest of Selma in the Black Belt, the department stopped white town officials from de-annexing a block of land where a subsidized public housing project—expected to serve primarily blacks—was about to be built.

"Vote dilution still exists to a substantial degree," concluded Gerald Jones during an interview in his Washington office. A black lawyer and Southside Virginia native, Jones had headed the Justice Department's voting section since it was created in 1969 to help enforce the Voting Rights Act. "Judging from the level of places where we still have to send federal observers and from the number of objections, I'd say we're far from going out of business," he said.

By the 1980s, physical intimidation, long devastating to black southerners, lived mostly in memory. However, isolated incidents remained. The nation was stunned in January 1987 when black marchers in all-white Forsyth County, Georgia, were attacked by Ku Klux Klansmen. But an official system of tacitly approved violence had passed from the scene. Black sheriffs like Lucius Amerson in Macon County, Alabama, and Richard Lankford in Fulton County, Georgia, contributed to the demise. The Ku Klux Klan was alive, but a mere shadow of its former self. With rare exceptions, hooded terrorists and burning crosses were the stuff of history. As the 1985 Selma-to-Montgomery marchers passed through Dallas and Lowndes counties, state troopers who had blocked their way in 1965 served as guardians. During the 1965 campaign, three people—two white, one black—died. During the 1985 reenactment, there were no injuries; there was no violence. Troopers, including blacks barred from the force in 1965, formed a security wall as the line wound down Route 80 and later in the week ushered marchers safely to the state capital. In Montgomery, the group was received by Governor George Wallace, whose 1965 rhetoric had stirred the flames of white wrath. In 1985, Wallace, who ironically had depended on black votes for his 1982 election, personally welcomed leaders of the procession.

If violence had abated by 1985, however, some southern blacks argued that political and economic intimidation still thrived. Already-tenuous relations with the Reagan administration plummeted that spring as federal prosecutors launched a full-scale investigation of alleged voting fraud in the Alabama Black Belt. Blacks, who in years past had pleaded unsuccessfully for similar investigations of absentee ballot manipulation by whites, were dismayed when a twenty-nine-count federal indictment was brought against three black stalwarts of the civil rights movement in Perry County. Most prominent was Albert Turner, a large, rumpled man who had served as a pallbearer at King's funeral and who had been an organizer of Selma's "Bloody Sunday" march. Those indictments were followed by others in Greene County. As the cases stirred national attention, leading blacks fumed that a witch-hunt—aimed at confusing and intimidating black voters—was under way. Justice Department officials countered that the complaints had been initiated by black candidates, running against other blacks, and that they had no choice but to respond.

However, accusations of trumped-up charges gained credence as the fall of 1985 passed and, after five trials, the government had yet to gain a conviction. Dismay turned to outrage when government prosecutors—frustrated by earlier losses—used a series of strikes against prospective jurors to ensure that the jury in the sixth trial would be all white. Even then, the defendant Frederick Daniels, a Greene County voting rights activist, was acquitted. Not until several days later did an all-white jury convict Daniels' codefendant, Councilman Spiver Gordon of Eutaw, on four counts of voter fraud. At the sentencing, U.S. District Judge U. W. Clemon took the unusual step of urging Gordon to appeal, apparently because of constitutional issues raised by the seating of an all-white jury. In the end, two other defendants pleaded guilty to reduced charges and received two years probation each. To traditional black leaders, the indictments were politically motivated harassment, designed to limit black participation in Alabama's 1986 elections. To federal prosecutors, they were an attempt to stop some black leaders who were manipulating elections by defrauding poor and illiterate blacks of their votes. Either way, black voters were still being victimized.

Equally murky and unsettling were persistent reports of subtle economic intimidation against black voters, particularly in sections of the Mississippi Delta and rural Georgia. There were numerous accounts, sometimes in court, of plants that "happened" to close late on election day and of landowners who increased their election-day hires, only to keep those workers in the fields until after polls had closed. Typically, in a long-running court case aimed at breaking the white stranglehold on the county commission in majority-black Marengo County, Alabama, a black minister testified that blacks who are employed by whites—particularly black teachers in the Marengo County school system—"truly cannot get involved in the campaign because of their fear of [losing] their jobs."[9] Similarly, in a 1983 Mississippi voting rights case, Jake Ayers, a longtime political worker in Washington County, testified to the frustrations of getting poor black field hands to the polls. "I went to pick some people up this year and they were picking cotton," Ayers testified. "They had asked me to come and pick them up at 12 o'clock, and at 12 o'clock I was there, but the plantation owner had brought the people their food and when they got through eating, they just went right on back picking cotton. They couldn't come in to vote because they worked until after 6 o'clock."[10] There remained, said Gerald Jones, a sense among poor blacks in some plantation counties that "if you want to eat, you'd better not cross Mr. So-and-So" by voting.

Twenty years after Selma, social interaction between southern blacks and whites reflected revolutionary progress. The Whites Only signs had become museum relics. In stores and offices across the South, blacks and whites shopped and worked, side by side. No black child could be denied a public education equal to that afforded whites. In Selma, the street outside Brown Chapel had been renamed in honor of Dr. King. In Charleston, South Carolina, a portrait of Denmark Vesey, the leader of an aborted nineteenth-century slave revolt in that city, had been hung in the civic center. In Athens, Georgia, at the state university where troopers once accompanied black students to class, Heisman Trophy winner Herschel Walker had been a campus hero of the early 1980s. In Birmingham, where police brutality was once legendary and there was not a single black police officer in 1965, about three dozen blacks were on the force. In Atlanta, the amount of city business awarded black firms had grown from $41,000 in 1973 to $27.9 million in 1985.[11] In Richmond, Virginia, as in virtually every southern city, blacks held top personnel posts once open only to whites. "The freedom of movement is in such great contrast to the atmosphere of oppression," said the Reverend Jesse Jackson, as he pondered the southern transformation during a pause at his Chicago office on a frigid December morning. "People really believed in the apartheid social system. That's a lot of change in social dynamics in a short period of time."

Across the South, however, away from the workplaces and shopping centers, life for many remained almost as segregated in 1985 as in 1965. One could drive the streets of almost any southern town and stumble upon an invisible line dividing white and black residential sections. Outside major cities, there were few schools, fewer restaurants and almost no churches where blacks and whites mingled in anything approaching equal numbers. Private white academies, opened in opposition to school desegregation, flourished in many communities. Everywhere, segregated private clubs remained. That was as true of the Piedmont Driving Club, one of Atlanta's most prestigious, as for American Legion posts and Elks Club lodges in dozens of small towns.

Most disheartening of all, blacks—regionally, as nationally—trailed far behind whites in every economic measure. In the seven states, the eighty-two counties with a population 50 percent or more black told the financial story in bleak detail. Every majority-black county had a higher level of poverty than its state's average. In all but two of the counties, there were fewer high school graduates than in the average county statewide. All but fourteen had a higher unemployment rate than average. Worse, those counties where blacks had achieved political control tended to rank at the lowest end of the economic scale, even behind black-majority counties still run by whites.[12] In majority-black Tunica County, Mississippi, one of the nation's poorest, state representative Clayton Henderson conducted a driving tour of shanties served by outhouses and outdoor water pumps and of ditches or backyards where raw sewage is dumped. In Tuskegee, Alabama, Commissioner Ronald Green spoke of his frustration—and ultimate failure—in trying to attract industry to Macon County, which has the highest percentage of black residents (84 percent) of any county in the South. And in Atlanta, a city praised for its openness to black interests, the Reverend Joseph Lowery, president of the Southern Christian Leadership Conference (SCLC), lamented that the economic problems of blacks "seem to defy solution even here." Seated in the cramped Auburn Avenue office where King once held court, Lowery said he believed that, with time, most of the battles for political equality would be won. But economic equality is another matter. "Political power has got to work for economic power," he said. The question—how?—remained.

Amid this turbulent climate of change and inertia, one constant was the importance of the Voting Rights Act to black aspirations. In 1985, as in 1965, the law remained a central element of black progress. If its achievements had been less lofty than those originally forecast, it was still remarkable legislation, producing more tangible results than any other civil-rights-era law, transforming old ways into new as insistently as any single legislative act in American history. In literally hundreds of communities, large and small, black political gains would have been slowed or prevented without the act's insistence on federal monitoring of every change in state and local election laws. The restructuring demanded by the act did not always translate into smoother, less problematic government. And as race relations advanced, arguments against certain remedies—ward elections, for instance—picked up credence in some communities. But on balance, the Voting Rights Act was responsible for bringing vastly more representative government to the South. Based on a democratic ideal, that meant better government. Initially, the act's chief contribution was in clearing the way for blacks to register in droves. By the 1970s, the ability of the Justice Department to halt election law changes adversely affecting blacks had become paramount. And after revisions to the law were approved in 1982, a section forbidding any election procedure—old or new—that curtailed or denied black voting rights produced a rash of changes in local electoral systems.

When Congress passed the Voting Rights Act in the summer of 1965, it declared war on a system of black political exclusion in force in the South for three-quarters of a century. For a while after the Civil War, the southern electorate was predominantly black. Blacks sat in every state legislature, and twenty black southerners served in the House of Representatives, two in the U.S. Senate and one as governor of Louisiana.[13] But the departure of federal troops soon ended the protected state that had allowed black participation, and by the 1880s, violence, fraud, and economic intimidation were being used by white southerners to reclaim political control. In 1890, Mississippi led the way in formal disenfranchisement of blacks by adopting a state constitution that imposed literacy tests, a two-dollar poll tax and other restrictions. An estimated 123,000 blacks lost their right to vote almost overnight. Within a few years, almost every southern state had copied Mississippi's example.[14] In 1898, Louisiana fine-tuned its literacy test by granting an exemption and permanent registration to anyone whose father or grandfather had been qualified to vote in January 1867. None too subtly, the date incorporated whites and excluded blacks. Eleven southern states undercut black influence still further by eventually adopting all-white primaries. Since one-party government prevailed throughout the South, primary victories were usually tantamount to election. When Gunnar Myrdal, a distinguished

Swedish scholar toured the American South in 1942 researching his classic study, *An American Dilemma,* he concluded: "For all practical purposes, Negroes are disenfranchised in the South."[15] Ralph Bunche who contributed statistical work to Myrdal, projected that out of an adult black population of 3.7 million in eight Deep South states, no more than 90,000 voted in the general election of 1940.

That system of political exclusion began to unravel in 1944 when the U.S. Supreme Court in *Smith v. Allwright* banned the Texas white primary. Across the South, blacks celebrated. But, while registrations improved, other devises forestalled the dramatic improvement in black voting that many had predicted when the court ruled. Not until over a decade later, with passage of the Civil Rights Act of 1957, did the modern congressional push for black voting rights begin. The 1957 act gave the attorney general power to bring lawsuits to protect equal voting rights, and it created a six-member Civil Rights Commission to apprise the president and Congress of problems and progress. The act was furiously debated, but in the end, only a handful of lawsuits were filed by the Eisenhower administration, and the impact on black voting in the South was minimal.[16] When the act was amended in 1960, prosecutorial powers were expanded somewhat, but critics protested that enforcement authority was still too weak. The Civil Rights Act of 1964 added further touches—a sixth-grade education was made a presumption of literacy, for example—but the systematic overhaul sought by blacks still eluded them. Enforcement continued to depend on costly and time-consuming lawsuits. Even when plaintiffs won in court, local or state officials could often undo the victory by simply doctoring an election law.

The architects of the Voting Rights Act aimed at overcoming those limitations. What they fashioned was a two-pronged attack. On the one hand, they sought immediate improvement in black registration and voting by outlawing restrictive practices such as literacy tests and by providing for federal examiners and election observers. On the other, under Section 5 of the act, they looked toward long-term protection. The attorney general or a federal court would be required to certify that any election law change— no matter how minor—in designated states was not intended to undercut black voting rights and would not have that effect. The section would apply to jurisdictions that in 1964 had some type of literacy test and in which less than half of the voting-age population had registered or voted that year. Six southern states and a portion of North Carolina fit the formula.

The beauty of the new law was that the burden of proof had shifted from the people to local governments. No longer would those who feared that an election law revision would diminish black political clout have to go to court to prove their case. Instead, it would be up to local governments to demonstrate from the outset that the changes they proposed were nondiscriminatory. As President Johnson signed the law, using one hundred souvenir pens, his praise was profuse. The act, he said, during a televised noontime ceremony, was "one of the most monumental laws in the entire history of American freedom." And he pledged: "Today, we strike away the last major shackle of fierce and ancient bonds . . . Today, the American story and the Negro story fuse and blend."

The promised merger began almost immediately, as federal examiners were dispatched to many of the South's most recalcitrant pockets. Within the first year, forty-three counties in Alabama, Louisiana, Mississippi, and South Carolina had been visited.[17] Skeptics would later note that not a single registrar was dispatched to Georgia, home of Richard Russell, the powerful Senate Armed Services Committee chairman, until the end of 1966. Nor did notorious Sunflower County, Mississippi, home to Jim Eastland, Senate Judiciary chairman, entertain federal examiners until April 1967. Despite such gaps, however, the initial success in signing up black voters was dramatic. By mid-March of 1966, the *New York Times* reported that federal examiners had enrolled 100,000 people, and local registrars another 200,000, since passage of the Voting Rights Act. The most dramatic increases came in the three states first visited by examiners. In Mississippi, the percentage of eligible black voters registered jumped from 7 percent to 33 percent between 1964 and August 1966. In Alabama, the gain during that period was from 23 percent to 51 percent of eligible blacks. And in Louisiana, black registration rose from 32 percent to 47 percent.[18]

By the early 1970s, the emphasis of the Voting Rights Act was changing. The pace of black registrations had begun to slow, and federal officials were becoming increasingly interested in the ability of the new voters to influence politics in their towns and counties. Up until 1969, only one Section 5 lawsuit had been filed by the federal government.[19] That challenge had come in Bullock County, Alabama, a heavily black county in which blacks were just beginning to exercise the right to vote. When state legislators approved a plan extending the terms of county commissioners from four to six years, the Justice Department objected. The extension was, in effect, keeping Bullock County government in all-white hands for at least two added years, the department held. A federal district court panel agreed.

Throughout the 1970s and 1980s, the Justice Department would object to hundreds of changes that had either a discriminatory intent or effect, and Section 5 would become the pivotal clause in keeping black political advancement alive. As federal officials halted change after change, the objections gradually began to give blacks not only equal access to the voting booth, but also—far more importantly—equal access to political power. In the first four years the Justice Department's voting section operated, said Gerald Jones, the section chief, about five hundred proposed election law changes were submitted for preclearance. By 1985, the annual figure had skyrocketed to about fourteen thousand changes, dozens of which were stopped each year. The stories accompanying those raw numbers demonstrated the remarkable tenacity of whites in attempting to retain power. The objections also suggested why a law that focused only on voter registration or that depended for enforcement on local citizens challenging election law changes in court might easily have become a mockery. Critics railed that the federal government was promoting unfairly a guaranteed result—the election of blacks. Yet the electoral systems under attack, history had proved, already insured a guaranteed result—the election of whites.

Example after example demonstrated the act's importance. In Richmond, for instance, in a classic case, a 1969 annexation negotiated largely in secret by white officials produced a large pool of new voters. Most were white. Overnight, an emerging black majority was returned to minority status. The Justice Department objected. The eventual settlement allowed the annexation, but only if a ward plan replaced citywide, at-large council elections. The rationale was that some districts would inevitably have black majorities, and black candidates could presumably be elected. In 1977 under the new ward plan, the city installed its first black mayor and council majority. Had the annexation gone forward unchallenged and the system of at-large elections remained intact, there was no reason to expect that the Richmond council would have progressed beyond its tradition of token black representation. The annexation would not have stopped blacks from voting, but by increasing the pool of white voters, it would have been an equally effective way of ensuring that black ballots did not count.

In dozens of settings the Richmond story was repeated. Between 1965 and 1985, the department halted more than 270 annexations, and in sites from Alabaster, Alabama, and Adel, Georgia, to Shreveport, Louisiana, and Spartanburg, South Carolina, black voting strength was protected by the voting act.[20]

A second category of objections dealt with local and state redistricting. In a typical case, the Justice Department objected to a 1975 division of the Mississippi legislature that placed large concentrations of black voters into multimember districts with even larger concentrations of white voters. Under the system, blacks might vote en masse, but whites still retained the strength to outdo them. Had the state been carved into individual districts, some districts inevitably would have had black majorities and black candidates might have been elected. But by lumping several smaller districts into a larger, multimember district, the legislature could ensure white voting majorities throughout the state. Such techniques had been used for years to dilute black strength. Partially as a result, there was one black legislator in a state almost 40 percent black. Based on the Voting Rights Act challenge, Mississippi was eventually carved into single-member districts. When elections were held in 1979 under the new plan, seventeen black legislators won office.

Similarly, when the Virginia House of Delegates fashioned its redistricting plan after the 1980 census, the lawmakers managed to separate five contiguous, black-majority counties, located in the tobacco-and-peanut producing area south of Richmond. Each heavily black county was paired with a predominantly white area, and in the end, not a single majority-black district was produced. Again, federal officials objected, and the lawmakers were forced to redraw the plan.

A proposed legislative redistricting plan in Louisiana was also rejected when black-majority districts statewide dropped from seventeen to fourteen. In New Orleans, for instance, despite an increase in the city's black population from 45 to 55 percent between 1970 and 1980, the number of majority-black districts under the proposed plan fell from eleven to seven, while the number of majority-white districts grew from seven to eight.

At the local level, Barbour County, Alabama, posed a typical redistricting problem. County officials decided in the early 1980s to move from six single-member districts and one countywide district to seven single-member districts in electing county commissioners. On the surface, the idea appeared innocent enough. But the Justice Department found that in a county 44 percent black, not a single proposed district had been drawn to create a black majority. Similar objections halted redistricting plans in Macon County, Georgia; Caddo Parish, Louisiana; Copiah County, Mississippi; Columbia, South Carolina; Southampton County, Virginia; and about two hundred other sites in the states first covered by the Voting Rights Act.

Nor were annexations and redistrictings the only grievances detected by the Justice Department. A host of devices—from limiting registration hours to changing the method of selecting officials to altering the terms of their service—could and did reduce the political effectiveness of blacks. In Bishopville, South Carolina, for instance, the town council was traditionally elected by the voters at-large, and only a plurality—not a majority—was needed to win office. Almost half of Bishopville's population was black, however, and when blacks began to register to vote in substantial numbers, the white council acted in response. Council terms were staggered, so that only a portion of the members would be elected in a single year, and a majority vote requirement was adopted. The combination was seen as limiting the prospect for blacks to prevail against the entrenched white power structure, and the Justice Department objected.

In predominantly black Tunica County, Mississippi, blacks began to flex their political muscle in the mid-1970s. They elected a circuit clerk in 1975 and the first black school board member a year later. Soon thereafter, county officials proposed changing the office of school board superintendent from an elected to an appointed position. The Justice Department nixed their plan.

In Terrell County, Georgia, after blacks were ordered admitted to the local grand jury, city officials voted to change the tradition of allowing the grand jury to appoint board of education members. Instead, they called for at-large elections. The Justice Department objected.

An Alabama case involved Greene County, a majority-black jurisdiction in which the state's first dog-racing track was located. Initially, the local legislative delegation—which remained white—was allowed to appoint the members of the racing commission. The year after blacks gained control of the delegation, however, the Alabama legislature stripped them of that appointive power. The Justice Department objected.

On and on, hundreds of cases both major and minor proved that true political power could not always be achieved by casting a ballot, and that without federal oversight, many of the gains of black voters could easily have been erased.

If the registration provisions and Section 5 of the Voting Rights Act captured attention through the 1960s and 1970s, still another clause gained importance after the act was extended by Congress for the third time in 1982. Section 2, as originally written, said essentially that no voting practice would be allowed that limited the right of any citizen to vote due to race or color. But court decisions had created doubt about when and how that section could be applied. In 1982, Congress clarified its intention by spelling out that the act should apply whenever a law had a discriminatory result, regardless of whether those who framed the law had discrimination in mind.

As a result, across the South, longtime election practices began to tumble. The most vulnerable proved to be at-large election systems. While political scientists debate the point, most research seems to show that blacks fare better in smaller election districts than in at-large elections where minority strength is submerged.[21] Armed with the revised Section 2, citizens in cities and towns throughout the region went to court to protest that at-large electoral systems had a discriminatory result. Often, judges agreed. In mid-1984, the *Atlanta Constitution* reported that at-large systems in Georgia and elsewhere in the South were "toppling like dominos." Nowhere was the result more apparent than in Mississippi. There, major cities—including Jackson, Hattiesburg, and

Greenwood—switched from at-large to ward systems, either directly or indirectly as a result of Section 2 litigation. The 1985 municipal elections justified the effort. In Jackson, which had not had a black council member in the twentieth century, three blacks were elected to a seven-member council. In the other cities also, long-standing color barriers were broken. "Section 2 is probably the most important change in the Voting Rights Act since it was passed," concluded Louis Armstrong, a legal services lawyer in Jackson, several weeks after his historic election to the city council. And so, the evolution of a law tailored to meet changing needs continued.

As the first two decades of black influence in southern politics ended, men and women, black and white, rich and poor across the region told of the joys and frustrations of living within a society in flux. They spoke with no single voice and conveyed no unified message. In the eyes of some, the promise of the Voting Rights Act remained unfulfilled. The rewards of political office were too narrow, too intangible, not relevant enough to individual lives. To others, the psychological gain of being able to compete for office, of being addressed as "Mr. Mayor" or "Councilman," of having a say in public-sector job hirings or contract awards was enough. To many blacks, the Voting Rights Act was a godsend. To still other southerners, almost all of whom were white, it was an abomination, visited upon the South by hypocritical northerners. In the mid-1980s, some southern blacks retained the fervor of the civil rights era, protesting that continuing white oppression was the root cause of black ills. Other blacks saw such arguments as passé. They called for new approaches and even endorsed coalitions with whites. Already, particularly in major cities like Atlanta or New Orleans, blacks were being elected whose experience was not grounded in the old wars for equality. Whereas black preachers were once the dominant force in black politics, now less emotional types with degrees in accounting or public administration were coming to the fore. Politicians like Michael Lomax, the scholarly and urbane county commission chairman in Fulton County, Georgia, or Harvey Gantt, the architect and M.I.T.-trained city planner who was mayor in Charlotte, North Carolina, seemed leagues apart from more impassioned, grass-roots sorts like Bennie Thompson, supervisor in Hinds County, Mississippi, or Henry Kirksey, state senator from Jackson, an aging politician whose spirit in battling for black rights appeared ageless.

John Lewis and Hosea Williams, who walked side by side at the head of Selma's "Bloody Sunday" march reflected the diverging attitudes. Lewis, who grew up in rural Pike County, Alabama, was fifteen years old when he first heard Dr. King's Sunday morning messages broadcast from Dexter Avenue Baptist Church in Montgomery. He was eighteen when he rode the bus over to the capital to talk with King about integrating Troy State College. And he was twenty-five on the day in 1965 when he was flown from Selma to a Boston, Massachussetts, hospital with his skull cracked by a state trooper's blow. Twenty years later, Lewis spoke of change so profound that "you can see it. You can almost feel it. It's a different climate; people are more open, more hopeful. The Voting Rights Act, it liberated black people, and it liberated white people, and it liberated white politicians especially."

But Williams had a far different view of the 1980s. "Political power has not delivered to its constituents as we predicted it would," he argued. "We said, 'Your vote is worth dying for,' and sure enough, they went out and died. We said, 'You've got to vote ol' whitey out and ol' blackie in.' So they did. But things haven't gotten better. In too many cases, they've gotten worse."

Others, like Supervisor Thompson of Hinds County, combined Williams' frustration and Lewis' sense of underlying progress. "There's some tolerance between the races. That tolerance is not based on an acceptance of individuals. It's solely because it's the law of the land and it's not fashionable to be an out and out racist," argued Thompson, as he shifted his large frame and rested his arms briefly on a cluttered desk.

At thirty-seven, after devoting half his life to battling the state's white power structure, Thompson's suspicions of white motives remained intact. But he had developed a certain regard for the political system, and a sense that the quest for political power had not been in vain. "I'm optimistic, more than I was fifteen years ago. Then I wanted to change Hinds County and the country overnight. I've finally come to the point that I look back and see where Mrs. Jones wouldn't be living in a decent house if some of us hadn't taken an interest. Or her husband couldn't have gone to the hospital if we hadn't gotten an ambulance. Little

personal things don't make statistics, but they make it worthwhile."

By the mid-1980s, few whites in official positions spoke criti-
cally of the emergence of blacks as a political force across the
South. To be sure, there were exceptions, including Charles Coleman, the former county attorney in Edgefield, South Carolina.
When a black majority took over the local council early in 1985,
Coleman concluded: "This county's been here two hundred years.
It'll take more than this to knock it off its feet." Among ordinary
men and women, resentment over what many viewed as preferen-
tial treatment of blacks sometimes spilled over. "If it was whites,
every damn one of us would be picked up," protested Edna Smith,
a long-haired young woman perched with friends on an automobile hood as she watched the 1985 procession of Selma-to-Montgomery marchers. But the official view was more nearly that of
Betty Fine Collins, a white councilwoman in Birmingham. As a
result of black involvement, "the city has changed, much for the
better," said Collins, as she paused outside city council chambers.

What many white southerners did not hesitate to criticize was
the burden of federal oversight imposed by the Voting Rights Act.
Nine states and portions of seven others had become subject to the
preclearance section of the law, but no region had been so long or
so thoroughly scrutinized as the South. "I call it 'the Second
Reconstruction,' " fumed a white city attorney in Indianola, referring to the act. White registrars, business executives, and councilmen echoed his disgust with the cumbersome reporting requirements and the extended legal challenges that the law had entailed.
Perhaps no single point produced such rapid disagreement from
southern blacks. "The Voting Rights Act is the very basis of any
future success we have in equality and justice in this country,"
insisted Howard Lee, a black man and former mayor of Chapel
Hill, North Carolina, in a typical response.

Out of that patchwork of impressions and beliefs emerged a
group of stories that seemed in aggregate to tell the history of
southern black politics from 1965 to 1985. At different times and
in different places, events carried contradictory messages. But that
diversity was in keeping with the stop-and-go pace of racial progress. Those stories—from Atlanta and Charlotte to isolated Black
Belt counties—reflected currents in dozens of other communities

across the South. Details differed, but the themes of disappointment, progress, and hope were the same. And so, from those
disparate parts began to emerge answers to the questions of how
far and in what direction the road that began in 1965 at Brown
Chapel in Selma, Alabama, had led.

3. EDGEFIELD COUNTY
The Transition

ONE EVENING IN MAY 1985, the citizens of Edgefield County, South Carolina, staged a small human drama. The scene was unplanned and unrehearsed, and it was a marvel that so many arrived in time to hear the opening lines. To get there, a few had to push sixty miles an hour driving home from work in Aiken or Augusta. Some had to round up the milk cows a half-hour early. And more than one family simply left the supper dishes on the table and brought the baby along. What the people had to say was mostly improvised. And when the words tumbled out, they were ripe with tension and hostility. There was a cutting, confrontational edge that made people forget they were all neighbors, and remember, instead, that most of them were white, while only a few were black. Here and there, in an inflection, a whisper, a phrase, was a hint of something ugly and racial. And here, too, was a suggestion that some in the audience knew very well what was ugly and racial and would not stand for it. In the dialogue between whites and blacks, there emerged a certain poignance. And after awhile, it seemed—even in the groping and the anger—that something richly American was at work.

The setting of this exchange was the Edgefield County courthouse, a spartan brick building erected in 1839 at one corner of the square in the little, history-and-antique filled county seat town of Edgefield. Robert Mills, designer of the Washington Monument, drew the plans for the hilltop courthouse, and in keeping with the times, the slaves of local planters and merchants helped lay the foundation and erect the wide steps leading from the street to the second-floor courtroom. Inside, a gallery of portraits—twenty-two in all—suggests the unique role this rural county sixty miles southwest of Columbia has played in the state's and the nation's history. The county has produced ten governors, five lieutenant governors, and several U.S. senators, a national record according to a dusty issue of *National Geographic.*

Nor is there much argument that the list includes some of the most virulent foes of racial integration ever to grace this long-defiant region. "Pitchfork Ben" Tillman, governor from 1890 to 1894 and later U.S. senator, was a self-proclaimed racist who condoned terrorism against South Carolina blacks and presided over the dismantling of their constitutional right to vote. So effective was his work that not a single black person was registered in Edgefield County at the turn of the century, nor for almost fifty years thereafter.[1] Another native son, U.S. senator J. Strom Thurmond, was a symbol throughout the mid-twentieth century of southern resistance to racial integration. When southern delegates bolted the Democratic Party's convention in Philadelphia in 1948, protesting the civil rights plank in the party platform, Thurmond led the renegade Dixiecrat ticket. He won thirty-nine electoral votes for president. His twenty-four-hour-and-eighteen-minute filibuster against civil rights legislation in 1964 set a congressional record that endures. Strom Thurmond High School and a bronze statue in the Edgefield town square convey the respect of a grateful citizenry.

That backdrop made the local returns on election night 1984 all the more savory for Edgefield's eighty-seven hundred blacks. The vote count took place at the courthouse, under the watchful eye of Tillman, Thurmond, and a collection of stern-faced judges, lawmakers, and Confederate generals preserved in oils and canvas on the courtroom walls. Before the night was over, three blacks —a telephone company technician, a widowed teacher, and a textile worker—had made history by winning seats on the Edgefield County Council. Half of the county's residents are black. But since Reconstruction, no black person had served on the county council, and none had defeated a white for any local office. In an instant, blacks had gone from exclusion to a majority on the

five-person council. Their control was tenuous. A shift of a few
votes in one precinct might return the council majority to whites
two years later. But blacks almost certainly would never again be
excluded. A decade of voting rights litigation that had taken them
through the judicial labyrinth to the U.S. Supreme Court was
over.

Whites greeted the local revolution with a mixture of dismay
and resignation. Many simply expected the worst. There would be
mass firings at the courthouse. Taxes would soon soar. Services
would deteriorate. "An awful lot of our community was in a state
of shock. A lot of the white community had the impression that
something unfortunate had happened," acknowledged Bettis
Rainsford, a wealthy land developer and publisher of the county's
largest newspaper. Blacks, in contrast, were jubilant. Pointing to
the courthouse portraits, Dr. Thomas McCain, a normally re-
strained black educator and administrator who had led the long
and often discouraging ten-year battle, whooped: "Ben Tillman
just turned his face to the wall."

Tillman, Thurmond, and the rest were in spiritual attendance,
too, some months later on the night of May 7 when the council
convened its weekly session. Normally, the Edgefield County
council meets in a small room in the administration building next
door to the courthouse. The racial power shift, however, was
accompanied by an explosion of civic interest in local government.
Weekly council meetings quickly became as magnetic as Friday
night turkey shoots or the "Rollin' Thunder Mud Tracks" in
nearby Aiken. "Used to, we'd have the third reading of the budget,
and not even the newspaper would show up," said William E.
McBride, Jr., the only holdover member of the former all-white
council. In the months after blacks took office, almost every meeting was transferred to the larger courtroom. On occasion there
was standing room only.

May 7 was one of those nights. The courtroom was packed
with about ninety whites and no more than a half-dozen blacks.
The whites had been drawn by rumors afloat in the county for
several days. Word was out that the new council intended to
abolish rural fire protection. Few prospects are more frightening
to a farm family than a vision of its home engulfed by flames far
from city water. So whites, many of them in a testy mood, had
turned out to ensure that the fire fighting contracts would be

renewed. The few blacks in the audience knew nothing of the controversy. They merely wanted to talk about road paving. There was no warning that they were about to witness a pivotal episode in a small community's passage through the shoals of political change.

When the meeting began, the fire protection issue was laid out quickly by B. Lovick Mims III, a third-generation sawmill operator and the sole representative of Edgefield's monied, white establishment on the new council. The problem, said Mims, was that the cost of fire protection was up, federal revenue-sharing funds—used to cover past costs—were down, and collection rates from farmers who had used the service were abysmal. The choices, he said, were a tax hike or dropping the fire plan. "If you're going to dance, you're going to have to pay the piper," said Mims.

Across the courtroom, there was a chorus of complaints.

"This isn't fair. You've spent a lot of money the previous council didn't spend."

"Our insurance'll be canceled if you go through with this."

"What are you gonna do when somebody's house burns down?"

Speaker after speaker rose from the long wooden benches. Their questions were fielded mostly by the white members, Mims and McBride. Black council members added no more than an occasional comment. Tom McCain, transformed from black political activist into county administrator, sat behind the council, furnishing data. At last, Mims broke the stalemate with a proposal. During the next year, he suggested, the council would put a lien on the property of any homeowner who failed to pay for a fire call. Meanwhile, the county would dip into reserve funds to cover the bulk of the contracts. Council members would have a year to come up with a more permanent solution. There were murmurs of support. Satisfied citizens leaned back in their seats to await council approval. A few began putting on jackets, ready to start home.

Council Chairman Willie Bright, an NAACP activist and technician for AT&T, called for the vote. The white members, McBride and Mims, went first. Both replied firmly, "Aye." Next came Albert Talbot, a thirty-six-year-old black textile worker and barber. Hands folded before him on the table, Talbot answered quietly: "No." Mrs. Sara Williams followed. Her vote, almost inaudible, was the same: "No." Bright hesitated, glancing up and down the table. "I'm voting against it," he concluded. The tally was three to two, against.

The proposal was dead.

The vote was on racial lines.

There was a moment of stunned silence; then, near mayhem swept the courtroom. Many of the whites were on their feet, shouting. Bright, looking confused, tapped his gavel for attention, but the strokes seemed tentative and were drowned out in the uproar. Gradually, individual voices broke through the din.

"How can you vote against it, Mr. Talbot? I am shocked. I had faith in you," pleaded a white schoolteacher, who appeared almost in tears.

"What would it cost you?" shouted a man, his voice laced with disgust. "That's the easiest thing you could be doing. That's ABC stuff."

Another, increasingly hostile, added: "If that's the way you manage your money, what are you going to do with the rest of our money?"

Decorum had vanished. The meeting was in disarray. Bright's pleas for order were ignored. Nothing mattered except the demands of angry citizens for an explanation. Finally, the crowd hushed. In an electric, almost-agonizing silence, black council members and white constituents exchanged stares.

At last, Albert Talbot began to speak, tentatively, awkwardly. "I just don't see how we can afford it," he said.

Outrage greeted the remark. "How can you say that? We've got $800,000 in reserve," a man shouted.

Talbot paused, tried again. "Maybe we can negotiate some with the fire departments. I'd rather do that than see a big increase in taxes."

"What are you talking about?" came the sizzling reply. "Nobody's talking about raising taxes. I want another vote. My councilman didn't understand the question."

There was a chorus of support. "Vote again. Vote again."

Sara Williams, looking pained, dabbed at her forehead with a tissue. Lovick Mims had risen from his chair to pace the back of the courtroom. Dr. McCain eyed the scene grimly.

Talbot made a final stab. "Maybe we can get together . . ."

"GET TOGETHER?" a man screeched. "We won't leave 'til you get together. You'll get together now."

There was another silence, long and awkward, and then Chairman Bright offered a glimmer of understanding. "Some people are not as fortunate as you and I," he said, so softly that those standing in back strained to hear. "They might not have a home owner's policy. And what happens if their home burns down?" Can a poor farmer whose home is a shack worth a few hundred dollars pay five hundred dollars for a fire call? he asked. Bright raised questions, too, about the cost of the proposed contracts. Other counties, he said, were paying less.

At last, the council recessed into a closed-door executive session. When the members returned, Bright announced that the council would try to renegotiate the proposed contracts. There were no promises about what would happen if those negotiations failed.

"Stupid as hell," muttered an Edgefield town councilman as he bolted from the courtroom.

"I'm totally disillusioned," added the schoolteacher who had spoken earlier.

Amid sighs and grumbling, and obvious relief that the confrontation was over, the crowd went home.

Several strains were evident that May night at the Edgefield County courthouse. As this modern-day, southern community faced transition, there was no mistaking the racial tension, the degree of distrust and prejudice in some voices. "She *can* talk," sneered one woman after Williams seconded a motion late in the discussion. "Don't you know how to use a microphone?" a man whispered sarcastically as Bright's voice remained difficult to hear. Black council members seemed equally leery of whites. "It was horrible," said Williams the next day. "It was like they ganged up on us."

It was also clear, however, that some whites in the audience were intent on avoiding a political lynching. A well-dressed woman, picking up on Bright's explanation, pleaded: "There *are* people who won't have the five hundred dollars. We really have a problem here." She urged a community barbecue or a fireman's ball to raise money. Another white, the director of a local wildlife federation, insisted: "I still have confidence in this council. They may still come up with some solution."

What Edgefield County residents also saw that night was a new political majority with a vision that would not be a carbon copy of the old council's. In a hostile environment, black members had refused to be cowed. However unrefined their political skills, they clearly were aware of their power. Just as clearly, they were willing to use it. "Last night, they took a stand that was pretty bold," Councilman McBride said the next day. "They received a lot of abuse." The black council members might not yet have learned to manipulate a political meeting. "But they know what they want to do, and they stick together. Make no mistake about that," he said.

McCain, who had had advance warning of the tempest, acknowledged later that he tried to warn black members of what lay in store. He admitted also that the kind of political finesse he had hoped to see was missing. The encouraging thing, he added, was the resolve of the black council members. In earlier budget discussions, they had made several policy decisions—that the proposed fire contracts needed renegotiating, that outlying communities (particularly some small black ones) were not being well served, and that the county needed to think about developing volunteer fire departments. Those principles may not have been communicated well at the courthouse meeting. But black council members did not budge from them. "A lot of people would not have had the courage to try," said McCain. "In time, they'll do all right. They'll learn the techniques."

A postscript to the episode came several weeks later. When attempts to renegotiate the fire contracts failed, the black majority adopted a fallback position similar to Lovick Mims' original proposal. For blacks, it was an early lesson in the fact that change does not come overnight. "We'll take a year to work on this," said McCain. "I think most whites would tell you they're now satisfied."

Since 1965, when passage of the Voting Rights Act brought federal registrars into the South, and blacks in droves began to sign up to vote, dozens of communities like Edgefield have become test tubes for political change. Only a few decades removed from a time when blacks formed little more than a tenant-servant class, whites have been forced to grapple with the reality of black council members, tax assessors, sheriffs, and judges whose decisions affect their lives. The result is nothing short of a political revolution in pockets of a region where, just forty years earlier, Gunnar Myrdal wrote, "the Negro problem actually is a main determinant of all local, regional, and national issues, whether political, economic, or broadly cultural."[2]

Hancock County, Georgia, less than one hundred miles from Edgefield County, was the first in the South to install a majority-black local government. The transition in 1968 was followed by turmoil and allegations of corruption that seemed to confirm the worst fears of many whites.[3] But in other cities and towns, from Greene County, Alabama, to Surry County, Virginia, the power shift—if uneasy and even traumatic, at first—has evolved more peacefully. Gradually, both blacks and whites have become aware of the limits of political power. Change often is not so great as blacks dreamed or as whites feared. Still, the moment of change often remains emotionally charged. In community after community, including Edgefield County, whites have resisted the day when blacks would take a meaningful role in local government as long as legal channels would allow. And when change comes, more often than not through the order of a federal judge, the initial months are frequently a time of rumor and fear. Will the Confederate statue on the square come down? How many white employees at the courthouse will be fired? Will taxes skyrocket? Will whites be ignored when services—roads or sewer line hookups or fire hydrants—are disbursed? In short, will blacks treat whites with the same hostility and disregard with which they were treated for generations? All those questions and more were on the minds of Edgefield County whites on October 2, 1984, when Willie Bright, Sara Williams, and Albert Talbot won the Democratic primary, ensuring their election in November to the Edgefield County Council.

That the transition would be tense was probably ensured seven days later when the all-white, outgoing commission decided to give H. O. "Butch" Carter a two-year contract. Carter, the county administrator and a genial sort, had for twelve years occupied what many saw as the most influential post in Edgefield County. In an administrator-council form of government, Carter helped formulate many of the policies approved by council. He also decided how to carry them out. In his twelve years in the job, the council had never seen fit to give him a contract. But on October 9, there was a new political ball game, and white council members were determined to score while they were still at bat. At stake, they insisted, were loyalty and continuity—not spite. "We knew most of us were not coming back," said Councilman McBride. "They felt that somebody needed to be there who would add continuity."

Willie Bright saw the matter differently. He had been in the audience on the night of October 9, hoping to soak up some techniques and learn about his new job. When the council went into executive session at the close of the meeting, he had no idea that anything of interest was afoot. It was mid-December before the future council chairman discovered what had happened behind those closed doors. When he heard about Carter's contract, Bright was furious. He decided to respond in kind.

The first meeting of the new council, traditionally no more than a swearing in, was scheduled for New Year's Day. Bright sent notices of the time to Mims and McBride by registered mail. When the two white members arrived, they found a courtroom packed with blacks and a council majority determined to fire both Carter and the longtime county attorney, Charles Coleman. A meeting Mims and McBride had expected to be a brief interlude in a day of television parades and football bowl games was suddenly transformed into a fiery inaugural, stretching well into the afternoon. According to the next issue of Edgefield's *Citizen News,* Lovick Mims put up a valiant, if impromptu, fight. Black council members would not budge.

"You're setting a bad tone for the conduct of the business of Edgefield County, and if you keep on, you're going to polarize the county even further than it is now," warned Mims.

"The people have elected us to do a job and we should do it," replied Williams.

Mims objected that Butch Carter would almost certainly go to court over the canceled contract. The firing might wind up costing the county $75,000 to $80,000, he said.

It was Carter and the old council members who would be responsible if that occurred, the black members replied.

The county attorney was involved in ongoing litigation; his continued presence was essential, pleaded Mims.

"From here on out, I am responsible," countered Bright.

When the vote came, Carter was fired three to two. The tally on the county attorney was four to zero, with Mims abstaining.

If the first council meeting was racially polarizing, the next one was equally so. After a more than two-hour closed session, the council hired Tom McCain to replace Carter as county administrator. The move was akin to installing a conquering general as the governor of a defeated province. For more than a decade, McCain had been at the forefront of lawsuits aimed at desegregating institutions from local juries to Strom Thurmond High School to the county council. A soft-spoken educator with a master's degree in math education from the University of Georgia and a Ph.D. in educational administration from Ohio State University, McCain hardly fit the mold of a firebrand radical. But for many Edgefield County whites, his name was synonymous with racial strife in the county. "If he were a white man, I think he'd be Grand Dragon of the Ku Klux Klan," the fired county attorney, Coleman, once said with disdain.

What irritated whites even more was that the black majority hiked the administrator's salary $6,000 in hiring McCain. And to make matters worse, McCain's attorneys in the voting rights litigation announced that they were seeking $481,000 in legal fees from the county. The sum was almost one-fourth of Edgefield County's $2.1-million annual budget. "He's the one that's going to cost the county all the lawyers' fees, and he's the one that's going to be signing the check," complained F. Charles Lucas, a local businessman and town council member in Johnston, one of Edgefield County's two major towns.

Having carried out the courthouse coup, both McCain and the black majority seemed determined in the weeks that followed to quiet the storm, to walk softly. One employee, the county's purchasing agent, quit in protest over the Carter firing. Other whites grumbled but stayed put. In his first months in office, McCain hired seven people. Three were white and four were black. Hirings broke a long-standing color barrier in two offices, including the tax assessor's where no black had worked in the twentieth century. There was nothing remotely akin, however, to the wholesale turnover whites had feared. "Having come into this position with such controversy, I have chosen not to try to go overboard to usher in a number of blacks," said McCain.

Still, undercurrents suggested that the transfer of political power into black hands might have significant ramifications. McCain began to talk quietly about better controlling the thousands of migrant workers who are driven or hitchhike into the county each spring and summer to work for influential white peach growers. He hinted at displeasure over use of a community development block grant to bolster a dying, white-owned local industry. And in the May 7 meeting, on a matter as seemingly routine as fire protection, council members showed the potential for racial division. "I think it's going to be a difficult transition; you've got a good example here tonight," concluded Ken Kaltz, general manager of a local manufacturing plant, at the end of the troubled May council session.

The county undergoing that change is typical of rural South Carolina in some ways, unique in others. Leading in from Columbia to the north, Aiken to the east, and Augusta to the south, Edgefield County's roads are bordered by flat fields of peach trees, nestled in light, sand-colored soil. There is an aura of Old South romance and bygone days in the white-columned antebellum mansions, set far back from the highway and glimpsed through deep lawns of pine trees and spreading boxwoods. Time hangs suspended, too, over the unpainted shanties still startlingly visible amid new brick ranchers and renovated farmhouses. There are churches with names like Mt. Canaan, Philippi, and Macedonia. Car windows are plastered with Clemson tiger paws or University of South Carolina decals. Billboards promote Miss Debbie's Nursery School or admonish that "God is Good. He Gave Us Mothers."

The county's largest towns—Edgefield and Johnston—are picture-book studies in southern ambience and charm. Major streets are lined with two-story frame houses, their wide verandas made inviting with porch swings and rocking chairs or flower boxes full of geraniums and pansies. There are antique shops and small dry-goods stores, and such historic touchstones as the Plantation House Inn or the century-old corner grocery on the square in Edgefield. The county's fascination with its own history is underscored by a sign outside the grocery. Edgefield, it boasts, has produced "more Dashing, Brilliant, Romantic Figures, Statesmen, Orators, Soldiers, Adventurers and Daredevils than any other county of South Carolina, if not of any rural county in America."

Clearly, the most revered of the modern lot is Strom Thurmond. Thurmond was born on a December day in 1902 in a rambling, gray-shingled house on the Columbia highway. His father was a local lawyer whose clients included "Pitchfork" Ben Tillman. The younger Thurmond launched his political career in 1929 as Edgefield's superintendent of education. He proceeded to become a state senator, a circuit court judge, governor, and U.S. senator. When local citizens decided to honor Thurmond with a statue, they chose to depict him as a country lawyer. In sculpture, he is wearing a rumpled suit. His shoes are worn and cracked. Age lines show in his forehead, and his expression is benevolent, wise. Whites in Edgefield County say that is the Strom Thurmond they know. "He was certainly a segregationist. So was everybody else in the South," said Rainsford, the local newspaper publisher. "But he has made a metamorphosis."

Blacks have a different view. Thurmond may have dealt fairly with individual people, they agree. But the more critical test, in their view, is one's stand on broad institutional and social questions. The bottom line, said McCain, is that "I don't think Strom will ever see blacks as equals."

If there are varying opinions, black and white, of Strom Thurmond, there are also racially divided views of Edgefield County. A few blocks from picturesque, postcard settings are shacks occupied by black families still mired in the depressing poverty of years past. Barefoot children in classic poses stare through ripped screen doors or romp in dirt yards littered with broken toys and rusting automobiles. In 1980, whites earned $6,178 per capita in Edgefield County; blacks earned $3,294.[4] One of the most shocking examples of the disparity is on Brooks Street in Edgefield. There, only an old railroad bridge and a few hundred yards separate lovely colonial homes—including one once occupied by U.S. representative Butler Derrick—from destitution. In the early 1980s, a $1.8-million community development block grant was awarded to help clean up that poor black area, known as the Rosa Hill section of town. About half of the money was spent improving roads and sewer lines, upgrading an old gymnasium and face-lifting about twenty homes. But, in what remained a sore point with many local blacks, the rest of the money was diverted to help shore up an ailing industry. McCain maintained that had blacks held office at the time of the financial transfer, there at least would have been public debate about derailing the Rosa Hill project.

Generally, whites describe race relations in Edgefield County as good. Blacks are more wary. The divided views are similar to those recorded by Donald R. Matthews and James W. Prothro in a mammoth 1966 study of southern black voters. "Most whites . . . feel quite good about race relations in their home towns," Matthews and Prothro wrote. "Over one-third of all southern whites gave race relations a 'io' on a scale of 1-10. Negroes take a far dimmer view of community relations; their modal rating was '5.' "[5]

For Edgefield whites, "good" race relations appears to mean an absence of overt tension, general cordiality, and nonviolence. "The black people and the white people in Edgefield grew up together. They get along fine. They've never had any race problems. And if these agitators will let the people alone, they will never have any," said Senator Thurmond a few years before the first blacks were elected to the county council.[6] Blacks, meanwhile, are more concerned with an overall economic and social structure that they deem unfair. Bright voiced that view. "This is a hard county, but its not like an Alabama county," he said. "You don't have Bull Connor people. They don't knock you over the head, but they still control you. They do it with an ink pen, not a stick."

A century ago in Edgefield County, force was in vogue. In the mid-1870s, the local senator, state representative, clerk of the court, school commissioner, and probate judge were all black. The demise of that brief era was signaled in the 1876 elections, shortly before Reconstruction ended and federal troops were withdrawn from the South. Local whites devised the "Edgefield Plan," in which every Democrat was instructed to "feel honor bound to control the vote of at least one Negro, by intimidation, purchase," or some other device.[7] Several hundred armed whites fulfilled their part of the bargain by seizing two polling places—the Masonic Hall and the courthouse in Edgefield—and refusing to let blacks vote. Rifle and sabre clubs, described by one writer as a "terrorist arm of the Democratic Party," also flourished during that era. Ben Tillman was captain of the local club in 1873 when two of his men shot the black state senator from neighboring Barnwell in the head. When Tillman was elected governor in 1890, he pushed through more permanent devices to block black voting.[8] In a crowning touch, the legislature simply abolished local elected governments. Local commissioners thereafter were appointed by the governor, and the legislature controlled local purse strings. Black political involvement was crushed.

By the 1970s and 1980s, the era of race-baiting terrorism was long over. In its place was a mutually accepted separation of the races. In Edgefield County, blacks and whites maintained separate American Legion posts. The Pine Ridge Country Club and Golf Course had only white members. Churches were racially segregated, as was most social life. Still, there were signs of change. Wardlaw Academy, founded in response to public school integration in 1970, was alive but not flourishing. In 1985 the school— named for an Edgefield native who wrote the Articles of Secession, declaring the South's independence from the federal union—had fewer students than in its early years. Meanwhile, the public schools, unlike those in many Deep South communities, had retained substantial white support. In the fall of 1984, 34 percent of the 3,564 students were white. At Strom Thurmond High, the 1984–85 student body president and secretary were white; the vice-president and treasurer were black.

Despite progress, some blacks believed they saw ongoing racism in small incidents, like an episode involving the Johnston police force. When the police chief was hospitalized, the town council tapped a white deputy, rather than one of two blacks with longer tenure, to fill in for him. Blacks also complained that local newspaper coverage of the county council had become far more intense than when whites were in charge. And they believed the school board trustees had not tried hard enough to narrow the black-white gap in school hiring. In the 1984-85 school year, there were almost twice as many white teachers and administrators as black. The school board included six whites and one black member, and a lawsuit aimed at changing that mix was making its way through the courts.

Surprisingly, McCain as county administrator sided with those whites who said race relations in Edgefield County were basically good. "You hear talk about the county being polarized. There's no truth to that at all," he said. Seated in his county office, outfitted in a three-piece gray suit and a starched white shirt, McCain seemed a model of administrative efficiency. His bearing was almost militarily erect; his voice, quick, high-pitched and friendly. That day, memories of lawsuits and campaign strategies were behind him. Road paving requests, a county dental plan, and reports on revenue sharing and budgets crowded his desk. "People in this county have respect for each other," he said.

The setting and the remarks seemed a world apart from the day in 1981 when McCain stood before the Judiciary Committee of the U.S. House of Representatives and testified: "The Edgefield County power structure has used every trick possible to keep blacks from participating in the political process. These range from offering bribes to outright refusal to abide by the law."[9]

Tom McCain was in the sixth grade in 1952 when his family moved to a small black community in the south end of Edgefield County. He was quiet and only marginally studious. There was little to suggest that twenty-five years later, he would become a grass-roots political hero who would sue and be sued for hundreds of thousands of dollars, would give up job opportunities in Ohio and Atlanta to stay in a poor rural county, and would push to the Supreme Court and the halls of Congress in pursuit of his personal dream.

His father, John McCain, was a farmer and textile worker who spent his days opening bales of cotton at a plant in Augusta and then went home at night to farm the fifty-four acres he saved for years to buy. At seventy-nine, the elder McCain would boast: "I worked twenty-four years at one plant, and I didn't miss a payday. I farmed at night, and I didn't miss a crop." Emma McCain, meanwhile, busied herself raising eight children. Tom was fourth from the oldest, and his parents' chief memory is that he stayed out of trouble, rarely needing a swat from the hackberry switch that his father kept handy and showing none of the devilry of a brother who later became a preacher.

As their son evolved into a civil rights activist, seeming to challenge at every turn the white power structure of Edgefield County, the McCains sometimes wondered if he was following the right course. They feared for his safety. And his father, who at peak was bringing home about $55 a week, was stunned when seven school board trustees in the mid-1970s sued his son for a combined $245,000. McCain, in a pamphlet distributed throughout the county, had accused the board of lying and filing false papers with federal officials, and the trustees filed suit in protest. "I thought that lawsuit was an awful thing. If he had to go up against that, he'd be in trouble for the rest of his life," John McCain said. The lawsuit was later settled, without payment, out of court.

For Tom McCain, the long and sometimes tortuous path of political involvement had begun one night in 1969. By then, McCain had completed his master's degree and was teaching at Paine College. At church one evening, he heard about a meeting called by the school trustees to discuss desegregation of Edgefield County schools. He decided to attend. A meeting for white parents had been held the previous week. This session was only for blacks. At issue was federal insistence that Edgefield come up with a more integrated school system than the current freedom-of-choice plan had produced. When the meeting began, McCain recalled, "the auditorium was full of people. I sat and listened to the discussion. The school board was all white. The board said they'd gotten a letter from HEW [the Department of Health, Education and Welfare], and they were ordered to make a change. They didn't know exactly how they were going to do it. One parent asked, 'How will we know what the plan is?' The superintendent said, 'We'll work with HEW, and if a plan is approved, we'll call another meeting to tell you.'

"Something grabbed hold of me and literally picked me up on my feet. I was thinking, 'This board will go to Washington. They'll decide something affecting us. And then, they'll come back and tell us what happened.' Before I realized what I was doing, I was halfway up to the front. I asked the superintendent if I could have the microphone. He didn't know what I had in mind, and he gave it to me. I told the parents the previous statement was reason enough for the black parents to become organized. I said there was an all-white school board, and we should have a black person on the school board. I said we should organize and demand that we participate." McCain's actions were not premeditated, he said.

"Something came into that auditorium, and when I found out what I was doing, I was already halfway down to the front."

At federal insistence, the trustees prepared for full-scale school integration in the fall of 1970. School opened on schedule, but at Strom Thurmond High, not all was well. By mid-September, black members of the football team, band, and cheerleading squad were boycotting games in protest of the high school's name, its nickname ("The Rebels"), its fight song ("Dixie"), and the practice of waving the Confederate flag at school functions. McCain and others filed a lawsuit citing those trappings as "badges and indicia of slavery and second-class citizenship of Negroes." When seventy-five students staged a walkout in October, a local judge issued a restraining order against McCain and other plaintiffs. Finally, a compromise was reached. The name and nickname remained. The fight song and Confederate flag were dropped.

From there, McCain progressed to other complaints. He led successful lawsuits challenging the practices of excluding blacks from grand jury service and separating prisoners on the local chain gang by race. Then in 1974, after an unsuccessful bid for election to the county council, McCain and two other blacks filed a federal lawsuit charging that Edgefield County's at-large election plan unconstitutionally weakened the voting strength of blacks. Judge Robert F. Chapman of the U.S. District Court was named to hear the case. Chapman was a partner in a prosperous Spartanburg firm when he was tapped by the Nixon administration for the federal judiciary. Conservative, Presbyterian, a former chairman of the South Carolina Republican Party, Chapman was regarded by McCain's lawyers as unlikely to issue a favorable ruling. Chapman heard the case in late 1975, but a series of complications delayed his order until April 1980. Armand Derfner, a former Washington, D.C., attorney who specializes in voting rights cases, recalled his shock the day Chapman's order arrived by mail. Opening it, Derfner discovered that Edgefield County blacks had won the case. "I have never been more surprised in my life as a lawyer," he said. "I almost cried. I guess Chapman just couldn't believe the let-it-all-hang-out discrimination." Derfner's elation was to prove short lived.

Chapman's order suggested that he was, indeed, dismayed by conditions in Edgefield County. He traced a pattern of electoral exclusion of blacks. Until a Fourth Circuit ruling in 1948, Chapman wrote, blacks had not been allowed to vote in the Democratic primary in South Carolina, even though winning the primary was tantamount to election. Even after the decision, he noted, Edgefield blacks found it difficult to register, and threats were made against some who did. Until 1970, no black had served as a precinct election official, and even after that, inclusion was slight. Not a single black person had won office in a contested election, even though the county in 1970 was more than 50 percent black. Of 117 precincts, eight had never had a black poll worker. Only when the trial was about to begin did county officials start to hire blacks in any appreciable numbers. Even then, black employees were concentrated in low-wage jobs. Few blacks were appointed to the county's boards and commissions. And racial bloc voting by whites, Chapman said, was "on a scale that this court has never before witnessed."[10]

He cited an example. In 1974 Tom McCain had run for the county council and George Brightharp, another Edgefield black man, sought a seat in the state House of Representatives. The men, Chapman noted, had very different personalities and backgrounds. McCain was an activist; Brightharp was not. "These differences were wholly outweighed by the one common characteristic shared by McCain and Brightharp—their race," the judge concluded. In five mostly white precincts, the men received identical votes, and in six others, their tallies were separated by three votes or less.

Chapman went on to rebut those who said the legal system should go no further than guaranteeing the right to cast a ballot. In an opinion that explained the rationale of the Voting Rights Act, he wrote:

> Participation in the election process does not mean simply the elimination of legal, formal or official barriers. The standard is whether the electoral system . . . tends to make it more difficult for blacks to participate with full effectiveness in the election process and to have their votes fully effective and equal to those of whites. Blacks have no right to elect any particular candidate or number of candidates, but the law requires that black voters and candidates have a fair chance of being successful in elections. . . .
>
> If black candidates lose in the normal give-and-take of the

political arena, then the courts may not interfere. And under
no theory of the law can a court direct a white to vote for a
black or a black to vote for a white. However, if there is proof,
and there is ample proof in this case, that the black candidates tend to lose not on their merits but solely because of
their race, then the courts can only find that the black voting
strength has been diluted under the system and declare the
same unconstitutional.[11]

Chapman did precisely that. His ruling was issued on April 17.
Five days later, on April 22, the Supreme Court stunned civil
rights activists across the nation. Ruling in the case of *Mobile v.
Bolden,* the court said, in effect, that it was not enough for plaintiffs to show that a particular election system "resulted" in discrimination against blacks. What must also be shown, the court
said, was that those who devised the election plan had "intended"
to discriminate. The ruling had immediate implications for
McCain v. Lybrand. Chapman was convinced that Edgefield
County's at-large election system resulted in discrimination. But
the testimony had not shown that the authors of the plan intended
to discriminate. On August 11, Chapman vacated his earlier order.
Victory, so elusive to Edgefield blacks, had evaded their grasp
once more.

Faced with the difficulty of meeting the Supreme Court's *Mobile v. Bolden* standard, McCain and his lawyers decided to opt
for a new tack. Under the Voting Rights Act, any election changes
—no matter how minute—must be approved by the Justice Department. But a 1966 shift from gubernatorial appointment to
election of local commissioners was never submitted for approval.
McCain and his lawyers argued that Edgefield County's at-large
system should be thrown out on those grounds. A three-judge
panel from the Fourth Circuit ruled three to zero against them.
But on February 21, 1984, a unanimous Supreme Court reversed
the lower court decision. The justices found the 1966 filing omis-
sion illegal, in effect invalidating the county's seventeen-year-old,
at-large voting plan. The Supreme Court returned the case to a
federal district court judge in Greenville, directing that a new
election plan be drawn. On July 11, Judge William W. Wilkins, Jr.,
a former legal assistant to Senator Thurmond, ordered into place

a single-member district plan. Two of the new districts had a significant white majority and two a substantial black majority. The fifth had slightly more black than white residents, but whites held the edge among voters.

By 1984 there were 4,080 registered blacks and 4,568 registered whites in Edgefield County. Black registration had jumped from 270 in 1960 to 1,207 in 1968 and 3,507 in 1980.[12] With the improved showing, blacks expected easily to win the two majority-black districts on the newly formed council. But only in the final days before the primary did a few leaders begin to suspect that they might also pick up a third seat. Among the five districts, the narrowest black-white split was in Johnston. Fifty-four percent of the residents in that district were black, but among those old enough to vote, whites had a slight majority. Black candidates seldom win in such districts. Making a black victory seem even more unlikely was the fact that the incumbent white candidate was Charles Lybrand, longtime chairman of the Edgefield County Council. The portly operator of a dry goods store on Johnston's main street, Lybrand was part of the ruling clique that had worked to keep control in white hands. He was no favorite of local blacks. And, as they were to learn, he was also a man who had made a few white enemies in more than a decade of wielding power.

Black leaders turned for their candidate to Sara Williams. Known locally as "Miz Sara," Williams and her husband, who had died in 1980, were among the most prosperous of the county's black citizens. At one time, they owned a shoe store, a car wash, a laundromat, and a dry cleaners. Williams' comfortable brick home, with its backyard rose garden, its spacious kitchen, and double carport, testified to their success. A teacher for twenty-eight years, Williams had a public presence that was unassuming and solicitous. She also had a strong, unalterable sense of pride. Her father, a sharecropper who had learned to read from his only book—Webster's blue-backed speller—had decreed that his children would not cook or clean, iron or sew in a white person's house. "We worked real hard," she recalled, "but for ourselves."

When she agreed to run for county council, Williams did not know if she could win. She did know there was some disgruntlement with the way the county was being run. And she was mildly surprised when a few whites, as well as blacks, began to tell her of their problems in getting services. As election day approached, black leaders mounted a voter registration drive that proved more successful than expected, and they began to hear rumors that some whites planned to back Williams or stay home on election day. It was a startling development. "We had never planned to run this county to be frank with you," said Bright. "We didn't think we had enough people registered."

He was wrong. On election day, Williams polled 598 votes to Lybrand's 549. Nathaniel Jackson, head of the local NAACP, described the jubilation as he drove through Johnston the next day. "People would just throw up their hands, a V for victory. It made me feel real good after all we'd gone through," he said. "It made me proud of Dr. McCain. He had donated ten years of his life to that cause. This was a trophy that we handed to him."

On an overcast spring day some months later, Tom McCain sat in the rear of a battered, dirt-streaked Chevrolet Impala and toured the rutted backroads of Edgefield County. Normally, McCain drove his own silver LTD, but this day, Jimmy Fegin, the young white county road supervisor, was giving his new boss a tour of unpaved roads. Later, they would work with the council to develop paving recommendations. There are hundreds of miles of dirt roads in Edgefield County. The state had allotted money to pave 2.5 miles worth. For a county administrator, the issue posed a no-win proposition. A few people would wind up happy; dozens more would not. Yet McCain seemed content. He had, after all, spent a decade seeking the chance to make decisions such as this. Surveying the countryside, he fired questions at Fegin:

"Whose road is that, Jimmy? Who put the gravel on it?"

"How many families on this road?"

"Look, Jimmy, they've moved that garbage container. Why do we have three empty cans and one running over?"

A lady drove up to empty her garbage. McCain watched as intently as a salesman during a product demonstration. "We do provide a service," he concluded, satisfied as she drove away.

Along the route, McCain pointed out county landmarks. Outside Edgefield, a cinder-block, Spanish-style building with bars on the windows stirred his memory. Once, before a McCain lawsuit stopped the practice, the building had housed the county's all-black chain gang. "It was a dungeon," he said. By the 1980s, that grim past was all but forgotten. The county road crew used the building for a shelter on rainy days. Down another highway was Strom Thurmond High. Drill team tryouts were in progress, and the parking lot was peppered with youngsters, black and white.

Clearly, Edgefield County already bore the mark of Tom McCain. Six months after the election of a black-majority council, the county remained poised to see how deep his scalpel would cut. Some of the goals were concrete, others more general. He was determined, for instance, to foster a new equity in county services, and in numerous ways—from hiring at the courthouse to awarding of county contracts—he hoped government in Edgefield County would come to reflect more nearly the county's racial makeup, half black, half white.

There were indications that change would not come automatically, however. The episode involving the firefighting contracts had shown already that blacks had much to learn and that whites still influenced policy, even if they did not control it. All in all, concluded state representative Joe Anderson, a young, white Edgefield lawyer, "I would say a lot of white people have already found the walls aren't tumbling down. I also think some blacks are going to find things won't get better overnight."

Anderson's words proved prophetic. Two years later, Johnston whites turned out in force and elected a white industrial relations specialist to replace Sara Williams. The new council, took office in January 1987, with a three-to-two white majority. Once again, racial politics had turned the tide in Edgefield County. No one predicted a return to the past, however. The federal courts had established the right of Edgefield blacks to hold office, and two years' experience had cemented that reality in the minds of both blacks and whites. Black council members would continue in office. Black workers at the courthouse would remain. The county's first black-majority government had not met all its goals. But it had improved some services, while holding the line on taxes. That was no small feat. Many whites were surprised at and applauded the fiscal conservatism blacks had displayed. Even the man who replaced Williams reflected the changing times. He was not of the mold of a Charles Lybrand, and blacks expected to work with him. "Those days are gone," concluded Tom McCain.

Councilman McBride spoke of an even more startling change among his fellow whites. Whites might have a majority on the new council, but when members met to reorganize, they re-elected Willie Bright to lead them. Tom McCain was retained as well. In the past two years, McBride said, blacks and whites had begun to regard each other as individuals. "To start with, I didn't know them, and they didn't know us. I didn't trust them, and they didn't trust us," he said. But gradually, on most issues, they discovered a common bond—an interest in the welfare of Edgefield County and the progress of its people. The concerns of blacks and whites, they found, were not so dissimilar as each side had once believed.

In Edgefield County, the transition—not quite as blacks envisioned it, or whites either—had passed.

4. ATLANTA
The Mecca

THE ATLANTA of *Gone with the Wind* is, of course, an Atlanta that never truly was. By the 1980s, Margaret Mitchell's portrait had become as far removed from reality as a Disney fantasy. Aside from tourist attractions like Cyclorama, featuring the Battle of Atlanta, and the memorial carvings on Stone Mountain, the Old South images were meaningless to this glitzy and often complicated Sun Belt boomtown.

Reality in modern-day Atlanta is the concrete and glass shafts of the Omni International, a complex of office towers, hotel, restaurants, and sundry shops, rising like sleek cylinders amid the lavish hotels and high-rise office buildings that form downtown. There, David Franklin, an exuberant, cherub-cheeked lawyer and part-time political consultant, tilted backward in a cushioned desk chair and, with a rush of verbal energy, explained the nuances of local politics. To Franklin, who managed the 1973 campaign of Atlanta's first black mayor, there is, for instance, nothing startling in the fact that two brothers in the 1960s' civil rights movement, state senator Julian Bond and Atlanta councilman John Lewis, were vying in 1986 for the same congressional seat. Political competition among black Atlantans is the norm. In this sophisticated setting, black-on-black contests are no more surprising than, say, Franklin's pedigreed roots. Franklin's great-great-grandfather founded Paine College in Augusta and spoke to audiences in England. His grandfather was the first black member of the Presbyterian Board of Missions. Even in the era depicted by *Gone with the Wind,* Franklin's family tree included educated professionals. Among Atlanta blacks, such roots are not unique.

A visit to the midtown home of Stoney Cooks, a wiry, serious black man who is Mayor Andrew Young's closest friend and adviser, also offers an updated view of Atlanta. Cooks grew up in urban poverty. He came to Atlanta through the civil rights movement, joined forces with Young in the Southern Christian Leadership Conference, and by the mid-1980s had completed the transition to middle-class affluence. Today, telephone calls from across the city and around the globe pour into the sitting room where Cooks works, surrounded by familiar touchstones—an array of computer equipment, a collection of bold African art, a whimsical etching of Woody Allen. For Cooks, there are Third World conferences to plan in Tunisia and Atlanta. There are business deals to handle for Young. And there are dozens of conversations with city employees, community activists, and reporters who recognize Cook's political savvy. In Atlanta, Cook's saga of upward mobility is—for hundreds of young, black professionals—the norm.

Modern Atlanta is characterized by the free-for-all bartering and bickering that defines city council politics and gives biweekly council sessions the flavor of a Middle Eastern marketplace. Eleven blacks and seven whites sat on the eighteen-member body in 1986, and amazingly, their votes rarely separated along racial lines. To a degree seldom seen in biracial American politics, coalitions are based on common interests, not color. Nor does similar pigmentation necessarily breed camaraderie. When Mayor Young took staff members to the 1984 Democratic convention at taxpayers' expense, it was Ira Jackson, the black chairman of the council's finance committee, not a white, who called for an investigation and fumed to local newspapers: "I don't think it's right." Atlanta has a black power structure diverse enough to encompass City Council President Marvin Arrington, a child of Atlanta's black ghetto who escaped to become a shoot-from-the-hip, Emory-educated lawyer; Fulton County Commission Chairman Michael Lomax, a favorite of the city's artsy, wine-and-cheese set; Councilman Hosea Williams, the still-flammable street radical of the 1960s; and Andy Young, the ethereal minister and Martin Luther King disciple who in the 1980s has made it OK for prominent blacks to embrace capitalism.

The reality of Atlanta is also the gleaming glass and marble office building on Auburn Avenue that houses the Atlanta Life Insurance Company, reported in 1985 to have the highest net earnings of any black business in the nation. It is the H. J. Russell Construction Company, rated by *Black Enterprise* magazine as the country's third largest black business. It is dozens of black-owned firms that take soil borings, draw architectural plans, build airports, and bid on almost every type of city contract. And reality is the "minority studies" section in a crowded bookstore at the corner of Peachtree and Marietta streets in downtown Atlanta. The books in that area deal primarily with Arabs and Jews. There are no volumes about black history or black politics—or blacks, period. That is appropriate, for in this southeastern commercial and financial hub, blacks are neither a numerical nor political minority. Economically, they may still lag behind whites, but to a degree unparalleled anywhere in the nation, black people influence and even control the rhythms of life in Atlanta. "It's the mecca," said Geraldine Thompson, a top aide in the 1973–81 administration of Maynard Jackson, the South's first prominent black mayor of the twentieth century.

From Tupelo, Mississippi, and Andalusia, Alabama, from Raleigh, North Carolina, and Alexandria, Louisiana, they come—young black men and women drawn by the rich academic tradition of the Atlanta University Center, minority go-getters lured by the promise of corporate opportunities, blacks of all ages attracted by the Martin Luther King Center for Non-Violent Social Change and the history it represents. What they find in Atlanta is a bustling core city of 424,000 people, two-thirds of whom are black, surrounded by a suburban ring that boosts the metropolitan population beyond 2 million. Futuristic downtown hotels and sprawling complexes like the Peachtree Center suggest a prosperity that Chamber of Commerce statistics confirm. All but a few dozen of the nation's Fortune 500 companies have offices in Atlanta. Twenty-seven foreign banks conduct business in the city. Ten international airlines shuttle passengers to Japan, Europe, and the Caribbean. The Hartsfield International Airport is the world's second busiest. The number of new jobs created in the area in 1984 —100,000—was surpassed only by Phoenix nationwide. And Atlanta regularly leads the southeast in such prime indicators of economic health as retail sales, housing starts, and commercial construction.

More important to those blacks and whites who view Atlanta as a mecca of racial harmony, blacks share in the spoils. The wealth of black political talent in the city makes it the unofficial capital of American black politics. Here, the notion of a dominant black leader controlling a willing black electorate is totally foreign. Blacks may coalesce around a single black candidate in a critical contest, say for mayor, but in day-to-day dealings, factionalism among blacks is as public and widespread as political divisions among whites in most other cities. Such normalcy is an ongoing witness to the triumph of civil rights forces in this city. Economically, too, Atlanta is the model to which blacks throughout the South aspire. For the upwardly mobile, it is a city of promise in which the mayoral administrations of Maynard Jackson and Andy Young have set the economic pace. In 1973, the year Jackson was elected, a fraction of 1 percent of the city's business went to minority firms. By 1984, the figure had soared to 31 percent, putting millions into the pockets of black businessmen.[1] Seven of *Black Enterprise* magazine's top one hundred black firms in 1985 were located in metropolitan Atlanta; nationwide, only Chicago did as well. And the percentage of black Atlantans earning more than $50,000 a year in 1980 outdistanced the figure in other southern cities, including Birmingham, Charlotte, New Orleans, Charleston, and Jackson.[2]

The result, said Bill Campbell, is that scores of young black urban professionals enjoy the good life in Atlanta. Campbell is among them. The only black member of a prosperous six-person law firm, he came to the city by way of Vanderbilt University and Duke University Law School. In an attractively decorated downtown office, Campbell sat surrounded by photos of his wife and young son, framed citations, and memorabilia from the city council, on which he serves. "For a young person with something on the ball, there's only one place in America, and that's Atlanta," he noted.

It is a sentiment echoed by Michael Lomax, a slender, tweedy black academician who teaches English at Spelman College. Lomax also chairs the majority-white commission in Fulton County, where Atlanta is located. As cultural affairs director for the city

in the 1970s, Lomax developed a strong white following. His tastes
—the opera, gourmet food, Gary Hart for president—defy racial
stereotype. "Atlanta is the city in the nation where black people
have the most political and economic power and where they are
central to the decisions that are made," said Lomax, during a
break in a round of morning committee meetings. But he added
a critical caveat: "It's the city of opportunity for black people who
can immediately access it. To do that, you've got to have a professional degree. Atlanta is not a mecca for low-income people."

There is, as Lomax suggested, another reality in Atlanta, and
it is uglier than the civic boosters—black or white—generally
allow. There are in this mecca thousands of poor people, the bulk
of them black. Atlanta may boast of having many of the wealthiest
black residents in the South, but it is also home to many of the
poorest. One of every three black families lives in poverty; only
one of fourteen white families suffers similar misfortune. Six percent of the city's black households had income of more than
$35,000 annually in 1980, but a dispiriting 25 percent existed on
less than $5,000.[3] Black and white leaders have a longer, more
solid tradition of interaction and accommodation than in perhaps
any other southern city. But racial confrontation—whether over
mayoral appointments, the makeup of the police department, or
the lineup of guest performers at a summer concert series—never
seems far from the surface. Nor do a variety of measures, from
housing patterns to public school attendance, bear out the claim
that this is a city of rare racial tolerance.

When Karl Taeuber, a University of Wisconsin sociologist,
measured racial residential segregation in twenty-eight cities in
1980, he found only four cities with more segregated housing than
Atlanta.[4] The figures were similar in 1970. Taeuber's conclusion?
"I've always been puzzled by Atlanta," he said. "The city has such
a great reputation . . . all the civil rights leaders. It's almost as if
they decided not to rock the boat at home." Whites are also
becoming increasingly isolated from city schools. In the 1969–70
school year, 36 percent of Atlanta's public school students were
white. By the 1985–86 term, the figure had dwindled to a mere 7
percent. Prestigious social clubs like the Piedmont Driving Club
still have not abandoned all-white membership policies. And as
late as 1979, when the Community Relations Commission

surveyed fifty-three major white-owned corporations, they found only 3 blacks among 480 board members.[5]

A 1985 study by Georgia State University sociologist Charles Jaret put such statistics in perspective. Jaret compared income, education, and employment levels among blacks in almost four dozen metropolitan areas, including Atlanta. Census data, he concluded, simply do not support the argument that blacks are living better in Atlanta than anywhere else.[6] Paradoxically, Jaret also found that blacks were migrating more rapidly to Atlanta than to any other major metropolitan area. Clearly, there is about this city a mystique, a sense of promise and an expectation that the promise will be fulfilled. It was in Atlanta in the early 1960s, at a time when chaos ruled all around, that pragmatic white business leaders and a sophisticated black elite sat down and worked out an agreement for peaceful desegregation of public facilities. It was here that Maynard Jackson—an eloquent, French-speaking, three-hundred-pound bull of a man—broke the psychological barrier against electing a southern black to run a major city. Here, too, by sheer force of personality, Jackson defied insult and outrage to demand a greater economic role for the city's black residents. And it was here that Andrew Young spawned an image of an international city, a haven not only for America's black residents, but a capital of Third World interests. This is, as scores of residents readily attest, no utopia. Racial problems are real and plentiful. But after two decades of black influence in southern politics, Atlanta is still the city that leads the way, that defines the possibilities and that—in part, because of its advancement—most clearly illustrates the stubborn persistence of inequality.

"God must have loved us better than he did anybody else in the South," said Dan Sweat, the white president of a prominent downtown business association, Central Atlanta Progress (CAP). Searching for an explanation of what makes Atlanta different, Sweat added: "He put the white ones here and the black ones here. There are very few cities yet that have any significant black leadership. That cast us in a different light than any other southern city." How that came about was a product of traditions that began in the nineteenth century and continued into the twentieth.

The birth of this southern metropolis came in 1837. A spirited, frontier town—first called Terminus, then Marthasville, then

Atlanta—sprang up at the end of a railroad line running out of Chattanooga into the red clay reaches of north Georgia. Within a few years, other rail lines had formed a juncture at the site, and Atlanta's future as a transportation center for the southeast had been ordained. From the start, race figured in a variety of ways in the city's history. The town's early years were marred by the Civil War battle of Atlanta, a bloody confrontation in which the Confederacy lost some eight thousand men. A few years later, Atlanta became the state capital when hotel owners in Milledgeville, then the capital, refused to rent rooms to black delegates to a constitutional convention. By 1895, Atlanta had gained enough postwar vitality to host a regional extravaganza known as the Cotton States and International Exposition. The celebration helped establish Atlanta's credentials as the leader of a New South and was an early example of the determination of city fathers to present a forward-thinking image to the nation. The exposition also spotlighted a former slave named Booker T. Washington, who was chosen to speak at the dedication of a pavilion honoring black progress. In a now famous speech, Washington urged blacks to abandon notions of social equality and to forgo "artificial forcing" of privileges that, he argued, could come only through hard work.

During the late nineteenth century, Atlanta's black residents began establishing the colleges and businesses that would later distinguish their community. In 1867, as the city was emerging from the ruin of the Civil War, the American Missionary Society donated $350 for the purchase of an old boxcar, which became the first schoolroom of Atlanta University. Eventually, that black school joined forces with Morehouse and Spelman colleges, constructing a network of red-brick buildings on a barren, wind-swept Atlanta hillside. In time, Clark College, Morris Brown College, and the Interdenominational Theological Center joined too, forming the nation's most impressive consortium of black schools. Across the years, black scholars like W.E.B. DuBois, John Hope Franklin, and Horace Mann Bond passed through the center, leaving their mark on the institutions and on Atlanta. Their classrooms were seedbeds for black achievers, and the center spawned dozens of future educators, lawmakers, scientists, judges, and ambassadors.

Meanwhile, in a city where the black population never dipped below 30 percent, black businesses were gaining a foothold. Along Auburn Avenue, tagged "Sweet Auburn," a black commercial center of small barbershops and groceries sprang up, sandwiched between the more imposing headquarters of the Atlanta Life Insurance Company and the Mutual Federal Savings and Loan Association of Atlanta. By the 1980s, Sweet Auburn had hit on hard times. Once, however, the street rang with the sounds of cash registers and the pulsating rhythms of city life. *Fortune* magazine in 1956 proclaimed it "the richest Negro street in the world," and its leading proprietors were recognized throughout Atlanta.

Enlarged photographs in a first-floor museum at Atlanta Life offer a glimpse of the cultivated existence that Atlanta's prominent black citizens enjoyed only a few decades after the Civil War. Ladies in high lace collars and silk gowns sit primly on lawn chairs; stern and well-groomed men are at their sides. The houses are large and rambling, with an aura of southern charm. The scenes are like those described by newspaper columnist Celestine Sibley who wrote in 1963 of a black world "not many white Atlantans dreamed existed . . . the great homes, the country estates, the receptions and the teas and cocktail parties, the art collections, the superb cookery and in general the taste and intelligence" of the city's first black families.[7]

It was only natural that men and women with such educational and financial advantages would also take interest in city government. In 1921, black Atlantans showed their political clout for the first time by combining to help defeat an educational bond issue that slighted black schools. The message was clear. In a city where a third or so of the population was black, a united black electorate —though small—might tip the scales of power. By the 1940s, Atlanta's white power structure and its black elite had struck up an informal alliance unique in major southern cities. Their combined ballots helped assure white businessmen of control over redneck whites, while blacks were rewarded with forward-thinking, racially moderate mayors. Control clearly belonged to the whites, however, with blacks settling for whatever concessions they could get. Well before most southern cities, Atlanta had black policemen and a black member of the board of education. Still, Atlanta entered the 1960s as an essentially segregated city in which a major determinant of the quality of life was race.

When Martin Luther King, Jr., came home to Atlanta in 1960 after gaining national attention as the leader of the Montgomery bus boycott, he found a black community strained by generational tensions. King had grown up as a child of Atlanta's secure, church-oriented, black bourgeoisie. His new role was to find a common ground between an older generation—including his father—which had tacitly agreed to peaceful and gradual desegregation and a younger audience demanding more immediate change. The critical test came soon after his arrival. A group of Atlanta University students had approached the Chamber of Commerce in the spring of 1960 to protest policies at major department stores. There were Whites Only restrooms and lunch counters and rules that prevented blacks from trying on clothes before they were purchased. The complaints led nowhere, and that fall King marched at the head of a student protest against Rich's Department Store in downtown Atlanta. The young pastor and dozens of students were eventually arrested. The city, which Mayor William B. Hartsfield had dubbed "too busy to hate," came face to face with its own prejudice. As Christmas passed and many of those arrested remained in jail, a national audience began to form. City fathers found themselves squirming in the spotlight. Atlanta's much cultivated progressive image was endangered. Action was required. Prominent storeowners, recognizing the inevitability of change, agreed to desegregate downtown stores and lunch counters. The switch, it was decided, would take place that fall, thirty days after the court-ordered integration of Atlanta schools. The delay would ease the fears of whites already agitated by the school order. Black students protested the timetable, but King held fast, and the agreement stuck.[8] The solution would be touted as yet another example of the rare accord between black and white Atlantans.

That same autumn, Atlantans elected as mayor Ivan Allen, Jr., the prosperous owner of an office supply firm and a Chamber of Commerce type who fit easily into the city's mayoral lineage of honorable and enlightened men. Allen's chief opponent was Lester Maddox, a wizened little man who ran a local fried chicken restaurant and came to the political fore as a school desegregation foe. A high school dropout, Maddox would eventually shock Georgia progressives with his election as governor, but in 1961 the alliance of white business leaders and middle-class blacks that ran

Atlanta combined to keep Maddox out of city office. Had they failed, Atlanta in the 1960s might more nearly have duplicated the strife in other southern cities. The reward for blacks was a mayor who seemed to surprise even himself as his ingrained, upper-class paternalism toward blacks evolved into deeper understanding and appreciation of their cause. Surrounding himself with racial progressives like Robert Woodruff, the renowned developer of the Atlanta-based Coca-Cola Company, Allen emerged as a prime force in keeping the racial peace in an explosive era. On his first day in office, he ordered all White and Colored signs dismantled at city hall. Later, he instructed department heads to stop advertising separately for black and white employees. He gave black policemen the authority to arrest whites. And when Atlanta University students were refused service at the city hall cafeteria, he made them his guests, ensuring that they could eat. Allen's most substantive contribution to Atlanta blacks may have been his decision—albeit a reluctant one—to testify in support of President John Kennedy's proposal for desegregating public accommodations.[9] Allen was the first southerner to lend his voice in testimony, and his courage enhanced Atlanta's national image.

In 1969, as Allen prepared to leave office, it was apparent that Atlanta's old coalition of business and black interests had fallen on hard times. That year's mayoral race was the first to be held since the Voting Rights Act had opened the door to political involvement by the black masses. At the same time, the civil rights movement had heightened black sensitivities. An alliance between wealthy whites and black voters—many of whom were economically deprived—seemed increasingly farfetched. The result was a new coalition in which blacks, liberals, and Jews elected Atlanta's first Jewish mayor, a local businessman named Sam Massell who was not part of the establishment clique. In the first two years of Massell's administration, minority hiring by the city increased 19 percent. Massell also insisted on recruiting the city's first black department heads and directors of personnel and public works. What most Atlantans remember about Sam Massell, however, is the slogan from his 1973 race against Maynard Jackson. In a desperate attempt to retain office, Massell branded Atlanta "a city too young to die." Paraphrasing the old "too busy to hate" motto, he took out newspaper ads to herald the idea that election of

Atlanta's first black mayor might poison the city's future. The attempt signaled that the city was not without racial prejudice. Massell's message could not overcome the double-barreled force of an ignited black electorate and a white business community intent on his ouster. With solid black support and an estimated 22 percent of the white vote, Jackson took the election. The old black-business coalition had reunited. This time, however, the tables were turned. Blacks—who were 54 percent of the city's population—held the upper hand, and Jackson would spend the next eight years making sure that white businessmen understood that fact.

Maynard Jackson is a man of startling physique, ego, and talents, and his two terms as mayor would leave Atlanta forever changed. He would challenge white Atlantans to live up to their creed of racial tolerance, and there would be no doubt that the challenge came in the form of a demand, not a request. He would leave whites sputtering with fury and blacks chortling with glee over his administration. As mayor, he would prove to be bold, articulate, courageous, imperious, and bullheaded. Some six-feet-two-inches tall, with a shock of curly hair and a girth like that of a portly Buddha, Jackson could dominate almost any arena with his sheer presence. That his personality was equally domineering set the stage for a colossal battle of wills with corporate types unaccustomed to being pushed, least of all by someone black. He would ring up city council members before daylight to advise them of some latest plan or to chew them out for opposing his policies. He would entertain a courtesy visit from a prominent executive and proceed to berate the man for failing to appoint blacks to top-level positions. Once he kept Georgia's governor-elect waiting a month for an appointment. With stunning audacity, he delayed construction at the Hartsfield International Airport and threatened to halt it altogether if black businessmen did not share in the contracts. He intimated to bank presidents that the city could just as well take its money elsewhere if officials did not see fit to appoint a black or two to their boards. He declined to be listed in a volume entitled *Men of Achievement* because women were excluded. He steadfastly refused to show up at any private club—no matter how prestigious—that excluded blacks as members. He prompted local headlines like "The Man Who Did

'Great Things Badly.' " And by the time he left office, black-white relations in Atlanta were more tense than at any time in memory. Blacks had also become a more visible and vital part of city life than ever before.

A child prodigy who grew up in privileged circumstances in Dallas and Atlanta, Jackson launched his political career on the night of June 4, 1968. Then a young lawyer, he happened to be watching television when he was stunned to witness the murder of Robert Kennedy. By morning, he had resolved to respond by taking a dramatic step. Jackson decided to challenge in the fall election U.S. senator Herman Talmadge, an old-school Democrat. Jackson spent the next day raising the $3,000 filing fee and officially entered the race a half hour before the deadline. It was three months and one week until the election. Jackson was the first black man to run for statewide office in Georgia, and he polled a surprising 24 percent of the vote. Most impressive, he also carried Atlanta against Talmadge, a development that encouraged him to run for vice-mayor soon afterward.

As the 1973 race for mayor approached, the open bickering between Vice-Mayor Jackson and Mayor Massell left little doubt that a contest was in the offing. David Franklin, a longtime friend of Jackson's, had come home from a stint in the North to join Jackson's law practice and help plan for the mayoral bid. In the spring of 1973, Franklin commissioned a poll by Pat Caddell, who would later become President Jimmy Carter's pollster. The poll results, Franklin recalled, stunned even Jackson's inner circle. What they found was that Jackson—who won 45 percent of those polled, versus 21 percent for Massell—seemed almost a shoo-in for election. "It scared the hell out of everybody," Franklin said. "We took those figures to the banks, to the Coca-Cola people. So we were able from the start of the campaign to get commitments from business people."

Even as Jackson was putting together a coalition of blacks and established whites, there was new evidence that political control in Atlanta had shifted. The old-line black leaders who had negotiated with whites for decades were no longer in command of the black electorate. Meanwhile, prominent whites could no longer dictate the terms of their agreements with black voters. If evidence of the changing times was needed, it was provided by the blowup of a behind-the-scenes pact between the black elite and the white power structure. The two groups had agreed that prominent whites would back Jackson for mayor if prominent blacks supported Wade Mitchell, a white alderman and banker, for the position of city council president. The deal was cut, but black leaders soon found they had no way of delivering the black vote. Wyche Fowler, a liberal white attorney, had also entered the race, as had Hosea Williams, the fiery street organizer who sat in King's inner circle. Both men had black supporters who were not about to be dictated to by traditional black leaders like Jesse Hill, president of Atlanta Life, and Herman Russell, whose construction company was among Atlanta's major black businesses. Hill, Russell, and others had prepared a sample ballot, picturing Jackson and Mitchell, for distribution in black neighborhoods. But Jackson, aware of the animosity the ballot would stir, threatened to denounce it.

"Jesse came to me," Franklin recalled. "He asked, 'What are we going to do?' " The group had already spent $5,000 printing the endorsement ballot. Finally, the Jackson campaign supplied $5,000 for Hill to print a new ballot. The revised version pictured Mitchell, but in the space for mayor, it noted simply that the black community had "made up its mind." When the election was held, black voters split and Fowler was elected. The lesson of the incident was that the days of control by an elite few—black or white—had passed. Blacks were now the dominant force in Atlanta politics, and they were free to compete with each other on terms once available only to whites.

White business leaders in Atlanta had not known Jackson particularly well before his election, but they had assumed that his links to the black bourgeoisie would make him accessible and somewhat predictable. What they found was a mayor whose agenda differed markedly from their own and whose style was a cross between that of a committed idealist and an unforgiving dictator. By April, the *Atlanta Constitution* was noting that "some of the big money men report frustration after trying to get the mayor on the phone." And by September, the seams appeared to be fraying. Central Atlanta Progress presented Jackson with a seventeen-page letter and addendum outlining worries about business flight from the city. Citing reasons for the concern, they noted a "perceived attitude of the mayor as anti-white" and a "growing racial imbalance" in the work force. A few days later, former Mayor Allen—viewed by whites as the very voice of reason and responsibility—went public with a charge that black and white racism was threatening to "kill off" Atlanta. By the following spring, word of the troubles had reached as far as Europe. In London, the *Economist* produced a searing article that argued: "The grumbles and accusations have recently become so intense that they have threatened to shatter the self-confidence and strong sense of civic pride that have incubated Atlanta's lusty growth."[10] Attempts at damage control did not prevent a public outburst that September from John Portman, the talented architect-developer whose visions were a key force in shaping modern Atlanta. Large investors were shunning Atlanta because they "see a city tearing itself apart," Portman warned at a civic forum. Already, he said, he knew of two companies that had revised their plans to locate in the city and had chosen Houston instead.

The problem was, in part, unfamiliarity, in part, style. Jackson and the white business community simply did not know each other well. Nor was either used to cowing to the demands of someone else. The troubles were also a matter of philosophy. Whites felt they had been remarkably sensitive to the needs of black Atlantans. Jackson saw their much heralded largesse as little more than tokenism. White business leaders did not take readily to Jackson's attempts to open their eyes. "We'd be trying to get business in for jobs, very big deals, very sensitive deals," said Dan Sweat of Central Atlanta Progress. "You'd say to Maynard, 'We need a little session with you and the chairman of the board of the XYZ Company.' He'd say, 'We've got to have more people at the table.' He'd want the head of the Urban League, the head of the National Organization of Women. You just can't say, 'Everybody, come to the table.' " In a typical incident, not long after Jackson took office, Sweat and the CAP chairman, a prominent white businessman, paid a courtesy call on the new mayor. There was an exchange of pleasantries and an offer to help Jackson out whenever possible. Then Jackson began to speak. As Sweat recalls the exchange, Jackson said, " 'Let me tell you. I respect CAP. But . . . If I'm going to be able to deal with you, you've got to broaden your board.' And he started ticking off all these people he wanted on it."

No boardroom was too sacred, no company president too intimidating for the mayor to sit down and preach the gospel of black inclusion. The message was the theme of his administration, and Jackson did not hesitate to remind established business leaders of their duty. Nor did he flinch at informing them of what he viewed as his duty—channeling city business to those who complied and depriving those who did not. At one point, he suggested that the bulk of the city's banking business might go to the bank that came closest to meeting his minority hiring goals. At another, there was a hint that the city could take its banking business to Birmingham if local officers were unconcerned about minority participation.

If any single episode typified the Jackson years, it was his insistence on minority participation in the expansion of the Hartsfield International Airport. More than 42 million passengers pass annually through that regional transportation hub, with its subterranean people movers and its neon-lit escalators. The facility is a financial bonanza for the city, producing substantial revenues and enhancing Atlanta's image as the most up-to-the-minute, city in the South. As mayor, however, Jackson left little doubt that he was willing to sacrifice those benefits on the altar of minority business enterprise. If airline officials could not find a way to include black firms in the $400-million-plus expansion scheduled for the mid-1970s, then there would be no expansion, he decreed.

A major airport overhaul had been in the offing since the late 1960s, and by 1975, it appeared that work was finally about to begin. At the last minute, however, Jackson stunned airport officials by calling a halt. Where, he asked, were the plans for involving minority firms? Not to worry, airline officials replied. There would be a good-faith effort to make sure that black-owned companies were included throughout the building process. For Jackson and the city council, that was far from enough. The mayor wanted to see actual contracts, spelling out in detail the work to be performed, and including blacks in everything from drawing architectural plans to laying tile. The name for what Jackson had in mind was "joint venturing." Nor would he be satisfied with only token involvement by blacks. There would be a goal of 25 percent minority participation in each phase of the construction process.

Whites were first astounded, then outraged. Surely Jackson could not mean that blacks had to be recruited in specialized areas where, it appeared, black firms either did not exist or were not large enough to do the required work. Would contracts be let to companies with no experience? Would there be slipshod work and cost overruns? "There was extreme anger, disbelief, uncertainty, racism, bigotry, and questioning of ancestral background from major companies in the airline industry and the business community in this city," said Dave J. Miller, who was Atlanta's manager of airport planning and development under Jackson. Jackson and Miller listened to the complaints and then moved forward. They were convinced that minority firms did exist, that blacks could perform the work, and that they would never be allowed to try unless whites were forced to give them a chance.

At every step, roadblocks had to be dismantled. There were, for instance, no black architectural firms in Atlanta with enough employees to do one-quarter of the airport design work. That obstacle was finally eliminated when four small black engineering firms joined ranks to provide sufficient manpower. White-owned companies also had to be closely monitored to ensure that they were complying with both the letter and the spirit of the law. One paving company, for instance, wanted to "joint venture" by creating a minority firm with its own black employees. The black workers, none of whom ranked as high as a foreman, would own 51 percent of the new company's stock, while the paving company's white owners would have 49 percent. In another instance, a white firm seemed resigned to sharing profits with a black joint-venturing partner but appeared ready to cut them out of actually doing any work.[11] City officials, in response, insisted on contracts that spelled out what labor would be performed by minority firms. Meanwhile, the psychological pressure on Jackson to soften his demands was enormous. Newspapers criticized the construction delays, and a grand jury was convened to investigate whether there were corrupt motives behind the joint-venturing scheme. In the end, the airline companies who were financing most of the expansion agreed to Jackson's demands. Construction finally began in early 1977, and when it was completed in 1980, both the timetable and the budget had been met.

Five years later, there was twofold proof of the durability of joint venturing. The city council, convinced the idea was working, had upped the ante on awarding contracts. A new ordinance, thought to be the toughest in the nation, called for blacks to be awarded 35 percent of city contracts. The degree to which white Atlanta had come to accept the idea was also evident in the diminished controversy. "It's something accepted and rarely thought about," noted John Braden, public relations director at the Hartsfield Airport. "It's just a way of life." Critics argued that estimates on how much airport construction money wound up in black hands (22 percent, airport officials said) were inflated. But for the black firms that shared in the profits, including several whose stock soared as a result, even inflated figures were better than the alternative.

If final proof of the alienation between Jackson and prominent whites was needed, it was provided as business after business stonewalled on ticket purchases for Jackson's testimonial farewell dinner in late 1981. The affair was eventually a sellout, with Jackson and his wife receiving a new Cadillac Fleetwood and a trip to Hawaii, but few of those applauding his service were top executives of the companies marking Atlanta as a corporate boomtown. Nor when Jackson went job hunting did he throw in his lot with one of the city's prestigious white firms. Instead, he became a partner, operating out of Atlanta, with a group of Chicago-based bond counsels.

Despite the icy departure, Atlanta whites seemed to be viewing the Jackson years more charitably as time passed. Some acknowledged that blacks might not have made such significant strides if Jackson had been less determined and abrasive. To blacks, with whom Jackson remained a hero, that reluctantly reached conclusion was self-evident, a given. Along with Frederick Douglass, the nineteenth-century black abolitionist, they argued that power concedes power only when forced. It was Jackson's curse and his blessing to be Atlanta's transitional mayor. Only time would tell whether animosity had slackened enough to allow him to fulfill a dream of again holding public office. His challenge to white city fathers had been to share economic wealth. He was, so to speak, the first black man at the negotiating table. And it was perhaps fortunate that he was willing to pound his fist a bit, for such displays were simply not in the nature of his successor, Atlanta's second black mayor, Andrew Young.

Maynard Jackson as mayor was a warrior, aggressive,

uncompromising, always on the offensive; Andy Young is a diplo-
mat, a conciliator, seldom ruffled by the day-to-day tensions of the
job. Maynard Jackson was an ideologue, certain of his positions,
committed to a black agenda. Young is relaxed, nonthreatening,
open to dialogue. During Young's 1981 campaign, Jackson, typically strident, raised a racial stink by accusing blacks who backed
Young's opponent of being "shuffling, grinning" Negroes. In contrast, when Young next met his white foe's black campaign manager, who was a target of Jackson's thrust, Young hugged the man
and reminisced about officiating at his wedding. As mayor, Jackson would be on the phone at 6:00 A.M., berating city council
members who had dared disagree with him. Council members
complain that, with Young, the mayor's office has too little direction. "You'd go in to see Maynard with a letter you wanted him
to sign," said one downtown Atlanta executive, explaining the
difference in the two men. "You'd say, 'Good morning.' He'd say,
'What's good about it?' He'd go through the letter, rewrite it three
times, put you through agony. But when he got it signed, something would happen." By contrast, the man continued, "you love
to go over and meet with Andy Young. He's so pleasant. You say,
'Good morning.' He says, 'Sure is.' Then he'll sign the letter and
expect his staff to carry it out. Unfortunately, it doesn't always
happen."

There is one other critical difference in the men. Jackson was
embraced by Atlanta's business community when he first ran for
mayor; within months, the alliance was in tatters. Young, despite
his record as a congressman and U.N. ambassador, was shunned
by white businessmen when he sought the office in 1981. Within
months of Young's election, the same men could scarcely believe
their good fortune. They had traded a pugnacious bulldog for a
mild-mannered preacher. The new mayor's visions were global,
encompassing world problems, and he was not one to be readily
riled if someone else's view of the mundane, the ordinary (i.e.,
day-to-day events in Atlanta) differed from his. Even more surprising, Young's positions on key issues at home rarely did differ
from those of the corporate world. This man of the cloth, a civil
rights champion, and defender of the world's poor, saw a surprising number of solutions in terms of free enterprise. He could and
did make outlandish statements (the Ayatollah Khomeini was a

"saint," the members of 1984 Democratic presidential nominee Walter Mondale's inner circle were "smart-ass white boys"), but when it came to locating roads and industry and billboards, Atlanta's entrepreneurial giants had remarkably little to grouse about. It was not what either blacks or whites had expected, and it demonstrated a new dimension in the evolution of the black mayor. The day would come, Young's performance suggested, when stereotypical ideas about how black mayors act would be as meaningless as old notions of how Irish Catholics respond to public office. As usual, Atlanta was a step ahead of the pack.

In the tradition of Atlanta's black elite, the city's second black mayor was third-generation middle class. That is the generation, Young once said, which finally feels confident of its economic security and comfortable with its mainstream birthright. Young was raised in an integrated neighborhood in New Orleans, the son of a prosperous dentist, the grandson of a successful saloon keeper and grocer. At Howard University, from which he graduated at nineteen, Young was a premed student. But his thoughts turned to religion, and his path led to the Hartford Theological Seminary in Connecticut and ordination as a Congregationalist minister.

In 1961, Young moved to Atlanta and went to work for the SCLC. Emerging as one of King's top lieutenants, he was the button-downed counterpoint to the tempestuous Hosea Williams. Even in the 1960s, Young's looks were clean-cut, Brooks Brothers, white shirt and tie. If King needed an ambassador to the uptown whites in a given city, he was likely to send the young minister with the dark suit and the serene, nonthreatening manner. That style also aided Young in 1970 when he ran for Congress in an Atlanta district that was about 60 percent white. He lost, but on his second try in 1972 was elected. The success of a black candidate in a majority-white district in the Deep South was trumpeted across the nation. Stoney Cooks, who directed that campaign, insists that whites were given much more credit for racial tolerance in the election than they were due. "That's been misused," insisted Cooks, who—unpaid—has run each of Young's campaigns for elective office. Ninety-nine percent of blacks in the district backed Young, compared with only 6 to 12 percent of whites, Cooks said.

Young had just been elected to his third term in Congress

when he was tapped by newly installed President Jimmy Carter to become the country's first black representative to the United Nations. Enjoying an almost mystical relationship with the deeply religious president, Young quickly emerged as a force within the fledgling Democratic administration. Within sixty days, it was also clear that he was the most controversial member of Carter's foreign policy team. Young, who brought the United States an unprecedented measure of goodwill among Third World countries, also displayed an uncanny knack for ill-advised, off-the-cuff statements. Friends like Cooks, who was Young's executive assistant at the U.N., patiently explain that some of the remarks were taken out of context or misunderstood.[12] But what came through to the public was a stream of misstatements for which the State Department or Young himself seemed to be forever apologizing.

Finally, in the summer of 1979, Young went a step too far. Treading on official U.S. policy, he met secretly with a representative of the Palestine Liberation Organization. His stated aim—to delay a Security Council vote on Palestinian rights—seemed innocent enough, but the evidence that Andy Young thought he could ignore a sensitive, long-standing national policy could not be tolerated. A few days later, an unapologetic Young resigned. To many Americans, the departure came not a moment too soon. But other acquaintances saw in the episodes a measure of the unique makeup of the man. "There's a lot of naïveté in Andy Young," said one associate. "He basically trusts everybody. People are pure, and good, and created in God's image."

Most of Atlanta's monied establishment was considerably less sympathetic. To them, Andy Young had proved himself a loose cannon, unpredictable at best, untrustworthy at worst. Already shaken by the strained relations with Maynard Jackson, the business sector was in no mood to give another black mayoral candidate the benefit of the doubt. When Young announced his intention to seek the city's top office, the movers and shakers of white Atlanta responded with deafening silence. Young might once have been an acceptable congressman, but white leaders in 1981 were determined that the office of mayor return to white hands. Business types were already lining up behind an inoffensive state legislator and construction company executive named Sidney Marcus. In financial contributions and votes, the white elite would almost unanimously boycott Young's campaign. The city "too busy to hate" showed once again that it had plenty of time for racial friction. "It was the last hurrah of turning back the clock," said David Franklin.

Young's answer to the white establishment was Charles Loudermilk. The son of a North Georgia redneck, Loudermilk was a local poor boy who made good. His furniture rental business was by the 1980s the largest such enterprise in the world. Loudermilk, a conservative Republican who lives in style in a wealthy and powerful north Atlanta neighborhood, had come to know and admire Young during his congressional tenure. "I just liked his approach, his honesty, his thoughtfulness," Loudermilk said one evening as he sat in the spacious den of his azalea-framed mansion. He also expected Young to become the city's next mayor. Loudermilk had no hang-ups about supporting a black mayoral candidate, and he decided to join what he saw as a winning team. He mistakenly expected at least some of his friends to do likewise. Had Young had the option, he might have tapped someone with more established roots to head his financial effort in the white community. As it was, Stoney Cooks and Andy Young could count on one hand the number of financially prominent white supporters.

Loudermilk's first move was to set up a meeting of top banking officials through a friend at the Citizens & Southern National Bank. About fifteen people showed up, and the atmosphere was polite but cool. Within a few days, Loudermilk knew why. "A week or two later, I called to see what financial support they were going to give," Loudermilk said. "The president of the bank said, 'None. Absolutely none.' All the resources and time and efforts of the group were going to Marcus." It was not unusual for Atlanta's white business community to hedge its bets in an election, giving some money to each major candidate. But in 1981 in the race for mayor, the stakes were too high for such niceties. Andy Young was to be financially blacklisted, and—fortunately for the Young campaign—Loudermilk regarded that shutout as a personal insult. "I was very, very upset," he said. "They could have given me a small check. I'm a competitive person. I said to Andy, 'How much is it going to take to win.' He said, '$300,000.' I said, 'I'll personally underwrite $300,000. If we can't raise it, I'll pay it.' " Young's financial worries were over.

If Loudermilk provided the financial security for Young's

election, sheer numbers made Cooks confident from the outset that his man would sit in the mayor's office. Two-thirds of Atlanta's population was black, and black voters could be expected to turn out in force to retain control of city hall. Cooks had no illusions that Young would fare well among white voters. Nor did he doubt that race would be a significant factor in the election. Cooks maintains that if Atlanta is a black mecca, it is because of black strength, not white benevolence. Young hoped for substantial white support in the 1981 election, but Cooks never expected that more than 10 percent of Young's votes would come from whites. A postelection newspaper analysis concluded that 11 percent of whites voted for Young and 11 percent of blacks backed Marcus. To Cooks, those statistics are proof aplenty that racism continues in Atlanta. "Here was a candidate with international notoriety, been a cabinet officer, in Congress three terms, ran against an undistinguished state representative who had not a single piece of legislation you could point to, and he had a hard time getting any white votes," Cooks said, shaking his head. Further proof of animosity came in the charges and countercharges of racism that riddled the closing days of the campaign. In the end, Young won 55 percent of the runoff vote.

If the windup of the 1981 campaign showed Atlanta at its worst, the reaction once Young was elected was typical of the way in which pragmatism eventually prevails in this city. Inviting about sixty business executives to lunch at the downtown Merchandise Mart, Young spoke the magic words of reconciliation. He could be elected without white business support, Young said, but he could not govern. Whites responded by opening the pocketbooks that had been zipped tight during the election. An anonymous committee of businessmen agreed to extend the olive branch by retiring Young's $200,000 debt. A month after the election, peace reigned once again in Atlanta.

The postelection donations were rewarded far more handsomely than most Atlanta businessmen ever expected. Within days of Young's inaugural, reporters were writing of the free-flowing harmony between city hall and the business elite. "Those accustomed to fighting their way through the barred doors and the Byzantine layers of guardians surrounding Maynard Jackson are finding it hard to believe just how accessible Andy Young is," wrote *Atlanta Journal* columnist Durwood McAlister. Another story told of an astonished downtown executive who asked for a fifteen-minute appointment, only to wind up with an hour of Young's time. The unexpected compatibility did not stop with public relations. On practical issues, Mayor Young was also winning business acclaim. Late in his first year, Young came out in favor of a 1 percent local option sales tax. Such taxes theoretically take a larger share of income from the poor than from the rich, thereby hitting at Young's traditional constituency. Young also startled observers by siding with business over neighborhood interests during the great road battles of his administration. As a congressman, Young had opposed a plan to build a major thoroughfare through a northeast Atlanta park. But when the road resurfaced as part of plans for a Jimmy Carter Presidential Library and Policy Center, the mayor—despite neighborhood opposition—lent his enthusiastic support. In another incident, Young first vetoed a major expansion of the Seaboard System Railroad's Atlanta complex, arguing that expanded truck traffic would harm the surrounding neighborhoods. Young later endorsed a modified plan, however. Again, he angered local neighborhood groups that were opposed.

Meanwhile, the hallmark of Young's administration also had a business-oriented flavor. From his first days in office, Young was a globe-trotting mayor, jetting off to India or Nigeria, Zimbabwe or Singapore, outdoing President Reagan in international travel and prompting quips that Atlanta was the only American city with a foreign policy. Certainly, few American mayors could boast of having a "special assistant for international affairs," as did Young. Often, the travels involved Young's own business interests. Frequently, however, Young would take Atlanta businessmen along for the ride, allowing them to trade on his renowned popularity in Africa and other underdeveloped areas. Meanwhile, dignitaries and businessmen from around the world trooped to Atlanta for meetings and conferences and a glimpse of the city that Young dreamed of converting from the hub of Dixie into an international showpiece. How much gold accompanied the glitter of those global ventures remained an unanswered question. But Young seemed convinced of the value of his travels and unperturbed by criticism of his absences.[13] Two days after his 1985 reelection, following a campaign in which he was chided for leaving Atlanta untended, Young set off for China, the Soviet Union, and Hong Kong. Nor did he mince words when some complained that he had shifted from a people-oriented to a pro-business approach to government. "I've made my peace with capitalism," he said.[14]

Not everyone in Atlanta is pleased with the terms of the settlement, and many prominent black politicians do not hesitate to say so. "There's very little to distinguish his administration as one that has shown compassion for the poor and minorities," complained Bill Campbell, the young, Duke-educated black lawyer who sits on city council. Hosea Williams, ever one to fan the flames of controversy, agreed. "There's a feeling in this city that there's been a retrenching," he said. "I just think when Loudermilk and them paid off that $200,000 campaign debt, Andy got very careless about what he was going to do." And City Council President Marvin Arrington felt the need so acutely that he decided to chide Young during their inaugural ceremony in January 1986. "The masses have not reaped the benefit of the real gains in this city and nation," warned Arrington, who would happily follow Jackson and Young to become Atlanta's third black mayor.

More than a decade after Atlanta's transition from white to black political control, such sentiments reflect both the best and worst of racial conditions in the city. On the one hand, race is no longer the determinant of all alliances and policy positions. A black mayor links arms with the white establishment. Black politicians do not hesitate to criticize him publicly for the actions that ensue. At other times, those same critics may applaud the mayor, disagree openly with each other, or form their own coalitions with whites. Substance in day-to-day dealings has become more important than skin.

On the other hand, all too often in this regional mecca, problems are matters of race. The economic gaps for many, black and white, are no less acute than in other American cities. Ongoing battles over the racial makeup of the police and fire departments have plagued the city for years. In 1985, a federal judge ordered a white man installed as director of Cyclorama, the tourist attraction featuring a giant painting of the Battle of Atlanta, after a jury concluded that Young had bypassed him twice for the job because of race. In 1984, when severe problems surfaced at the Atlanta zoo, white workers blamed the troubles on cronyism by Young in hiring a black director. And when the Atlanta Convention & Visitors Bureau was seeking $5 million from the city, Young turned them down, pending the hiring of more black employees. Such stories are monthly, if not weekly fare in this city. Tales of black exclusionism also remain, as when Arrington refused to attend an Emory University board meeting because it was held at an all-white social club, or when residents speak of the I-20 highway as an imaginary dividing line between black and white Atlanta.

If black Atlantans do chance to become complacent about their status, they need only look to surrounding counties to realize how fragile their equality can be. In 1985, for instance, in nearby Cobb County, there was a firebombing of a black family that dared to move into a home in a previously all-white area. And many residents believe that several counties have refused to join Atlanta's mass transit system because the easy access might prompt blacks to move there. "People say, 'It'll bring the niggers down here,' " acknowledged Dennis Mullen, a white Atlanta policeman who lives south of the city in neighboring Clayton County.

Hosea Williams confirmed this contradictory image of his city. His tiny city hall office reverberated with anger as, eyes closed, hands clasped, he spouted out frustration that has scarcely dwindled in twenty years. "Atlanta has the falsest image of any city in this nation," he fumed, tugging at a beard grown white with middle age. "Rich as it is, there is still more low-rent housing per capita, more homeless and hungry."

For every Williams, however, there is in Atlanta a Michael Lomax. Creasing his brow in thought, Lomax argued that no city —east, west, north, or south—has abandoned racial politics or achieved racial equality. "Race and ethnic identity in American politics is very much present always," he said. What is significant is the degree of emphasis on race, and by that measure, Lomax believes Atlanta is remarkable for both its honesty and its harmony. There is no question, Lomax said, that racial feeling can surface in Atlanta, as in 1985 when the Fulton County commission was considering adopting a goal of 20 percent minority participation in awarding contracts. "You saw all the old racial red herrings," he recalled. Nor is there any question that residents often manage to look beyond race, as when he was elected chairman by the majority-white commission. "For all its faults and blemishes, Atlanta continues to struggle toward being a city where black and white people deal better with one another than anywhere else," he concluded.

The magic of Atlanta, then, perhaps is in that struggle. Racial incidents have arisen throughout the city's history. They continue today. But across the decades, the city's racial tapestry has never truly come unraveled. Unlike a Birmingham or a Selma, the city has put no one in authority, black or white, who was willing to tug hard enough at the thread to set that breakdown in motion. There is, apparently, too much that is healthy and pleasant about the notion that things work in Atlanta. The city is not color-blind, but for all its failings, it has managed with determined frequency to act in ways that were.

5. MACON AND LOWNDES COUNTIES
The Rural South

IN 1974, ON THE DAY the mayor and the councilmen christened the Tuskegee Industrial Park with flowery speeches and a stone slab marker, Jim Roberts stood in the doorway of his rustic, pine-sheltered grocery and watched. Promises of new industry and jobs and a better life drifted across the highway in the small Alabama town, and Roberts felt the breeze of change. "At least I was hoping so," he recalled. Thirteen years and hundreds of thousands of federal dollars later, the marker had been joined by an electrical substation, water hydrants, a high-pressure gas line, an airport landing strip, and a single, industrial-sized building— everything, in fact, but industry. By the start of 1987, only one small, black-owned firm, employing about 55 people, was operating. A second, previous tenant had shut down a year earlier. Mostly, the park remained in its natural state, a preserve of wild oats, scrub brush, red-clay dirt, and towering pines. Across the way at Roberts' grocery, life continued its slow, unfettered pace. Dreams of lathe operators and computer technicians pulling up for gas or a Mello Yello—maybe even, a week's groceries—had long since died. Business was scant. Prosperity remained as elusive as ever.

To some, the tale of the Tuskegee Industrial Park is a metaphor for the unending struggle of life in Alabama's Black Belt, a dozen or so counties stretching like a cummerbund across the lower half of the Cotton State. The area's name evolved from its soil, a black dirt so rich that for local aristocrats in the era when cotton was king, the land might just as well have been pure gold. Only later did the label come to apply to the skin tone of the thousands of men and women whose sweat combined with the soil to produce that wealth and who shared almost none of its riches. The Alabama Black Belt, in turn, is twin to portions of the Mississippi Delta, eastern North Carolina, southside Virginia, southcentral Georgia, eastern Louisiana, and the coastal plains of South Carolina—in all, eighty-two counties in the seven states—in which in 1985 blacks equaled or outnumbered whites. With few exceptions, theirs is a shared story of economic deprivation, of industrial underdevelopment, of financial patterns still clutched to a rapidly vanishing agricultural past.

In most of those counties, whites in the mid-1980s still run local government. But in twenty-one, including Tuskegee's Macon County, a combination of constitutional challenges, Voting Rights Act litigation, and sheer numbers have produced a result unheard of just two decades earlier: blacks govern. In the Alabama heartland, Macon County, east of Montgomery, and Lowndes County, just south of the capital, tell in microcosm the story of what happens when blacks win political office in the rural South. The result in those counties, as in others, is a mixed bag of spiritual emancipation and economic setback, of white flight and deinstitutionalized segregation, of failure and success. Economically, educationally, and socially, Macon and Lowndes counties are at the opposite poles of progress among rural counties governed by blacks. The poles, however, are not so far apart, and the pair show all too clearly how the shared trait of blackness often outweighs other considerations in determining a community's quality of life.

Macon County has long been a social and cultural haven for black southerners. In 1881, a former slave named Booker T. Washington was commissioned to start a school there for the training of black teachers, and in a one-room, wooden shanty, Tuskegee Institute was born. Over the years, faculty and students at the Institute—from Washington and George Washington Carver to Ralph Ellison and Lionel Ritchie—have walked Tuskegee's wide, oak-shaded streets and paused in a town square where the gabled, yellow-brick courthouse is still protected by a rifle-bearing Confederate soldier. In their wake lies a sense of vibrancy and pride,

if not wealth. A famous campus statue of Washington lifting a veil
of ignorance from a dazed and barefoot slave suggests the institute's perception of itself as a force of enlightenment in the lives
of the region's black dwellers. While most Black Belt counties trail
far behind the rest of the state in educational levels, Tuskegee has
a higher percentage of college graduates than all but five Alabama
locales.

Such resources have bred a tradition of independence and
assertiveness that has placed Macon County in the vanguard of
political change throughout the area. Black councilmen were
elected in Tuskegee as early as 1964, and Alabama's first black
sheriff and state legislators resided there. Macon County also
boasts another distinction, however. With 27,000 residents, only
16 percent of whom were white, the county in 1980 was the blackest
in the South.[1] All its assets could not overcome that single statistic
in dictating the economic status of its population. The financial
position of Macon County blacks, relative to whites, is easily the
best among southern Alabama counties with large black populations. But the gap is still striking. Black family income is only 60
percent of that for white families and the ratio of black to white
poverty was almost three to one. As the wild, undisturbed spaces
in the Tuskegee Industrial Park testify, a decade-long push to
attract major industry has failed. The reason, many Macon
County residents suspect, is a matter of complexion.

Lowndes County, by contrast, is grimmer and more remote.
Its gently rolling highways lead through a collection of dusty
hamlets and snake-filled swamps. Even in springtime, as muddy
fields are beginning to green and clumps of yellow jonquils liven
the roadsides, there is a bleakness to the landscape and an eerie
cast, born of miles of trees draped in gray shawls of Spanish moss.
In Lowndesboro, where many of the county's wealthiest whites
live, there are regal old homes, set off by towering oaks and rows
of flowering shrubs. But the down-in-the-heel dormancy of towns
like Hayneville and Fort Deposit seems more in keeping with the
county's pulse. The soil there, so the saying goes, is so rich that
a peg-legged man could take root. But in Lowndes County, as all
across the Black Belt, land that once boasted acres of cotton lies
idle, and the handful of whites who dominate the local economy
have turned to timbering or cattle for income. Seventy-five percent

of the county's 13,250 residents are black, and their destitution is such that Lowndes ranked in 1980 as the fifth poorest county in the nation. Six out of every ten local blacks lived below the poverty line. Fifteen years earlier, when a young native West Indian named Stokely Carmichael arrived in the county with a sleeping bag and a few dollars in his pocket, the numbers were even worse. Carmichael, along with a local construction worker and father of eight named John Hulett, put Lowndes County on the national map in 1965 when they founded the Lowndes County Freedom Organization. The group became a model for freedom organizations throughout the rural South and evolved into the once-dreaded Black Panther Party.

Despite such historic and cultural differences, the common bonds between Macon and Lowndes counties are greater than those that separate them. Like other black-majority counties, they share a history of violent oppression, limited resources, and un-developed skills. Two decades after the Voting Rights Act ended a century of disenfranchisement, they demonstrate the limits of that act in changing social traditions and long-standing economic patterns. In 1985, blacks controlled every seat on the Macon County commission and school board. They had dominated both bodies since the early 1970s. The town council in Tuskegee had one white member, and county government boasted only two white elected officials, the tax assessor and the probate judge. In Lowndes County, meanwhile, blacks held four of five commission seats and the same number on the school board. There had been a black school board majority since 1978 and black control of the county commission since 1980. Strong black influence in county government dated to the early 1970s. The results of that black control are far less striking than Carmichael or Hulett or dozens of others would have forecast in the days when their lives were consumed with the quest for political power. Indeed, some residents—black, as well as white—fear a correlation between the presence of black officials and some of the counties' continuing problems.

Psychologically, to be sure, the entrenched, degrading fear that once defined life for blacks, particularly in Lowndes County, is gone. Sheriff Lucius Amerson in Macon County and Sheriff John Hulett in Lowndes, both black, have helped usher in a new respect for equality under the law. Whites who once roamed the region with a pistol in the glove compartment or a rifle in the pickup gun rack was no longer free to make targets of those with whom they disagreed. That change, like the simple ability of blacks to hold office, signal a tremendously important shift. "Twenty years ago, there was a general fear in the minds of a lot of people. There were a lot of gun-carrying people," said Eli Seaborn, superintendent-elect of county schools, when asked to sum up the differences produced by the previous two decades. Now, he said, the tension produced by the threat of violence is gone. "People don't give it a second thought."

Socially and economically, however, the degree of change in Macon and Lowndes counties could give comfort to segregationists who once plastered the word "Never!" on trees and fence posts across the countryside. Social institutions might be officially desegregated, but they are not integrated. Public school classes in both counties are overwhelmingly black. In Lowndes County, 13 whites went to school with 3,277 black children in 1985, creating a 99.6 percent black school district. In Macon County, the student body is 95 percent black, consisting of 253 whites and 4,909 blacks. That county's largest high school, according to the local superintendent, had "two whites, and one of them is a Puerto Rican." In both counties, whites frequent private academies or find ways to enroll their children in neighboring county schools. Segregated private academies for whites are so institutionalized that in 1984 Macon County's all-black governing board offered to share some of its profits from a new, state-regulated dog track with the all-white Macon Academy.

Both whites and blacks expect private, segregated academies to remain a feature of local life. "I think they will be," said Linda Bargainer, the white tax collector in Lowndes County and the mother of three children who had attended Fort Deposit Academy. Many local whites are not quite so adamantly opposed to integration as they were twenty years earlier, she said, but those same individuals believe the quality of local public school education is abysmal. Their fears were reinforced in 1983 when a stunning 48 percent of Lowndes County's juniors failed the language section of a state competency exam written at the ninth-grade level. Forty-six percent failed at math. "You just put your priorities in order and decide which things you want the most," said Bargainer, explaining the willingness of white parents to pay $100 or more per month for a private school.

Nor are schools the only example of continued segregation. In 1985, visitors to Fort Deposit, Lowndes County's largest town, a onetime frontier outpost with a reputation for toughness, had two options at lunchtime. They could eat a sandwich in their car or they could drive several miles to the interstate highway. There were no cafés in town. The reason, explained Mayor Ralph R. Norman, Jr., who is white, was that "folks won't open one up" in an era in which both blacks and whites must be served. Similarly, the county's major financial institution, the Fort Deposit Bank, had no black officers or board members. In a county only 25 percent white, bank officials had never hired a black person in a noncustodial position. "We don't have any policy. We just hire the most qualified people," explained John Ellis, the bank's president. The local cattleman's association and its ladies' auxiliary, the Cowbelles, were segregated, as were churches and clubs. Local newspaper pictures of school groups, social organizations, employee outings, and beauty pageants showed a thoroughly segregated way of life.

"The social life," concluded Mayor Norman, "is not integrated at all. If anything, there's less contact than there used to be." A retired insurance salesman who emitted a rumpled congeniality, Norman recalled times as a child when black quartets would sing at his church. "Now, we wouldn't do that. It'd just cause problems. You'd have some people in the church who wouldn't like it." Similarly, he said, there is a nutrition program in town that serves both elderly blacks and whites. No one forces members of the two races to sit separately, but they do, he said. "The federal government changed life here, but they didn't change it the way they thought they were going to. You can't change social action by law."

Economically, as well, black control has not produced hoped-for progress. The experiences in Lowndes and Macon counties bear out the warning of Charles Bullock III, political science professor at the University of Georgia. "Even when blacks win political control, they may be severely constrained in the economic changes which can be achieved," Bullock wrote in 1975.[2]

"The counties with black voting age population majorities are among the poorest in their respective states, and redistributive policies rarely bring them to more than parity with other counties." In 1980, median family income for Lowndes County's black residents was $7,493, compared with $18,350 for local whites. Black income as a percentage of white income had improved slightly, from 33 percent to 41 percent in the previous decade, but the shift satisfied few black residents. Continuing widespread poverty is reflected in the absence of hotels, fast-food franchises, or chain stores and in the worn and drowsy appearance of towns like Hayneville and Fort Deposit. In timeless tradition, a half-dozen white families and a few companies own the bulk of the county's land. The sort of depression-era shanties depicted in James Agee's *Let Us Now Praise Famous Men* mostly have given way to modest frame dwellings, but destitution still exists along backwoods trails and on isolated, hard-scrabble plots. In Macon County, residents are more prosperous. The median income of black families in 1980 was $10,423, the highest in the Black Belt. The square in Tuskegee is bustling. There are several fast-food restaurants not far away, a sleekly modern town hall, and a comfortable, black-owned motel just off the interstate highway. Even so, median income for white families is—at $17,500 in 1980—substantially higher than for blacks. And black income has actually slipped from 63 to 60 percent of that earned by local whites between 1970 and 1980.

The failure of the Tuskegee Industrial Park to attract industry is, to many, a symbol of the economic hurdles still facing black-run counties. When the park opened in 1974, Macon County blacks were still in the first, heady stage of running local government. Optimism about their ability to overhaul the local economy was at its peak. The marker designating the entrance to the park reflected that euphoria. "The Pride of the Swift Growing South —City of Tuskegee Industrial Park. Johnny Ford, Mayor," it read. For the next decade, attracting a major industry would remain a priority of Ford's. But as time passed and prospect after prospect slipped away, Tuskegee's internationally traveled mayor began to talk more about the importance of retail growth and the stability of the local employment rate, which remained among the best in the Black Belt. He was less likely to mention the fact that the Tuskegee Institute and the local Veteran's Administration

Hospital remained, as they had been for generations, the main-stays of the local economy, or that the percentage of county residents working in manufacturing jobs was in 1980 the second lowest in the state. The major addition to the local economy was the state-regulated Victoryland dog track, which opened in 1984 and promised to inject several million dollars annually into local governments.

Both Ford, a suave and urbane former aide to Bobby Kennedy, and Ronald Green, the college-trained administrator who headed the Macon County commission, spoke of the frustrations of trying to attract white-owned industry. While Ford bristled at the suggestion that the industrial park had failed, he acknowledged: "For something to come to Tuskegee, they've got to be convinced. You know and I know who owns most of the industry in this country." One of his first acts as mayor, Ford recalled, was to schedule an appointment in Montgomery with an official of the company that operated the Big Bear food chain. Big Bear had been planning to build a store in Tuskegee, but when news of the change in city government hit the streets of the capital, doubts began to surface. "The first thing I had to do was go meet with him," Ford said. "I had to assure him. He was planning on building a new store. When they heard the mayor was black, then he was about to change his mind. So I had to assure him that it would be okay."

Next came a sewing factory. There again, the company had been thinking about locating in Tuskegee. But when officials heard about Ford, they were less sure. "So I had to go and assure them," he said. "Just about every commercial outlet we have, I had to personally, as mayor, assure them that it was okay to locate in a community that was predominantly black. Kentucky Fried Chicken, I had to just talk with the man, discuss it. Burger King, I had to say, 'Hey, come on.' "

As a former economic developer for the county, Green estimated that he had contacted some three hundred firms about locating there. While no company officer told him directly that the large minority population was a handicap, Green had no doubt that it was. A top official in former Governor Fob James' administration suggested to him that industry—fearing unionization and labor troubles—shied away from counties with a population that was more than 30 percent black, he said.

That opinion was supported by evidence presented in a 1983 court case involving a firm in Roanoke, Alabama, several counties away on the Georgia border.[3] Material subpoenaed from the Amoco Fabrics Company, a subsidiary of Standard Oil of Indiana, suggested that Amoco officials would not consider locating in an area where more than one-third of the residents were black. Internal memos and depositions described the search for a plant site. In one memo, the man in charge of the plant location project informed Amoco's president that several Georgia counties had been eliminated from competition "on the basis of high minority or high industrial employment." In another instance, the plant locator reported that Cordele, Georgia, was rejected "because minority population was considerably higher than previously reported." In a deposition, an industrial development executive employed to aid in Amoco's search said he was told not to consider counties with a minority population over 35 percent. And in other court papers, the fabric company's vice-president for manufacturing said bluntly: "Our experiences are that the lower the concentration of minorities, the better we're able to perform and get a plant started up." In a subsequent survey of industrial development specialists in various southern states, the *New York Times* found wide agreement that worries about unionization and worker reliability prompted various industries to steer clear of majority-black counties, particularly in the 1960s and 1970s.

Through little effort of county fathers, and primarily because of proximity to Montgomery, one stroke of good fortune did befall Lowndes County. The General Electric Company, attracted by cheap land, availability of the nearby Montgomery airport and related factors, decided to locate a $350-million plant within the county. Scheduled to open in early 1987, the plant was expected to employ about 250 people in producing commercial and industrial plastics. There were mixed opinions, however, on how much Lowndes County would profit. Company officials admitted that upper management was almost certain to live in Montgomery. A thirty-seven-year moritorium on paying local taxes had been granted through the Montgomery Industrial Board, which represented local interests in negotiations with GE. And most jobs were expected to bypass Lowndes County's unskilled work force. In early hiring, a company spokesman said that only 3 to 5 percent of the jobs were going to county residents. Certainly, there would be spinoff benefits. GE had already made a $25,000 award to the local vocational-technical center and had allotted $100,000 toward a four-year program designed to improve the work skills of high school students and others. However, the gifts were only a fraction of the company's multimillion dollar tax break, and skepticism about major change remained widespread. "The new plant coming in here will never help Lowndes County," said Frieda Cross, who with her husband ran the local newspaper, the *Lowndes Signal.* "They're looking for educated employees. The people who are on welfare are not educated," she said.

Such complaints cut a familiar refrain throughout the rural South. During the 1960s and 1970s, the region as a whole had outpaced other areas of the country in industrial growth. But the pattern of expansion was an uneven one. Rural areas had benefited little, and if the county was also majority-black, the likelihood was that its industrial progress was least of all.[4] In some cases, businesses simply chose to locate in metropolitan areas where transportation and communications systems were more reliable and work forces better trained. In others, low-wage industries that might once have been candidates for settling in rural areas were producing their wares overseas. But in still others, some industrial relations specialists said, companies feared that the poor schooling and high dropout rates often equated with rural, black counties might hamper hiring and that unionization might become a greater threat than in settings dominated by whites.

For Macon County blacks, the local industrial park is proof aplenty that such discrimination is real. Theirs is a county in which local residents are unusually well educated for the rural South. A major interstate highway runs through the county. There is an aggressive mayor with national political ties in the county seat. And the federal government has contributed millions of dollars toward improving local life. The combination has not put Macon County blacks on an equal financial footing with the county's whites, nor the county on an economic par with most of its majority-white neighbors. "If whites had been willing to overlook color, there's no reason in the world why that county should not have been an oasis, culturally, economically, and otherwise," concluded Jerome Gray, field director for the state's major black political organization, the Alabama Democratic Conference.

Dramatic, overwhelming change was what many blacks had in mind when they began the quest for political power in Macon, Lowndes, and other Black Belt counties. The pursuit of that power in individual sites followed varied routes. Yet even when the populations differed, experiences often overlapped. Wide gaps in education and sophistication separate some Macon County blacks from those in Lowndes County, and those differences are reflected in the counties' political histories. On the one hand, Macon County's odyssey was highlighted by precedent-setting lawsuits and negotiations between blacks and whites. Lowndes County's route, like the locale itself, was courser and tougher, overshadowed by violence and the threat of force. On the other, Macon County did not escape turbulence. Murder occurred there, as well. And in the 1980s, shared memories of political violence, totally foreign to most Americans, still shaded the surface calm in which both communities moved. Intertwined with those histories were the stories of two men—Tuskegee's Johnny Ford and Lowndes' John Hulett. Each was the dominant political figure in his county, and each reflected the separate, yet unifying qualities of the localities they represented.

Johnny Ford grew up in Tuskegee in the days before prominent whites had packed their bags and moved to Opelika or Montgomery or some other spot where they were less likely to find themselves beholden to a black mayor or their children enrolled in heavily black schools. In those days, and to a lesser extent in these, there were four groups of people in Macon County—the wealthy whites who lived in gracious, lattice-trimmed houses set back from the roadway in yards of wildflowers and boxwood hedges; professional blacks, attracted to Tuskegee by the institute or the Veterans Hospital, bringing with them touches of big-city culture and both a fascination and disdain for the more simplistic surroundings they found; low-income whites, who were able to inject into the equation some of the meanness found in neighboring counties; and poor blacks, whose poverty and illiteracy were as acute as that anywhere else in the South. The populace was much aware of those castes, and at times the chasm between professional and low-income blacks was as great as betweeen blacks and whites.

By 1985, Ford was Tuskegee's best-known citizen, commanding an audience far outside the boundaries of his hometown. He was chairman of the World Conference of Mayors, and Ronald Reagan, he said, called "from time to time." His office walls featured a mosaic of photographs, recording moments with presidents and would-be presidents. Such mementos seemed light-years removed from the tumbledown neighborhood where Ford grew up amid the lowest of Tuskegee's castes, poor blacks. The only child of a father who worked as a nursing assistant at the VA hospital and a mother who did domestic work for both black and white families, Ford recalls with clarity his segregated upbringing and the moment when his political ambition was born. Standing outside the city park in downtown Tuskegee one day in the mid-1950s, he watched white children swimming and playing ball in an enclave protected by a fence topped with barbed wire. A plaque over the gate carried the mayor's name, and in his thirteen-year-old mind, Ford conceived the idea that if one mayor could put up a barrier, another could take it down. He would become, he resolved, Tuskegee's mayor.

Had he but known, legal maneuvers that would one day help make that dream a reality were already being set in motion. The population in Tuskegee had long been majority-black, but black voters used whatever limited clout they possessed to influence white councilmen, not to elect members of their own race. In the 1950s, however, a few whites began to squirm at the notion that blacks might one day rise up and claim political office. They decided to redraw the city boundaries. When they were finished, almost every black resident had been excised from the city limits and any danger of a political coup had been forestalled. Charles Gomillion, a professor at Tuskegee Institute and a leader in a local black civic association, decided to file a lawsuit in protest. In 1960 in a landmark decision in the case of *Gomillion v. Lightfoot,* the U.S. Supreme Court ruled that racial gerrymandering was, indeed, unconstitutional. Four years later, the residents of Tuskegee marched to the polls and installed on the town council the first two black men to win public office in Alabama since Reconstruction.[5] By then, Macon County had become the first county in the South in which a majority of the registered voters were black. In keeping with the moderate leanings of Macon County's black leadership, Gomillion and others agreed to run biracial slates for office in 1964 and 1966. Two incidents marred the attempts at harmony.

In one in January 1966, Sammy Younge, a Tuskegee Institute student working with SNCC to register Macon County voters, was killed by a white man when he tried to use the restroom at a local gas station. A riot ensued, and there was a second explosion later in the year when the white man was acquitted of second-degree murder charges. Partially as a result of the ensuing black anger, Lucius Amerson—who was not included on the biracial slate—was elected sheriff in the fall of 1966.

Against that mid-1960s backdrop, Ford fled north. He worked for awhile in the slums of New York's Bedford-Stuyvesant section, signed on as a political adviser to Robert Kennedy and—after Kennedy's death—came home to run for office. In 1972, his time came. He decided to challenge C. M. Keever, a local white store-keeper who had been mayor for about eight years. Personable and photogenic, Ford campaigned Kennedy-style, drumming up enthusiasm with door-to-door handshaking and open-air rallies. But even in the majority-black city, he believes, his election would not have occurred without the protection of the Voting Rights Act. Gazing out an office window overlooking the street that once divided the black and white sections of Tuskegee, Ford described one of the ways in which the act influenced his election. "They had put all the voter registration days in the summer when the students were away," Ford recalled. "There were about 3,700 students. On the last day of registration, the football team, the cheerleaders came back early. We got a bus and loaded up the entire football team, right? Two-hundred-and-fifty pound tackles. We ran the bus to the courthouse. They just literally scared those little white folks to death. So they just locked the door. They would not register anyone. This was a violation of the Voting Rights Act, so we filed a lawsuit. We took it to the federal district court in Montgomery. The judge ruled in our favor . . . . The voting registrars were ordered to open up again Monday. We registered about 150 students." The next day, out of 4,000 votes, Ford won by 127.

He took office on October 7, and the transfer of power from white to black in Macon County seemed complete. Keever, in an act that symbolized the capitulation of local whites, simply packed up and left town. J.A. Parker, the president of the Alabama Exchange Bank, headquartered on the square in Tuskegee, was one of the prominent whites who remained. Over a decade later, Parker recalled the frenzy with which whites sought to block the advent of black power and the disappointment when they failed. "They took all the steps they could to avoid it happening," said Parker, a small, congenial man whose office door stands open to drop-in visitors. "They scared voters with what they could expect if it was all blacks—inefficiency, jobs being bought and sold. They played on prejudices like George Wallace did."

By any standard other than race, however, the mayor Tuskegee had acquired hardly seemed radical. More pragmatist than ideologue, Ford took as his hero Booker T. Washington, a man whose conciliatory and self-effacing philosophy enraged more militant blacks. In a 1974 interview, Ford described what he admired about Washington. "He was production oriented. He didn't preach violence or hatred or bigotry. He didn't preach racism . . . . His philosophy was 'cast down your bucket where you are.' " Ford seemed unconcerned that, in his own words, Washington "was known as one of the biggest Uncle Toms that ever lived."[6] Adopting Washington's philosophy, Ford was to find, could work some wonders in Tuskegee, but not all the miracles he sought.

In Lowndes County, too, opposition to black political power ran deep. In early 1965, there was not a single black registered voter in Lowndes, a county then about 80 percent black. John Hulett, a small, compact man whose resolve matched his steely, muscular build, broke that barrier by registering on March 17. He became the pebble that started an avalanche. A few nights later, Viola Liuzzo, a white Detroit housewife, set out for Montgomery after depositing in Selma a group of people who had completed the Selma-to-Montgomery march. She intended to ferry a second set of marchers back that night, but her plans were interrupted. Liuzzo never reached Montgomery. After a frantic, high-speed chase through the darkened countryside, a car carrying four Ku Klux Klan members, one of whom turned out to be an FBI informer, pulled alongside her green Oldsmobile. Shots were fired and the car with Liuzzo, fatally wounded, at the wheel plunged into an embankment.[7] Three of the Klansmen were eventually convicted in federal court of violating Liuzzo's civil rights, but not before the first of the Klansmen to stand trial was acquitted of murder by an all-white Lowndes County jury. So bruising is the

memory of that trial that—two decades later—a local white official who sat on the jury still carried a copy of the judge's instruc-
tions in his wallet. O.P. "Buddy" Woodruff, a white farmer and
former commissioner who was appointed probate judge after his
predecessor retired in late 1984, drew out the paper, worn into two
pieces and yellowed with age. He read aloud the words, instruct-
ing jurors to acquit the Klansman if they found that the testimony
of the informer provided the only evidence of guilt. "I've carried
it for twenty years," Woodruff said of the judge's charge. "When
I would travel, there were so many questions. Eventually, this
would come up."

Lowndes County again became the focus of unwanted national
attention a few months later. The county, one of the first to be
visited by federal registrars after the Voting Rights Act passed in
August, had been a focal point of black voter registration efforts
throughout the summer. In one episode, about thirty people were
arrested in a picket line that had formed outside the ramshackle
collection of storefronts facing the railroad track that runs
through the center of Fort Deposit. Among the mostly black
protesters were two white men, Jonathan Daniels, a seminarian
from New Hampshire who had come South for the summer, and
Father Richard Morrisroe, a priest in a mostly black parish in
Chicago. After a week in jail without bond, the group was unexpectedly released on August 20. As Daniels and Morrisroe walked
with two black girls toward Varner's Cash Store across from the
austere old courthouse in Hayneville, a part-time deputy sheriff
named Tom Coleman blocked their path. There was an exchange
of words, and Coleman began blasting away with a shotgun. Daniels died instantly. Morrisroe survived, paralyzed.[8]

The murders were deeply affecting for both Stokely Carmichael, the newcomer to rural Alabama, and Hulett, who had
grown up amid the rampant poverty of Lowndes County. Carmichael arrived in Lowndes County two days after Liuzzo was
killed. Throughout the summer, as SNCC's representative, he
worked with Hulett and others to register hundreds of black voters, and when Daniels was added to the list of slain civil rights
advocates, Carmichael erupted in anger. "We're going to tear this
county up. Then we're going to build it back, brick by brick, until
it's a fit place for human beings," he told listeners at an evening

rally a few days after Daniels' death.[9] The words could have been Hulett's own. The time had come, Hulett agreed, to take control of a power structure that left blacks and their allies unprotected.

The avenue Carmichael and Hulett chose would be creation of their own power base—the Lowndes County Freedom Organization. The group took as its symbol a taut and snarling black panther. Later, when the movement had reached west to California, Carmichael and Hulett's creation was dubbed the Black Panther Party, and it became—with its militancy and outrage—a symbol of fear in a nation torn by the struggle for civil rights. Years afterward, his hairline receding, his still-wiry frame clad in the brown shirt and tan pants of a rural sheriff, Hulett sat in the office he had occupied since 1970 and recalled the years of struggle. The black panther, insisted Hulett, was not intended to strike fear. "It was only an emblem," he said. "The press named it the Black Panther Party. We formed a parallel party because when we started filing for office, the Democratic Party upped the fees from $50 to $500. We chose to do our own party so we wouldn't have to pay the fees."

By 1966, a year after Hulett walked into the registrar's office and insisted on his right to vote, blacks had a voting majority in Lowndes County. That spring, when it became clear that they intended to use their clout to oust white officeholders, the local Democratic Party devised a plan. Nominations would be made through a convention, rather than the usual primary, and the filing fees—as Hulett noted—would be hiked dramatically. Those efforts were rewarded in November when the entire freedom organization slate went down to defeat. Many blacks did not vote, and others were not yet ready to break with the tradition of supporting whites. Two years later, black candidates were again defeated after a strange episode. The local probate judge, Harrell Hammonds, a wealthy white landowner who had long befriended blacks, refused to release the names of the Lowndes County Freedom Organization's candidates prior to the election. To do so, he insisted, would jeopardize their lives. Only after the local Democratic Party threatened a lawsuit did he renege and release the names. In 1970, the long-sought breakthrough finally came to Lowndes County. Three black candidates were elected to the offices of coroner, circuit clerk, and sheriff. As Hulett donned the sheriff's badge, whites steeled themselves for the dreaded transfer of law enforcement authority to a man whose organization, at least nationally, had taken on revolutionary overtones.

It seemed fitting, given the county's violent past, that the first major position won by blacks was that of sheriff. Just as Ford's polished demeanor was an appropriate reflection of the county he represented, so John Hulett seemed a proper ambassador for Lowndes County. Rough-hewn, uneasier than Ford in the spotlight, Hulett, with his soft voice and reticent manner, was a legendary figure in the Black Belt. After years of attention, however, he still disliked being photographed, and even discouraged reporters from sitting in on his talks to schoolchildren. The day he took office in 1971, Hulett met the silent defiance customary when blacks were elected in those years. The former sheriff and his two white deputies simply left. It was up to Hulett to learn the job by trial and error. Across the county, whites feared a breakdown of police protection and watched warily during Hulett's first months on the job. "You didn't know how it would turn out, whether he would answer the calls of white people," recalled Frieda Cross. "But everytime anyone called, he answered promptly." Mayor Norman was even more explicit. "Some people didn't think they'd be more than a first-class monkey," he said, referring to the county's first black elected officials. Hulett was aware of the suspicions and the concern that his affiliation with the Black Panthers hinted at a disregard for the law. But he was no revolutionary, and after a few months of performing the job he was elected to do, "people started falling in line," he said. Ominous predictions that whites would take up arms to block his serving in office never came true.

It did not take long to establish in both Lowndes and Macon counties that there were limits to what political power could achieve. For Ford, an early lesson came in the form of the statue of the Confederate soldier, which was presiding in timeless fashion over the small green in the center of Tuskegee's town square. A pledge to dismantle that unwelcomed reminder of a grim past was part of Ford's campaign for mayor. Once elected, however, he discovered that disposing of the statue was not so easy a task. The Daughters of the Confederacy, it turned out, owned the statue and the land on which it rested, and they were not disposed toward removing it. Eventually, the women offered to give Macon County the park—if they would move the statue to a white cemetery and construct a government complex in keeping with southern traditions.[10] The last demand was so costly and so vague as to be unworkable. In 1985, the statue remained.

When Ford took office in 1972, there were less symbolic priorities as well. Chief among them was improving the economic lot of his town and county. As director of the local Model Cities' program, Ford was already familiar with various avenues for attracting federal funds. The new mayor had also rubbed shoulders with white politicians during his days in the north, and he was not opposed to using those connections or other practical political lessons he had learned. He knew, for instance, that as a southern black Democrat, his support would be much appreciated in certain quarters. When George Wallace stood for reelection in 1974, Ford ignored the governor's segregationist past and backed him. Earlier, Ford had broken with most black voters by endorsing Nixon over George McGovern in 1972. In Neal Peirce's study, *The Deep South States of America,* Ford matter-of-factly explained: "If they're looking for a favorite fellow to give some extra money to, I'll certainly take it. It's business with me—no emotion. What you must do is penetrate the system and, once within the system, learn how it works."[11]

Ford learned well. In a 1983 report on progress in rural Alabama, the U.S. Civil Rights Commission reported that between 1970 and 1981, Tuskegee received over $30 million in federal and state funds to help prepare the city—directly or indirectly—for industry.[12] When money for schools, law enforcement, health facilities, and the like was added, Ford estimated that the first thirteen years of his administration had produced $60 million in outside grants. The industrial park had been purchased and built with federal funds. An adjoining airport serviced by a small commuter line had similar funding. An antiquated water system had been replaced by a modern water facility pumping about 4 million gallons a day. A new, $16-million sewer system served the county. An updated electrical distribution system allowed Tuskegee to sell electricity throughout the county. "That was all done with federal dollars," said Ford. "We've been fortunate in getting federal resources to develop the infrastructure of the city for physical, social, and economic development."

What state and federal dollars alone could not do was convince white businessmen and industrialists that they should also invest private funds in Macon County. At the Tuskegee Industrial Park on a warm spring day in 1985, Johnny King described the impact of white skittishness on black fortunes. Nearby, about two dozen employees of King's firm, C&K Manufacturing, sat stitching light olive fabric into Army dress shirts. A few months later, King's company would run out of contracts, but for the moment, his workers and the employees of a small, high-tech firm that also filled military orders were the park's only residents. The building in which they worked seemed dwarfed by the quiet, undeveloped surroundings. Talking above the whir of the machines, King complained about the difficulty of attracting industry to Macon County and of starting a minority enterprise. Area banks turned down his applications for establishing a $100,000 line of credit, and it was only through a government-supported revolving loan fund that the business finally got under way. "You take the white boy," King argued. "He can go establish himself a line of credit because he grew up in the environment. He played with the bank president's son, and if they can do it for him, they will. But me? I've got to put up my whole life and sign a contract in blood."

In Lowndes County, also, political power had its limits. By the mid-1980s, the pace and approach of government continued to seem as unhurried and languid as ever. In many ways, the managing of public affairs was no better, no worse. Until state auditors pushed them to change, county commissioners—as they had for years—turned out little more than a skeleton budget, based more on past habits than current needs. It was 1984 or so before the commissioners finally began to call in various officials and ask them how much money they really needed to do their jobs. "Before, they just didn't have a bookkeeping system," said Linda Bargainer, the white tax collector. Black-run commissions, like the white-run ones before them, "had receipts, just all piled up." Tax Assessor Elbert Means, who was emerging as the resident black critic of the county's black-run government, complained about the results of that approach. "The county commission, they have no idea what I do here, and this is 90 percent of their monies," he said. "I've never been called to a budget hearing. We're not accountable for nothing. We do what we want to do."

Voter registration rolls, long swollen with individuals who no longer lived in Lowndes County, reflected the lackadaisical approach to government. In the mid-1960s, one writer recorded that no blacks and 118 percent of whites were registered to vote in Lowndes County. By 1985, it appeared that both black and white registration were in excess of actual voting-age population. Asked for a registration count, Probate Judge Woodruff sifted through various drawers before coming up with a figure of 12,400 eligible voters. That number was 750 less than the total population of a county where a sizable chunk of the residents were children.

And so, in numerous ways, from absentee ballots to job openings, change and permanence walk hand in hand in Macon and Lowndes and neighboring Black Belt counties. Voices of optimism blend with voices of dispair. "Political gains have yet to translate into economic gain. Blacks in Lowndes County have little reason for optimism," concluded the U.S. Civil Rights Commission staff when they visited the county in 1983. And in Macon County, they warned: "Segregation, white economic power, and the decrease in federal assistance may impede future progress and development within the county." Still, both the commission and local residents could point to some positive change. Basic services in both counties are vastly improved. Twenty years earlier, few black homes in Lowndes County had running water. By 1985, most did. Earlier, the county had no sewers, except in Fort Deposit. By 1985, sewer systems served substantial portions of the county. Through the local health department clinic and the Lowndes County Health Services Association, medical care was more readily available to poor people. In Macon County, the pattern was similar. Water, sewer, and health services were all improved.

While social institutions do not fully reflect the change, there are also important adjustments in attitudes. Blacks are more confident of their place in the mainstream; whites, however reluctantly, are more accepting as well. "A lot of people didn't think the Nigras would ever be able to do anything," admitted Fort Deposit's Mayor Norman. "Now they can see that they have." The comparable black view was expressed by Willie Moore, a retired waiter at Tuskegee's Veterans Administration hospital. As he pumped gas for pocket money at a mom-and-pop grocery on the edge of town, Moore fairly radiated his joy at the modern state of affairs. "Since that march in '65, it's a different world," he said, wiping his hands on an oil-streaked cloth. "Everything's better." In the old days, before black officials ran the county, he said, most black people steered clear of white enclaves like Notasulga. "They used to arrest you over there if you went through," he said. But no more. "This county here, it's just about right," Moore concluded.

So long as blacks and whites have equal access to major institutions, neither group seems particularly perturbed by the lingering social segregation. Members of the races meet on the sidewalk or in the courthouse in Hayneville and Tuskegee, and as they have done for generations, pause to chat about the weather or the general demise of affairs in Washington. But people, black and white, do not go visiting in each others homes. They do not worship together or educate their children in the same classroom. "That's just the way life is," said Hulett, and with the possible exception of schooling, "it doesn't bother me a bit." What does perplex black officeholders throughout the region, however, are poverty statistics that seem to defy improvement. Hulett might be the dominant politician in the county, but he does not hesitate to say that politics has failed to produce the changes he and others expected. "Until people become economically strong, political power alone won't do. For most people, it's like it was sixteen years ago," when he took office, Hulett said.

Challengers to the established black leaders, like Means, see the economic failure as one of technique. If whites were given a greater role, if blacks were more careful about budgets, if both were more demanding of results, then perhaps jobs would follow, they argue. Talking at a locomotive's pace, Means ticked off his list of complaints: "Nothing has changed in this county that we —whites or blacks—had a hand in. Any change here was stuff that was passed down from the outside. We have not had any industry come. The school board's at an ebb. There's an alarming rate of illiteracy." All too often, the young people who come into his courthouse office to purchase automobile tags are unable to write, despite being recent high school graduates, Means said. In a school system run by blacks, he added, the blame can no longer be placed on whites.

In the midst of that ongoing political debate, there is growing suspicion that the failure of Black Belt counties to improve economically is a systemic problem, almost beyond correction by local officials. With similar woes plaguing the full sweep of majority-black counties, it seems clear that more is needed for correction than simple shifts in local personnel. Increasingly, state departments of industrial development are being called on to devise specific strategies to aid poor black counties. One suggestion urges inexpensive, commuter transportation systems for counties, like Lowndes, which are in close proximity to urban areas. Other proposals call for increased involvement of blacks on state industrial boards and more specific help in setting up utilities and other services needed to attract industry.

Despite the immensity of the task, across the Black Belt men and women continue to hope that economic and social barriers might someday crumble as political ones once did. Mrs. Euralee Haynes, who retired in 1985 as the first black superintendent of schools in Lowndes County, believed that might happen when the GE plant finally opened. "GE could come in here and give us the money to build a school of the future," said Haynes one late spring afternoon, just weeks before she would leave office. Her administration was only then recovering from its pitiful showing on the 1983 competency exams, but Haynes' focus was on the future, not the past.

A day earlier, a white family had enrolled their three children in the public schools, citing the high cost of private academies. Their addition boosted white enrollment in the entire school system from ten to only thirteen, but Haynes was delighted. "Economics can do a whole lot of things. That's one reason we got three kids back," she said. Just as Haynes saw in those three white faces hope that the era of private academies might be passing, so she argued: "GE could change the whole complexity of the system. Who knows?"

The scenario seems as unlikely as did Haynes' enthusiasm over an infinitesimal shift in student population. But hope can never fully be discounted in such settings. Just twenty years ago, the notion of blacks holding political office also seemed an impossible dream.

6. BIRMINGHAM
The Mayor

IN MEMORY, he is five years old, a plump, serious boy with his father's eyes and his mother's nose and a manner so disarming that some relatives have taken to calling him "Papa." The year is 1940; the place, Livingston, Alabama. Around him drifts a serene and finite world, its boundaries stretched by Saturday morning wagon rides into town, its days peopled with cousins and aunts whose tenant shacks are a corn field or cotton patch away. Already, he is being fitted into an economic vise. He rides a mule bareback to the spring, wrapping small fists around the handle of a bucket that he lugs back to his sun-parched parents. His tiny fingers snatch course, white puffs of cotton from opened bolls and deposit the prize in a rough, woven sack. He is as unaware of the poverty that surrounds him as of the threat, now spreading past Europe, of global war.

On this clear, late-summer evening, the boy is about to encounter change. He is bidding his first farewells. Goodbye to the kerosene lamp-lit rooms he has known, to the paneless wooden windows that latch fast at night, to the walls papered with pages from old catalogs. Goodbye to the Nixon family, whites on whose land his father has sharecropped and whose ancestors were half brothers and half sisters to his own, darker-skinned great-grandmother Ann. Goodbye to the wide, fertile fields of cotton, peanuts, and potatoes. With his mother, Mary Ernestine, and his brother, James, the boy climbs into the back seat of a cream-colored automobile. The car is the pride of his Uncle Joe Nathan, who drives. His father sits straight and alert in the front seat, his strong, talented hands at rest. A mattress is fastened to the roof of the car. The inside is loaded with boxes so that the boy can hardly see out. He and his brother vie for a glimpse through the windshield of unfolding horizons. The towns pass—Livingston, Eutaw, Tuscaloosa. A warm wash of night air and the songs of insects fill the car. He sleeps. A jerk. A start. The car stops on a city street.

He is in Birmingham. The magical city spreads before him. A few miles away, rust-colored stacks spew out black smoke as thousands of grimy, sweat-drenched workers labor at U.S. Steel's Fairfield mill. Soon, his father will join them at the plant, the largest steel-making facility in the South. Further away, to the east, is Red Mountain, with its telltale red soil, its iron-ore rock formations, and its statue—fifty-five-feet high—of the god Vulcan, wild-eyed and triumphant in his discovery of iron. All around in the Jones Valley, an uneasy, simmering brew of ill-educated, economically insecure immigrants, poor whites and often poorer blacks, fuel this brash, upstart industrial metropolis. The boy sees nothing but the house, his new home. He dashes through the rented rooms, three of them, linked one to the other in shotgun fashion, so that a bullet fired through the front door might pass undetected out the back. He marvels at the electric lights, opens the icebox door, plans where he will sleep. Outside, there is a ferocious clanging, and the boy rushes to the high front porch. The noise is from a streetcar, his mother tells him. He does not know what a streetcar is, nor that the Vinesville line will one day carry him uptown to a world and a life beyond anything he can imagine.

Thirty-nine years later, on a November day in 1979, former Alabama governor George Wallace, then governor Fob James, U.S. senator Howell Heflin, and a slew of dignitaries converged on a bunting-draped stage in downtown Birmingham. They had come to witness one of the more extraordinary events in the history of a city long tormented by racial strife. Less than two decades earlier, the town had been derisively labeled "Bombingham" and "the Johannesburg of the South." Some fifty racial bombings, culminating with the deaths of four Sunday school students in May 1963, had plagued the city over the years, and the ingenuity and brutality of city fathers in enforcing racial segregation had proved ludicrous even by southern standards. So, the installation of the first black mayor of Birmingham was a scene that both state and national dignitaries were unwilling to miss. As schoolchildren waved tiny American flags and the Alabama symphony performed the rousing score of Purcell's "Trumpet Voluntary," a shy, deferential man whose credentials included a University of Oklahoma doctorate in invertebrate zoology, stepped forward for the oath of office. Reporters from the *New York Times,* the *Chicago Tribune,* and elsewhere scribbled notes as Richard Arrington savored the moment by recalling his family's odyssey from Livingston three decades earlier.

"Sometime in 1940 my father, who had spent his adult life as a sharecropper in southwest Alabama, decided that better fortunes for his family lay in coming to Birmingham," Arrington began. "He had no money to pay the bus fare for the 110-mile trip . . . so he asked his brother, who had already come to Birmingham to work, to send him bus fare. . . . He came to this city and found a job in the steel mill and immediately moved his family to a duplex house in the western section of the city." And now, like others, his parents had lived to see their children attain undreamed-of positions of responsibility.

Already, when Richard Arrington came to office in 1979, there were black mayors in Atlanta, New Orleans, and Richmond. Mayor Maynard Jackson of Atlanta was midway into his second term; in New Orleans, Ernest "Dutch" Morial, a former civil rights lawyer and judge, had completed a volatile first year in office. Across the South, in small towns and isolated counties, dozens of other black men and women were dismantling the bastions of a segregated past. Still, perhaps no other southern black politician's story testifies so eloquently as does Arrington's to a spirit of human triumph and the resilience of the American political system. It is not only that Arrington mounted a rags-to-riches rise, from a cotton patch in the Alabama Black Belt to the laboratories of a recognized university to the helm of the state's most populous city. It is also that his ascent came in Birmingham, a city long synonymous with the most hateful and demeaning features of a discredited way of life. If, as blacks began their third decade of active participation in southern politics, Atlanta was the model for what a city could become, then Richard Arrington was the model for individual success. By the mid-1980s, with no legal or—apparently—political obstacle separating him from a third term in office, beginning in late 1987, Arrington had become as entrenched as any figure in southern municipal politics. White businessmen who had feared disaster when his inaugural coincided with the continued demise of Birmingham's steel industry, were solidly behind him. Continued downtown construction had staved off fears of a dying commercial core. The mostly black Jefferson County Citizens Coalition, founded by Arrington in 1977, was steamrolling its way through elections as successfully as any comparable political group in the nation.

Yet the price and limits of change remained painfully clear. Some of the themes were familiar, repeated in setting after setting as blacks continued their push for equality into the 1980s. Arrington's avid pursuit of economic parity for blacks had produced minimal and sometimes embarrassing results. Only a handful of blacks had been named to major commercial and banking boards within the city. More than once, Arrington's attempts to steer city contracts to minority firms had resulted in newspaper stories highlighting his own political and even financial links to the companies involved. Nor had Arrington's dramatic successes in Birmingham made him any more immune than other ambitious black politicians to lingering racism outside the city's boundaries. Arrington's fondest political dream was to challenge Senator Jeremiah Denton in the 1986 United States senatorial election. It was not, he finally concluded, a race a black man could win. If such economic and political limits were typical regionally, another aspect of Birmingham's evolution seemed unique. By midpoint in the mayor's second term, some longtime liberal whites—voices of moderation in the race wars of the 1960s—had become outspoken critics. Their complaint was that this mild-mannered scientist and former academic dean had become a political kingmaker and boss. Arrington dictated who was elected to the Birmingham City Council through the Citizens Coalition, and he dictated city policy through the council's majority-black membership, they said. Admirers responded that Arrington had been evenhanded in his treatment of whites, even as he pursued the goals of his primary constituency, blacks. But the mere fact that a charge of exclusionism had been leveled was for a Richard Arrington—indeed, for any black son or daughter of the Birmingham of the 1940s, 1950s, and 1960s—the greatest of ironies.

To southern blacks, Birmingham in the mid-twentieth century was more than a name or place; it was the very symbol of racial separatism. Martin Luther King, Jr., viewed the Birmingham of the 1950s and 1960s as "the most thoroughly segregated city in the country."[1] And Virginia Van der Veer Hamilton, professor of history and department chair at the University of Alabama in Birmingham, also wrote that "Birmingham in the 1950s was the nation's largest and most rigid bastion of segregation."[2]

There was proof aplenty. As elsewhere, both public and private facilities—schools, churches, restaurants, theaters, hotels, hospitals, and cemeteries—were racially segregated. But there were even more ingenious twists. In one incident, Birmingham whites banned a book featuring both black and white rabbits. In another, they tried to stop white-run radio stations from playing the music of black artists. The Metropolitan Opera refused to perform in the city, and the Southern Association's baseball team left town in protest.[3] In 1961, when the city was ordered to integrate its recreational facilities, officials simply shut down sixty-eight parks, thirty-eight playgrounds, six swimming pools, and four golf courses.[4] Separatism was enforced by both random and official violence. Arthur D. Shores, the city's first black councilman and for more than a decade the only practicing black attorney in Alabama, for instance, saw his home bombed twice in 1963 and in another incident, found a box with forty-eight sticks of dynamite set to go off at his house.

Long-standing animosity between the police department and black residents also had a devastating psychological impact. Among blacks, the prevailing sentiment in police-community relations was neither respect nor dependency, but fear. The city's first black police officer was not hired until 1966, and by 1976 only 5 percent of the force—twenty-eight officers—was black.[5] The chilling impact of that segregated system is recalled by Arrington as one of the most distinctive features of growing up black in the Birmingham of the 1940s and 1950s.

"We grew up in fear of the police," Arrington said, as he sat —legs tucked beneath him—on a plush tan sofa in his spacious city hall office. Typically, the mayor was meticulously outfitted in a tailored black suit and white silk shirt. His small white mustache and thinning dark hair were carefully groomed. Relaxed and at ease amid the understated elegance of the room's polished wood floors, its deep-grained paneling and recessed lighting, Arrington seemed an unlikely candidate to have experienced the bruising incidents of which he spoke. A bookshelf to one side of the formal sitting area held the standard treasures of a family man and sports enthusiast turned politician. There were snapshots of an infant daughter and young son, an autographed basketball and football from city teams, a framed photograph of former president Jimmy Carter. Only a wall etching of Martin Luther King, Jr., pensive, his mouth pressed against folded hands, his eyes focused on some indiscernible spot, separated the scene from dozens of mayoral offices across the country. In that setting, Arrington's high-pitched, reedy voice was calm and even. His gaze was direct, his face lit by a half-smile. Yet, as he spoke, there was no mistaking the significance he attached to a series of police-related memories, both for their impact on him personally and for what they said about the larger Birmingham community. "We grew up listening to the stories of adults—you didn't know whether they were true or not—of how the police would call you over to their car and hit you over the head," he said. "It was an issue that haunted me all my life. Even when I was a teenager, my mother could not rest 'til we were home. I was a freshman in college, and if I was not in by 11:00 P.M., my dad had to go find us. My mother never said, 'You're going to get in trouble out there.' It was always the police, afraid of what the police were going to do. . . . I grew up never having a favorable experience with a police officer."

If Birmingham blacks had long been aware of their contemptuous treatment by police, the nation at large was forced to confront the issue in the spring of 1963. In April of that year, King began a series of fateful marches that would not only bring appalling photographs of police brutality into living rooms across the land, but would also—for the first time—underscore to the nation the potential destructiveness of unbridled black rage. At issue in the demonstrations was the desegregation of downtown department stores and public facilities, as well as public- and private-sector hiring. As King led singing, chanting legions of blacks through Birmingham streets, Police Commissioner Eugene "Bull" Connor

—a former baseball announcer and twenty-year veteran of city government—obtained a court injunction to stop them. King refused, and on Good Friday, he and others were jailed. Still, the marches continued. An increasingly incensed Bull Connor met them with snapping police dogs, electric cattle prods, and high-pressure fire hoses. A nation watched transfixed as columns of children were driven back by the force of the water and as police dogs lunged at kneeling demonstrators. The outraged response brought local black leaders and some seventy-seven of the city's most prominent whites to the bargaining table.[6] Within a week, an accord was reached, but the night after the settlement, the hotel where King had stayed and his brother's home were bombed. The attacks set off a rampage unlike anything the country had yet witnessed. Groups of enraged blacks roamed the streets for several hours, breaking windows, setting fires, and smashing cars. "The rules of the game in race relations were permanently changed in Birmingham during the predawn hours of Mother's Day, 1963," one historian wrote, recording the militancy of Birmingham blacks during that melee.[7]

Any doubts about the urgency of tackling Birmingham's racial problems were erased a few months later when a bomb shattered the Sunday morning stillness at the Sixteenth Street Baptist Church. Located diagonally across from the Kelly Ingram Park, where many of the spring marches began, the yellow-brick church with its twin spires and blue neon cross was a rallying point for civil rights activists. Paying the price for that involvement on the morning of September 15, 1963, were the four young girls who died in the bombing. Chris McNair, a professional photographer later elected to the Alabama legislature, lost his oldest child, Denise, that day. The episode, he recalled twenty-two years later, "had a devastating effect on me personally." But it also inspired "a soul-searching, awakening time for the nation," he said. "Birmingham wasn't that much different than any other town. This town was just dumb enough to offer the friction that was needed for that kind of thing to succeed. The whole nation was corrupt."

The week before the Sixteenth Street Baptist Church bombing, Richard Arrington left Birmingham for Oklahoma, ready to begin work on a doctorate. From an early age he had intended to go to college. "Nobody in my family had ever gone to college, but my parents always told me I was going to," he recalled. Arrington was less sure about how to get there or what to do after he arrived. In high school, he studied dry cleaning in a vocational program considered far more practical for young black boys than English literature or Latin, and when he enrolled in Birmingham's all-black Miles College, the height of his ambition had been reached. A freshman psychology teacher, however, took an interest, suggesting that he had an aptitude for science, and another teacher —a biologist—began preparing him for graduate study. "I didn't even know what grad school was at the time," Arrington recalled. He quickly learned.

After earning a master's degree at the University of Detroit, Arrington was persuaded by Dr. Lucius Pitts, the magnetic new president of Miles College, to return to Birmingham. The association with Pitts—Brother Lucius to the Miles College faculty—was a turning point in his life, Arrington believes. "He would tell me and others what we had to do in this city in terms of providing black leadership," Arrington said. "He convinced us we had a role to play in the community, beyond what we did professionally." Previous Miles College presidents had watched skittishly as students began to speak out about racial segregation; Pitts, in contrast, helped them to organize. When two black women were roughed up by police in a neighborhood near the college, Pitts convened a meeting of black leaders. Arrington was tapped to draw up the list of grievances. The act was his first direct involvement in the civil rights movement, and it defined the role he would play. It was not in Arrington's nature to march or deliver rousing protest speeches. What he could best contribute was behind-the-scenes legwork, drafting statements, and developing position papers. That he did.

By 1966, when Arrington again returned to Birmingham, this time with a doctorate in hand, much of the racial furor had cooled. Still, "even though we had gotten off the streets, there were problems," he recalled. When black leaders formed a community action committee in the late 1960s and again presented whites with a list of complaints, including police brutality, Arrington was part of the group. One result was the formation of Operation New Birmingham. That alliance of civic leaders and businessmen launched a series of Monday morning breakfast discussions that continued into the 1980s. The meetings provided Birmingham's first significant biracial forum. Whites dominated the organization, however, and in a 1974 interview, Arrington expressed continuing black concerns. Operation New Birmingham "has wanted to say who the black leaders are going to be in this town, and they have annointed blacks with whom they could deal," he said.[8]

One such man, many felt, was Arthur Shores, who had been appointed as the city's first black councilman when a vacancy occurred in 1968. Despite his distinction as a civil rights attorney who had represented King and others, Shores was a congenial and humble man who posed little threat to the white leadership. His sense of fairness led him to find admirable traits even in such avid segregationists as Bull Connor and George Wallace. "Bull was a loudmouth, but it was politics," Shores maintained two decades after Connor's historic confrontation with Birmingham blacks. At age eighty-two, Shores still kept office hours and liked nothing better than to reminisce about bouts with his old adversaries. "Bull would tell me, 'Whenever you have anybody in the city jail, if you feel they should be out 'til you have a trial, just tell 'em I said to let your clients out.' " Shores said he believed Connor was a racist "in a way," but that George Wallace—who pledged to preserve "segregation forever" when he began more than two decades of off-and-on control of the governor's mansion in 1963— was not. "I tried a case before him when he was a circuit judge twenty-five years ago down in Barbour County," Shores said. "The case lasted a week and there was not a decent place I could eat. The governor sent out for food, and we'd eat in his chambers." Wallace simply used the race issue for political advantage, Shores argued.

Richard Arrington joined Shores on the council after the 1971 elections. He had been tapped earlier that year by a group of blacks anxious to cultivate some younger and more aggressive political leaders. His low-key style appealed to enough whites to elect him, and the leadership void into which he walked helped ordain his success. In politics, Arrington said later, "timing is everything." It was his good fortune politically to emerge at a moment when Birmingham blacks were longing for an official voice to focus attention on the city's continuing racial problems.

What neither blacks nor whites fully realized was that this quiet, refined academician had long been incensed by police treatment of blacks and that he would not flinch from speaking out when the opportunity to do so came. Ironically, the first brutality complaint handled by Arrington involved a white man. Soon afterwards, other people began to appear at his door, and Arrington did not hesitate to bring them or their problems before the council. If someone was bruised or beaten, he was particularly anxious that they be seen. The police brutality issue, Arrington said, "became the foundation of my whole political career. It was an issue I did not have to compete with other elected officials on. None of them wanted to touch it. . . . All of a sudden, I had as close as you could get to 100 percent support in the black community."

By 1979, the overtures for Arrington to run for mayor were mounting. Both he and his second wife, Rachel, were resistant, thinking that the time had come for him to pursue his longtime plan of becoming a college president. David Vann, Birmingham's incumbent white mayor was moderate to liberal on racial issues, and Arrington felt no particular concern about seeing the city in Vann's hands. In the early summer, the Arringtons left town for vacation. They returned to find the city in an uproar over the police shooting of twenty-year-old Bonita Carter, a young black woman who had been in the gunman's car during a convenience store shoot-out. Carter, who was unarmed, died from three shots in the back, fired by a policeman. Outraged blacks insisted that the policeman be fired, but Vann refused disciplinary action. The mayor's only move was to take the officer off patrol duty, citing concerns for the man's safety. Arrington recalled a 9:00 A.M. meeting in which he and other blacks begged Vann to reconsider. The mayor refused and, with the police chief at his side, promptly announced the decision at a 9:30 A.M. press conference. The response was an outbreak of the city's worst racial violence since the 1960s. In Kingston, where the incident had occurred, there were clashes between groups of blacks and Ku Klux Klansmen. Young blacks hurled bricks at passing cars, and snipers took aim at the police. For the first time in his life, Arrington decided to join a protest march as an estimated four thousand people descended on city hall. A group of black ministers meeting at the Trinity Baptist

Church summoned Arrington and informed him that they intended to draft him to run for mayor. "We feel you owe it to the black community," he recalled their saying. Arrington sat down and wrote out a statement. Only a few weeks remained until the first round of the mayoral elections, but he would run.

In that race, Arrington first defeated Vann, who could not withstand the loss of black support, and went on to face Frank Parsons, a white lawyer and travel agent, in the runoff. The contest was characterized by racial innuendo and division. On election day, a record 72 percent of Birmingham's black voters went to the polls, and Arrington swept into office with a two-thousand-vote margin. A *Birmingham Post-Herald* analysis concluded that 90 percent of whites backed Parsons and almost every black voter supported Arrington. The new mayor inherited not only Birmingham's legacy of a racially troubled past, but also an electorate repolarized by the events of recent months. Arrington also faced the universal dilemma confronting "first" black mayors—how to address the soaring expectations of long-powerless blacks without further alienating whites whose continued involvement was imperative for a healthy economy. "You're dealing with expectations when you first come in," said Arrington. "There are the expectations of the black community that expects you to do much more than you can do, and the expectations of the white community that expects the very worst, that has all kinds of fears."

Six years later, Richard Arrington presided over a city that astonished no one so much as itself. Problems were there for all to see, but the achievements seemed paramount. A city of 284,000 people (56 percent black), radiating to a metropolitan area of almost 1 million, Birmingham had survived both economic and racial trauma. Driving west toward Tuscaloosa, U.S. Steel's giant Fairfield Works—once the hub of a smoky, bustling corridor, now a largely idled collection of rust-colored smokestacks and towering railyard tipples—stood as a reminder of an economic era that had passed. To the east, the statue of Vulcan still rose from Red Mountain's iron-crusted depths, but the Roman god's right arm no longer held aloft a just-forged spear. Reflecting a new era, the hand bore a green light promoting traffic safety. Once, a sign on the old Chamber of Commerce building downtown had boasted:

"Everything to Make Steel—Iron ore, Coal, and Limestone—are all within Gunshot of this building." Americans had identified the city as "the Pittsburgh of the South." One of every three jobs was reportedly linked to iron and steel production, and those who visited the town found a conglomeration of iron foundaries, machine shops, blast furnaces, and mines. By the mid-1980s, the largest employers in a diversified economy were the University of Alabama at Birmingham and a series of communications companies. U.S. Steel, which once issued paychecks to some thirty thousand Birmingham-area workers, was down to a payroll of twenty-five hundred after a temporary shutdown in 1982. The company had recently invested about $1 billion in a seamless steel pipe mill, but operations were high tech, a world apart from the gritty furnaces and production lines of years past. Downtown, high-rise bank and office towers mingled with aging, yellow-brick buildings where the industrial magnates of the 1930s and 1940s held sway. Nearby neighborhoods, with their modest homes and tiny yards, reflected Birmingham's working-class makeup and the stamp of urban poverty. But the city's core was alive. It had not been abandoned by white financial interests.

Racial progress was equally apparent. Two decades after Birmingham shocked the nation with its racial intransigence, blacks and whites in this onetime war zone seemed to have reached a workable, if imperfect, peace. White businessmen ran unsolicited ads in support of a black mayor. Biracial groups, uniting some of the city's most distinguished white leaders with neighborhood representatives for poor blacks, met regularly. Blacks, once excluded from city hall, controlled the city council, even as major departments continued to be run by whites. The city's commitment to black hiring and contracting was dramatically changed, but whites had not been excluded. Certainly, problems remained, and they were not minuscule. Whites were still leaving the city for more segregated suburbs. The white population in city schools continued its decline, from 53 percent in 1960 to 18 percent in 1985. Voting patterns still showed solid blocs of black versus white voters. Private clubs and service organizations were only beginning to open their doors to blacks. The downtown Birmingham Rotary Club had taken in two black members and the Kiwanis Club had three. Corporate boards had only token integration, and

blacks and whites who met during working hours seldom social-
ized together in the evening. Yet few places in the South—or the
nation—seemed in 1985 to present such contrast from 1965. Birmingham's racial problems might be no less than those in dozens
of other cities, but astonishingly, they were no greater.

What did seem larger than usual was the influence of the
man who had led in orchestrating change—Richard Arrington.
To many, the very notion of Arrington as machine politician
seemed ludicrous. This, after all, was a man who still emitted an
aura of shyness, who returned Sunday after Sunday to the tiny
Primitive Baptist Church he attended as a child, who liked nothing better than a meal of turnip greens and corn bread, who
infinitely preferred an evening at home with a good book and
Ray Charles on the headphones to an uptown cocktail party or
a handshaking, baby-kissing session at a local mall. His strength
lay in the methodical, organizational skills associated with a
scientifically trained mind, not in any charismatic draw or particular knack for manipulating power. So bland was Arrington's
image that his wife felt moved to insist: "He's not a dull man.
We tell jokes. He wears casual clothes. People don't believe
that." Comparisons to former Chicago political boss Richard
Daley, which surfaced in Arrington's 1983 reelection campaign
and stuck, were nothing more than a political ploy, produced by
that year's opponent, protested the mayor. "Look at Daley as a
personality, a man who pulled all the strings. I have nothing like
that," he said. But Arrington's laughing dismissal gave way to a
hint of satisfaction as he added: "It's amazing. People begin to
believe what they hear after awhile. Legislators call me and
think they can't get their bills through without my support. If
you constantly say somebody's powerful, even when they're not,
a lot of people believe it."

Arrington's lock on power was not achieved overnight or without trauma. The most openly divisive racial confrontation between his administration and white residents came in 1981 and
involved electoral politics. That year, Birmingham voters were
due to elect five of the nine members of the city council. About
three weeks before the October election, the *Birmingham News*
reported that Arrington appeared to be pushing for a black majority on the city council by endorsing an all-black slate for the

vacancies. Whites at the time controlled six council seats and blacks, three. Having lost the top city post two years earlier, whites were unwilling to see their control at city hall erode further, and they mounted an enraged protest against the appearance of racial bias on Arrington's part. The mayor argued that he had done nothing different than whites who had simultaneously endorsed an all-white slate. "It was an example of fear feeding upon fear," he said.

Tensions heightened in mid-October as the *News,* under the headline "Arrington 'Machine' Thunders," reported that the five Citizens Coalition candidates had easily catapulted into the ten-person runoff field. "If ever there was any doubt about the power of Mayor Richard Arrington's political machine, it was laid to rest Tuesday," the postprimary newspaper story read. A few days later, whites vented their wrath by doubling the normal turnout for an off-year election and defeating four of the black candidates. The number of whites on council jumped from six to seven, and Arrington was handed his first—and only—major political trouncing. The message did not go unheard. The Citizens Coalition, as well as prominent white endorsement groups, would make sure in future years that their slates included at least token biracial representation. Not long after the 1981 election fiasco, Arrington also began a conscious effort to build bridges to whites, particularly in the business community.

"What I had to decide as mayor was not whether I was going to pursue civil rights goals, but how to do it," Arrington said. "If I alienated all the white leadership, I began to realize that it was going to be twice as hard to achieve the goals. And so, I decided to sort of change my approach, to try to win people over."

Two of Arrington's major goals when he took office were to expand city hiring and contracting involving blacks. The state of minority hiring was indicative of how much segregation still existed in Birmingham. In 1966 the city had only 9 classified black employees out of a total of 1,689. Most unclassified workers, who held menial janitorial or grounds-keeping jobs, were black. Nine years later, in January 1975, the city still had only 155 blacks among its 2,233 classified workers. The police and fire departments were among those most resistant to change. In the decade after Birmingham's first black police officer was hired in 1966, blacks inched up to a mere 5 percent of the force. By August 1981, the city was majority black, but just 13 percent of the 651 officers were black. Blacks held no rank above sergeant, and only 3 of the 131 sergeants were black. There were similar conditions in the fire department. In 1976, eight years after the first black firefighter was hired, 2.1 percent of the force was black. By August 1981, the figure was still below 10 percent. None of the blacks held a rank position.[9]

Against that backdrop, the Birmingham branch of the NAACP and several individual blacks in early 1974 brought employment discrimination lawsuits challenging the city and Jefferson County. The U.S. Justice Department joined the plaintiffs a year later. In January 1977, a federal district court judge in Birmingham found that various hiring policies in the police and fire departments did discriminate against blacks. The ruling was upheld on appeal, and a second trial directed at other personnel board policies began in August 1979, just prior to Arrington's election. By that fall, the various parties in the lawsuits had launched serious negotiations to work out a settlement. Once elected, Arrington lent his blessing. "I said we were not going to pay out any more fees to fight what we knew was a losing cause," he recalled. A consent decree, calling for increased hiring of women and minorities, was entered in August 1981. By mid-decade that agreement was, ironically, under attack by some of the same Justice Department officials who had helped negotiate it, but the impact on city hiring had been appreciable. In the police department, for instance, 130 officers had been hired since the decree took effect. Of those, 67 were white and 63 black. Twenty-seven whites and 23 blacks had been promoted to sergeant, and 7 whites and 3 blacks to lieutenant.[10]

Still, Arrington had also shown that it took more than a black mayor to produce dramatic hiring changes in a city governed by civil service regulations. Most of the high-ranking positions in city hall were still held by whites. The only black department heads were the city attorney and the director of streets and sanitation. "Under civil service, I have to wait 'til there's a vacancy; you can't just fire people," explained Arrington.

A second, related goal of Arrington's as he came to office was to expand the number of city contracts awarded to minority firms and to encourage the private sector to get involved in minority enterprise. At midpoint in his second term, the mayor would cite those attempts to turn political power into economic gain as the most frustrating aspect of his years in office. Arrington's hands were partially tied by a state supreme court decision forbidding minority contract ordinances, popular in other states. Meanwhile, his overtures to the private sector were hampered by the city's conservative banking climate and by citywide difficulties as Birmingham made the transition from an industrial economy to a more diversified one. Asked what local blacks had to show economically for his tenure, Arrington replied: "Quite frankly, we don't have very much."

If the change was less than Arrington hoped, there had still been some economic progress for blacks. The most measurable results involved city contracting. In the mid-1970s, before Arrington took office, the city adopted an ordinance calling for 15 percent of public works projects to be awarded to minority firms. In 1976, prior to the ordinance's passage, less than $1,000 had been awarded black firms out of city contracts totaling millions.[11] The new rules rapidly came under legal challenge from the Associated General Contractors. In 1980, the Alabama Supreme Court sided with the contractors. It ruled that giving preferential treatment to black firms violated the state's competitive bidding law. The decision was appealed to the U.S. Supreme Court, and city officials were stunned when the high court refused to hear the case. The rejection left the fledgling Arrington administration with no choice but to try to stimulate voluntary compliance with the banned ordinance. "For two to three weeks, we just held up on awarding contracts," recalled Roger A. White, Birmingham's contract compliance officer. "The contractors started worrying about payments. Finally, the utility contractors came to the mayor and offered a plan to voluntarily use minorities. We agreed. That was the beginning." In 1985, for the fifth consecutive year, the city met an informal goal of awarding more than 10 percent of all public works contracts to minority firms.

Measuring progress in the private sector was more difficult. As in most American cities, the black-white income gap in Birmingham remained discouragingly wide. The 1980 census reported that 6 percent of the city's white families lived in poverty, compared with 28 percent of black families. Median income for white families was $19,550; for black families, it was $11,425. Given that disparity, one longtime dream of Arrington's was creation of the MESBIC (Minority Enterprise Small Business Investment Company), which would provide venture capital for minority firms. Repeated efforts by Arrington to fund the MESBIC fizzled, however. Soon after he took office, Arrington met with the presidents of four of the city's leading banks—AmSouth, SouthTrust, Central, and First Alabama—and asked them to put $250,000 each into the low-interest, lending pool. That seed money was to provide the leverage for another $4 million in borrowing capital, Arrington hoped. Arrington believed that the bank officials were committed to the project's success. The mayor received several progress reports and, when the MESBIC fund reached about $700,000, suggested that the group file for federal licensing. No one filed. "Finally, it just dawned on me that they weren't going to do it," Arrington said.

"I don't know why four or five people should be asked to conceivably take major losses over a city policy," responded Wallace Malone, Jr., chairman of the board of SouthTrust, Alabama's second largest bank holding company. "It sort of took on the aspect of banks lending money to a lot of people who were not qualified to borrow the money and did not have the wherewithal to ever pay it back." Others saw the banks' failure to respond in a different light. Ed LaMonte, executive secretary to Arrington and his top white aide, underscored the administration's disappointment. The MESBIC's failure, he said, stemmed both from the underdeveloped state of minority business in Birmingham and the legal problems encountered by the city in trying to mandate minority contracting. But it also said something about white business attitudes, LaMonte argued. "There was not an exceptional effort made to say, 'This is a fault in our community, a weakness. We are all well served by making special efforts."

By the mid-1980s Birmingham residents were hard-pressed to name more than a handful of major black businesses within the city or more than a token number of black representatives on corporate boards. At its upper echelons, the black economic structure remained remarkably similar to that of the mid-1970s. A.G. Gaston, whose insurance company, bank, realty firm, radio station, and assorted other investments had earned him millions, remained—even as he passed ninety—"the" man to see in black corporate circles. Besides Gaston's endeavors, there were successful black-owned janitorial and limousine services. Most other black businesses fit traditional categories—funeral homes, building contracting firms, and mom-and-pop operations. Six years after Arrington took office, two blacks sat on the seven-member Federal Reserve Bank Board. Louis Willie, Gaston's right-hand executive, was a board member for the Alabama Power Company, and there were blacks on the corporate boards of AmSouth Bank and South Central Bell. Asked for other examples of blacks on prominent boards, Willie shook his head. "I just ran out of gas," he said. Still, Willie said, that disappointing record must be placed in its historical context. When he came to Birmingham from Texas three decades earlier, "I didn't even know there was a Federal Reserve Bank Board," much less expect to become its first black member. "The ground is now much softer for planting other seeds," Willie said.

As 1986 began, there was little doubt that Arrington and the city's first black council majority, elected late the previous year, intended to do all they could to speed the process. Arrington had avoided the dramatic showdowns in which Atlanta's Maynard Jackson threatened to halt airport construction or withdraw city funds from various banks if minority concerns were not addressed. But there were hints that the new council—with backing from Arrington—intended to act more aggressively in forcing white businesses to deal with the economic needs of blacks. "We're starting to discuss these items with all the individuals who come before us to ask for support," said William Bell, an administrator at the University of Alabama at Birmingham and the newly elected council president.

Arrington's growing assertiveness on economic matters stemmed partly from the ease with which he won reelection in 1983. As that campaign approached, Birmingham's economic health was of paramount concern to both blacks and whites, particularly when the jobless rate soared to a stunning 16.7 percent in January 1983. Since the 1960s, the city had begun to cultivate a more diversified economy than in the days when steel production and related mining interests reigned. But Birmingham remained enough of a blue-collar town that it was hard hit by recessionary trends in the early 1980s, and when U.S. Steel temporarily closed its doors in the summer of 1982, the shutdown was a blow to the community. Voters, however, seemed to accept the mayor's argument that the city was a victim of national trends, not mismanagement. (Indeed, by November 1985, the city's jobless rate had dropped to 6.1 percent.) Meanwhile, Arrington stressed that a wave of downtown commercial construction was under way, and he touted his efforts to develop a series of industrial parks. Most of all, he capitalized on the goodwill developed with white businessmen, particularly during the second half of his first term.

Business sentiment was highlighted in an election-eve newspaper ad, featuring endorsements of Arrington by board chairmen or presidents of several of the city's most prosperous firms. Such stamps of approval sealed the fate of his white mayoral opponent, John Katopodis. A Harvard-trained educator and councilman, Katopodis was generally viewed as a liberal until he became city hall's resident critic of the Arrington administration. Throughout the campaign, Katopodis railed against Arrington's mounting influence, rehashing the bitterness of the 1981 councilmanic campaign and drawing parallels between Arrington and Chicago's Mayor Daley. It was to no avail. Arrington whipped Katopodis by almost twenty thousand votes.

At least part of Katopodis' rhetoric—the claim that Arrington was becoming all-powerful politically—stuck, however. Two campaign developments underscored Arrington's growing clout. First, on a rainy election day in the wake of a relatively quiet campaign, Arrington and the Citizens Coalition turned out a stunning 76 percent of the city's registered black voters. The figure not only set a record for blacks, but also outstripped white voter turnout by about 10 percent. After the debacle two years earlier, the coalition was clearly taking no chances. Second, not only had solid bloc voting insured Arrington's reelection, but the coalition-backed council slate had done just as well. Four of the six men endorsed by the coalition won outright; two others faced each other in a runoff election.

As the 1980s evolved, other incidents bolstered Arrington's image. There was, for instance, his decision to back Walter Mondale over Jesse Jackson, the favorite of many Alabama blacks, in the fight for the 1984 Democratic presidential nomination. On Super Tuesday, the day Mondale faced possible annihilation in a series of primaries and caucuses, the Citizens Coalition rolled once again. Spurred by entreaties that a vote for Mondale was a sign of confidence in Arrington, Birmingham's black voters gave Mondale an edge that figured prominently in his Alabama victory. "Many voters are very comfortable with Arrington's leadership," sighed the Reverend Abraham Woods, a Jackson supporter and the local head of the SCLC, after Jackson's defeat in the city.[12]

Nor was Arrington's growing stature diminished by articles such as a February 1984 dispatch describing the mayor as the city's "secret weapon" at the state capital in Montgomery. According to the report, the mayor had driven downstate for a private meeting with Lieutenant Governor Bill Baxley, pulling from the ashes a bill giving Birmingham a horse-racing track. It was the second such resurrection orchestrated by Arrington, and it prompted state senator Earl Hilliard of Birmingham to comment in a news report: "Political power is the perception of political power. Everyone in this state feels the mayor has a great deal of influence over the black vote. . . . People believe he has power, and believe me, he does."[13]

Proof surfaced once again in the 1985 races for city council. Almost two dozen candidates, including seven members of the Citizens Coalition, filed for five seats. When the tally was taken, four of the coalition's candidates led the balloting. A fifth coalition member, a newcomer to council politics, was forced into a runoff with Bettye Fine Collins, a white woman who was a former school board chairman and had served on council since 1981. Collins, a forthright and sometimes combative woman who—through the Urban League and other groups—had long cultivated solid black ties, made no secret of her outrage at not being rewarded with coalition support. "The thing that hits me, it doesn't matter where you've been and what you've done. It's whether you're going to swear allegiance to a person, the mayor. That is not good government," she said. Collins flaunted her independence during the campaign and proved on election day that the coalition was not invincible. But her twenty-five-hundred-vote victory had its price. Tension between Collins and some black council members was striking. "Don't call me Ms. Collins, please," snapped council member Linda Coleman, after a clerk misidentified her at a meeting in early 1986. And council president William Bell quickly cut off a reporter asking him to respond to a criticism raised by Collins. "I don't comment on what Ms. Collins says," Bell replied.

If the 1985 elections once again demonstrated the polling power of Arrington and the Citizens Coalition, their most far-reaching consequence was the emergence for the first time of a black voting majority on council. While Arrington had lost few major battles during his first term-and-a-half, most observers expected the transition to immunize him from any but the most minor policy defeats, again tightening his rein on the city. Many of those who had once scoffed at the label "Boss Arrington" were beginning to see some validity in it. "It is becoming more and more an accurate statement," said David Herring, a senior vice-president of the First Alabama Bank of Birmingham and the council president until his ouster by Bell after the 1985 elections. Most blacks and some whites seemed to have little problem with the cementing of Arrington's power. For instance, Jimmy C. Lee, board chairman and chief executive officer of the nation's largest, family-owned Pepsi bottling operation, located in Birmingham, saw that clout as the inevitable consequence of Arrington's having performed well. "He is certainly building quite a political structure of which he seems to be the leader," said Lee, who is white. "There's nothing wrong with that. He has a tremendous amount of white support."

But individuals like former councilwoman Nina Miglionico and John Katopodis worried that whites could come to feel alienated and inconsequential in city government, just as blacks once did. Such a feeling clearly dictated the decisions of Miglionico and Katopodis not to seek reelection to the city council in 1985. Their combined tenure was over thirty years, yet both felt local government was so dominated by Arrington that they could play one of only two roles—a rubber stamp or a voice in the wilderness. Particularly for Miglionico, a tiny, spunky lady who had three crosses burned on her lawn in the 1960s and whose role in easing racial tensions in that era doubtless exceeded Arrington's, the departure was laced with irony and some sadness. With a shrug and in a resigned voice, she described her view of Arrington's attitude: "Getting a black majority on the council was more important than keeping people with 'black hearts.' I was introduced many times as having a 'black heart.' I'm not being critical. I'm merely saying people's priorities can be different." Her own priorities, Miglionico insisted, were not far removed from Arrington's. Yet, despite her long record of civil rights activism, she did not win Citizens Coalition backing in 1981 and had appeared to have little hope of doing so in 1985. "The danger comes if whites feel it's not necessary for them to go to the polls, that the black coalition has spoken and they will elect. That has a civic dampening," Miglionico said.

Another danger, some said, was that Arrington—long viewed as scrupulously honest—would become lax in mixing private friendships or business deals with public responsibilities. The *Birmingham News* throughout 1985 reported a series of small incidents that seemed to suggest that the lines of separation were weakening.[14] In one episode, the mayor awarded a business partner an unbid city contract, possibly worth $240,000, to perform architectural work at a downtown auditorium. As mayor, Arrington is authorized to hand out contracts worth thousands—and even millions—of dollars each year for architectural, legal, and other consulting services. Those contracts do not have to be bid, and Arrington has made no secret of his interest in using them to expand city work done by minority firms. Arrington argued that the city had contracted with the architect to do preliminary inspections on the auditorium months before the two men became partners in a marketing and sales firm. It was understood from the outset, Arrington said, that the same architect would be used if the city decided to proceed with the renovation. Such episodes prompted the editorial staff of the *News* to call on Arrington to avoid "even the suggestion of impropriety." The mayor described the hubbub as overblown but agreed that he intended to become more cautious.

Addressing the larger issue of his domination of Birmingham through the Citizens Coalition and a majority-black council, Arrington insisted that he was being credited with more power than existed. When the newly elected 1985 council dumped Herring, who is white, as its president and installed Bell, who is black, Arrington maintained that he was as surprised as anyone. The turning point for Bell came when two black members, who had previously committed to Herring, decided under considerable pressure to switch. None of that pressure came from him, Arrington said. Similarly, Arrington said he had taken little direct role in determining Citizens Coalition endorsements in recent years. But few observers either inside or outside the coalition doubted that Arrington could sway events when he chose. Some, including the mayor, said it was only a matter of time until the coalition— no longer glued together by the imperative of breaking down racial barriers—began to fray. But, barring a major misstep, it seemed unlikely that any significant split would occur while Arrington held office. No other black Birmingham politician could come close in commanding white business support. That fact helped Arrington cement his hold on black voters, just as continued solidarity among blacks boosted Arrington's stock with white businessmen.

"The mentality here is that as long as the economy's good and the blacks are quiet, everything's good. But that doesn't speak to whether there's truly been racial progress," complained Katopodis. As legitimate as those concerns might be, even the criticism hinted at Birmingham's progress. To say that an economy that had undergone a radical transformation was healthy was no small achievement. To say that blacks in a city that had symbolized the worst of southern apartheid were generally satisfied with public policy seemed revolutionary as well. There were valid worries about increasing alienation among white voters, but as long as the business community remained willing to invest in the city, those problems did not seem insurmountable. Certainly, if the newly elected black-majority council hoped to maintain a biracial city, its enthusiasm for black economic activism would have to be tempered by extending olive branches in other directions. It was a lesson that Arrington professed already to have learned, and his guidance would doubtless be crucial.

Many people had contributed to Birmingham's improved racial climate, but none more than Richard Arrington. To the hard-edged, brittle climate of the 1960s, he brought a competence and quiet dignity that disarmed those who said no black man was capable of running Alabama's largest city. His even-tempered, nonthreatening style and academic background were perhaps the perfect antidotes to the hysteria that had so captivated earlier generations. As the city's ambassador to the rest of the nation, he epitomized a new Birmingham, less wedded to a brutal past than to an optimistic future. His challenge in the close of the 1980s was to manage his extensive power as effectively as he had managed its acquisition. No one could fault Arrington for pressing forward in the area most resistant to change, black economics. But the route was not without risks. The ongoing task was to strike a balance between black and white interests, at least until that day when such distinctions had blurred.

That such a day had yet to arrive was clear from Arrington's soundings on the 1986 U.S. Senate race. He was repeatedly told that if any black man could successfully challenge Denton, it was he. The unstated corollary was that, of course, no black man could. Arrington's conclusion was that he might win the Democratic primary through a combination of black bloc voting and the ballots of Republicans, who would support the challenger they perceived to be the weakest opponent for Denton. Alabama voters are not required to register by party. But Arrington simply could not envision a situation in which he would win the general election. Race, he believed, remained too potent a force, too ingrained in the subconscious mentality of too many voters. To ease his disappointment, Arrington in early 1986 helped found the Alabama New South Coalition, a predominantly black statewide voter group. When he also became its first chairman, there was widespread speculation that the mayor was angling to run for some major statewide office. Arrington insisted otherwise. His goal was the U.S. Senate, he said, and if he could not run against Denton in 1986, it was most unlikely that he would challenge Senator Howell Heflin, a Democrat, when Heflin's term expired in 1990. "Time is against me; I'm not as young," he said. What Arrington did hope the New South Coalition might do was to make some younger black person's stab at major office more feasible. "I'd like to remove those artificial ceilings on ambition imposed by race," he said.

Certainly, his own achievements and ambitions had soared far beyond the imaginings of anyone who happened to see a car, mattress on top, and a small face peering from the back seat, speeding toward Birmingham on a summer evening in 1940. He had become Mr. Mayor, a marvel to some, a thorn to others, but the undisputed political leader in a city that once would have scorned his service. His hope was that, as part of his legacy, no one else would have to travel quite so far.

7. RICHMOND
The Tensions

IT WAS ONE OF THOSE sticky, sweltering days when the ice cream
vendors along Main Street do a bumper business and the stockbro-
kers, lawyers, and bankers who have made this street a state
symbol of monied aristocracy and unchallenged power send out
for sandwiches and iced tea. Ninety miles to the north in Washington, President Jimmy Carter's energy plan was in trouble, stalled
by the summer doldrums and a controversy over price controls on
natural gas. Overseas, U.S. efforts to mediate peace in the Middle
East and Rhodesia were stalemated, and the diplomatic corps was
lamenting the latest Arab terrorist bombing in Tel Aviv. Back in
the Old Dominion, Virginians were in shock. The GOP's Senate
nominee had died two days earlier in the crash of a small plane,
and mourning supporters were sadly turning their sights to John
Warner, a rakish former Navy secretary, and Elizabeth Taylor, his
celebrity wife. On Richmond's Main Street, however, as twilight
softened the leaden heat on this evening of August 4, 1978, and
bookkeepers, tellers, and secretaries straggled home, there were
even more pressing concerns.

The group filing into the spacious and austere meeting room
on the first floor of the United Virginia Bank building, at the
corner of Tenth and Main, represented the corporate giants of
Virginia's capital city. Collectively, the net worth of the dozen or
so executives was an estimated $50 million. When they spoke,
governors and senators, as well as newspaper editorial writers and

city bureaucrats, usually listened. It was not whimsy that brought these titans together on an evening when most would rather be enjoying drinks at the downtown Bull & Bear Club or heading for a leather-bound easy chair in the luxurious, all-white neighborhoods of Richmond's West End. Instead, they perceived that a racial storm, as well as a potentially dangerous challenge to their own influence, was about the erupt. Their mission was to squelch that insurrection quietly, before Richmond's 219,000 residents—half black, half white—ever realized what had occurred.

Four guests, three men and a woman, also made their way to the bank building that evening. They had driven in from jobs in less prestigious sections of town, and most had never set foot in a private, Main Street meeting room. It was not hard to tell the insiders from the invitees. There was, for instance, the matter of pedigree. Henry Marsh, the spokesman for the group, was a whispery-voiced minister's son who happened to make his living defending black Virginians in civil rights cases. Claudette McDaniel, a flamboyant social worker, had grown up and still lived in a section of the city sometimes referred to as "dogtown." Chuck Richardson, who sported a distinctive, shoulder-length hairstyle, was a Vietnam veteran, then working on a degree in urban planning. Walter Kenney, a post office employee and national postal workers' union official, completed the foursome. Marsh, it so happened, was Richmond's mayor; the others were members of the Richmond City Council. If family roots did not set the guests apart, there was at least one other telltale distinction. All four were black. Everyone else in the room was white.

The white businessmen quickly laid out the agenda. Two days earlier, they knew, Henry Marsh had secretly approached Richmond's white city manager, Bill Leidinger. As mayor, representing a five-member black majority on a nine-member council, Marsh had delivered an ultimatum. The black members of council no longer felt comfortable working with Leidinger, Marsh said. It was time for the city manager to go. The black majority, hopeful that Leidinger would depart quietly, had offered him sixty-to-ninety days' notice to find a new job. What Leidinger, a forceful and independent manager who had no intention of leaving meekly, had done instead was to take to the telephone, informing corporate allies of this latest council outrage. And now, those men wanted to know, what in heaven's name did Henry Marsh and his colleagues have in mind? Did they not understand that so precipitous an act might shatter the fragile racial harmony that this city had carefully constructed since the Marsh majority came to power seventeen months earlier?

"I came here to listen," replied Marsh, his tone soft, yet firm. If his fellow council members were unaccustomed to rubbing shoulders with the economic elite of this tradition-bound city, Marsh did not suffer a similar handicap. He knew, at least professionally, most of the men in the room, and his law practice thrust him daily into adversarial relationships with influential white lawyers, judges, and officials. What Marsh had no intention of doing was acting like some lackey who had been called on the carpet for insubordination. He wanted the men in the room to know that he was not afraid of their anger. Nor, though he did not say so, did he expect to be persuaded by their arguments. His reply was simple. "I came to listen and learn. You're an important part of the constituency of the city I was elected to serve, and I'll take your views into consideration," he said.

Those views were quick in coming. Leidinger had been an outstanding city manager, some said. His expertise and skill would not be easily replaced. Leidinger enjoyed the respect of the business community, others added. He had done nothing to warrant the firing. The messages soon became more pointed. Business support was essential, someone warned, if the council majority had any notion of achieving its dream for an office-hotel-shopping complex that would revitalize downtown. There were veiled references to construction projects that might never materialize and businesses that might never set up shop if race relations were allowed to deteriorate. And then, there was the chilling message that Marsh carried with him years after the episode had passed. If Leidinger was not retained, the council members were told, "blood will flow in the streets of Richmond."[1]

"I'll get back to you," Marsh replied. The meeting disbanded. And then, Marsh did something that said to admirers that he was no one's "boy," and that to critics demonstrated an incredible arrogance. He simply packed up his family and left for a long-planned camping trip. By the time news of the impending firing broke three days later in Monday's editions of the *Richmond*

Times-Dispatch, Marsh was nowhere to be found. His black council colleagues, less polished than the mayor in their public dealings, were mum on the subject. For the next week, the controversy raged unchecked. At a press conference, Leidinger said he had "absolutely no intention of resigning." In an interview, Henry Valentine II, a leading participant in the Main Street meeting as well as a former vice-mayor, said Marsh "is not satisfied with being mayor, but wants to be king."[2] Not until August 15, eight full days after Richmonders became aware of the dispute and began to take sides, did Marsh issue a detailed public statement outlining philosophical and policy differences with Leidinger. By that time, opinions were already formed. Many of the white city fathers were in a fury. Lines had been drawn that would lead to years of political turmoil in this, the first southern city to elect a black-majority council to do its business.

When Marsh and four black allies captured control of the Richmond City Council in a special election on March 1, 1977, the news of their victory ricocheted across the South. Atlanta would soon follow, but for the moment Richmond—the beloved capital of the Confederacy—was the only major southern city with a black majority at its helm. The election prompted lamentation and glee. Those who envisioned the city eroding into the James River saw their fears reinforced by a banner headline in the Richmond *Afro-American* a few days later. "Power to the People," the newspaper proclaimed, raising a verbal clenched fist to a city and state steeped in the virtues of patrician, oligarchic rule. The paper's response was both a measure of the momentary euphoria among blacks and a foreshadowing of the bitterness to come.

A decade later, Richmond's experience had become a forceful study in the limits of black political power and in the pitfalls of trying too hard, too fast to force political change. To some, the first phase of Richmond's story, when Henry Marsh served as mayor from 1977 to 1982, is a tale of one man's arrogance and his failure due to an abuse of power. To others, who weighed Marsh's resolve and purpose more sympathetically, it is more nearly the story of the limits of one man in tackling a city's financial power structure and a reminder that political influence is less weighty than economic clout. As Marsh learned, a black mayor can afford to go only so far in alienating Main Street. If that threshold is ever reached, the mayor's days in office are probably numbered, as were Marsh's.

In two ways, Richmond's political evolution stands apart from those elsewhere in the South. First, the depth and persistence of acrimony on the Richmond council after blacks took control were unique. Dozens of key votes—involving appointments, redistricting, utility bills for the poor, school appropriations, a residency requirement for city employees, expense accounts, and more—broke down along racial lines. A former city attorney estimated that the city spent roughly $200,000 between 1978 and 1984 defending council members in lawsuits filed or encouraged by other council members.[3] At times, public threats and insults seemed commonplace. It would be six years before the hard-line, factional voting relaxed somewhat.

Equally novel when it occurred in 1982 was the election of a second black mayor whose power base rested mainly with whites. Roy West, a black middle-school principal and political novice, never heavily involved in civil rights activities, that year attracted mostly white votes in winning one of nine ward seats. Taking office on a pledge to end council bickering, he promptly joined with the four-member white minority to elect himself mayor. The move was a stunning setback to the Marsh-led black majority. White conservatives could scarcely believe their luck; black liberals were appalled. As time passed, most Richmond whites, including the bulwarks of Main Street, seemed delighted with West's performance. Blacks, however, remained divided over his leadership. The controversy reflected a growing national split between civil-rights-era black leaders and coalitionists willing to work in tandem with whites. It mirrored, too, growing economic differences among blacks. West, elected to a third term in 1986, represented a middle-class district; Marsh, a poor one.

Against that backdrop, Richmond also served as an example of the limitations of black politicians in effecting dramatic change. Black progress in Virginia's capital had, perhaps inevitably, fallen shy of the expectations many black residents had in March 1977. The political shift had brought a tide of black faces to city hall and a spate of city contracts to minority-owned firms. But the transfer of power from whites to blacks had proved more painful and the acquisition of power less absolute than many blacks envisioned. A voting majority at city hall had done nothing to erase segregation in the high-toned neighborhoods of west Richmond, where household income is four times that of the city as a whole. Nor had it eliminated the knots of unemployed black men, standing idly at midday amid the abandoned houses and garbage-strewn lots of the East End. It had not stopped a steady erosion of white support for public schools, which in 1985–86 were 86 percent black. And it had not reduced the number of black Richmonders who lived in poverty. Median income for Richmond's black families in 1980 was $12,643; among white families, $21,215.

And yet, for all this, Richmond and its residents—both black and white—had moved stubbornly forward. The city "will die if the Negroes take control," one influential writer for the afternoon newspaper, the *News Leader,* predicted before blacks won political control.[4] Instead, in the mid-1980s, Richmond as a whole was flowering economically, even as blacks continued their struggle to turn political clout into economic gain. A newly completed hotel-convention-shopping complex, featuring one of James Rouse's glass-and-steel pavilions, was prompting hopes for downtown revival. And the design, bridging Broad Street, the traditional dividing line of black and white Richmond, was a tribute to dreams of a more racially unified city.

As in other cities where blacks had won political power, the racial shift on city council had given Richmond blacks a role previously unknown on boards and commissions and in city offices. City boards from the housing authority to the planning commission had gone from majority-white to majority-black membership. Whites still held a disproportionate share of the top-paying city jobs, but the gap was narrowing. Of the thirty highest ranked positions, blacks held twelve in the spring of 1985, versus four in 1977.[5] Black role models included the city manager, the fire chief, and several city department heads. Meanwhile, city construction contracts awarded black firms were up from 3 percent in fiscal 1981 to 30 percent in fiscal 1984, according to purchasing officials. Even though "blacks expected a lot more to happen, things have changed for people who have the resources and know-how to get around," concluded Randolph Kendall, Jr., executive director of the Richmond Urban League. "Poor folks," he added, "they're still looking for a place to stay."

The city that Marsh and his allies took command of in 1977 had never been associated with the race-baiting vitriol of some quarters of the Old South. Throughout Richmond's history, the attitude of white leaders toward blacks was most often benign and paternalistic. Meanwhile blacks—less tortured than many of their brothers and sisters to the south—often settled for minor, incremental gains. For some, there was even a measure of prosperity. Before the start of the Civil War, about 20 percent of Richmond blacks were freed slaves. The nation's first black-owned bank and its first black insurance company were founded in the city.

Still, there was never any doubt about the insistence of whites on both their own supremacy and on racial separation. Throughout Richmond's history, incident after incident spoke to the forced inequality of blacks and whites. William Byrd, father of the city's founder, dealt extensively in the African slave trade. When George Wythe, signer of the Declaration of Independence and a Richmond resident, was poisoned by his grandnephew in 1806, a law forbidding the court testimony of a black person against a white protected the murderer. Ironically, Wythe had drafted the law. The only witness was a longtime servant of Wythe's, a black woman.[6] By the mid-nineteenth century, Richmond was second only to New Orleans as the nation's largest slave market. At least five slave dealers served on Richmond's common council before, during, or after the Civil War.[7] And the white view of black inferiority was reinforced by such rules as an 1859 city ordinance forbidding blacks to walk in Capitol Square, unless accompanied by a white.

Between the end of the Civil War and the turn of the century, some thirty-three black men served on the city council.[8] However, the turn-of-the-century adoption of a new state constitution effectively disenfranchised blacks. Richmond's black voters did not score another major victory at the ballot box until Oliver Hill's election to the city council a half-century later in 1948.

The racial tensions that would erupt after Marsh's election began to form in the mid-1960s. By then, both blacks and whites were becoming increasingly aware that the days of unfettered white political control in Richmond were ending. It was simply a matter of the numbers. In 1930 the city's population had been 71 percent white and 29 percent nonwhite. By 1965 the estimated gap had narrowed to 54 percent white and 46 percent nonwhite. Projections called for a fifty-fifty split by 1968. In a much-quoted editorial, the Norfolk *Virginian-Pilot* pointedly described the political situation. "One hears whispers more and more these days that something must be worked out before June 1968," the editorialist wrote. "The June 1968 deadline is . . . the point, according to computations by experts on population shifts, when Richmond comes face to face with the possibility that Negroes could take over control of the City Council. This is the reason behind a hectic search, now underway, for a means to re-establish a white majority in the city's population."[9]

A special commission of the state legislature lent its support to the cause of white supremacy. The Aldhizer Commission in 1969 recommended an amendment to the state constitution that would have allowed the city to expand its boundaries into the heavily white suburbs every ten years. Both the House and Senate gave their blessing in 1969, but final approval was blocked a year later.

Meanwhile, city officials were hard at work trying to shape an annexation agreement with neighboring Chesterfield County. In 1965 city and county representatives embarked on a series of private meetings that would extend over five years, eventually resulting in Richmond's annexation of twenty-three square miles and forty-seven thousand people. About 97 percent of those individuals were white, and their inclusion tipped the city's racial balance back toward whites. The acquisition also produced a legal challenge that over the next several years would take black Richmonders and city officials before a half dozen judicial bodies, culminating with the U.S. Supreme Court.[10] In a case unique in municipal annals, the proceedings would result in blockage of local council elections from 1970 to 1977.

The emphasis during the 1960s annexation negotiations, according to later court testimony, was strictly on increasing the number of Richmond's white residents. Several of the Main Street executives who summoned Henry Marsh and his allies to the 1978 upbraiding over Leidinger's firing played key roles in the talks. Meetings were held in private homes, some as far as fifty miles from Richmond, in secluded restaurants, and in parked cars.[11] As the 1970 city council elections approached, discussions between

Mayor Phil Bagley and Irvin Horner, the chairman of the Chesterfield County Board of Supervisors, intensified. At last, on May 14,
agreement was reached. In court Horner later testified that Bagley's abiding interest was in numbers (How many residents would
the annexation produce?), not in the impact on city services or on
Richmond's tax base. "He only asked me to verify how many
people were in the area of the line we drew," Horner said.[12]

Using the new boundaries, eight whites and one black—Henry
Marsh—were elected in 1970. Among the losers was Curtis Holt,
a disabled black construction worker and high school dropout
who finished seventeenth in a field of twenty-eight candidates. A
public housing resident and occasional preacher, Holt was largely
unknown to the city's established political leaders, both black and
white. He was, however, convinced that whites had manipulated
the 1970 electoral process, and that the black middle class had
capitulated in its duty to expose that moral corruption. Holt knew
practically nothing about the Voting Rights Act. He was almost
penniless, and he did not even know the name of a good lawyer.
But he was convinced that right was on his side. Over the next few
years, Holt's resolve would transform him into a grass-roots
southern black hero. His personal dreams and ambitions would
never be realized. Fifteen years later, his economic lot would
remain sadly unchanged. But Holt's actions would forever redi-
rect the course of life in Virginia's capital city.

"A lot of people thought other bureaucrats learned me what
I learned. It didn't work that way," said Holt a year before his
death in 1986. Holt was a North Carolina youth who left school
in the tenth grade to earn a living. But it did not take a diploma
for him to add up where his votes came from in 1970 and to realize
that precious few of them came from the annexed area. "I got to
thinking that the annexed area had got a multitude of votes and
I just got a little scraping of the barrel. I decided to go to the
NAACP," he said. The reception Holt received was not warm.
Standing outside the association's headquarters on East Clay
Street after being turned away, Holt began to pray. What came to
him, he said, was a directive. "Go home, open the telephone book
to lawyers, and before you gets *(sic)* to Z, you'll get an answer."

That formula led Holt to the office of a young white lawyer
named Cabell Venable. Venable was the offspring of a well-con-

nected Virginia family. But he was also getting started in law practice and was anxious to make a name for himself. If Holt had an innate sense that the annexation was morally unfair, Venable had an inkling that it could not withstand legal challenge. Holt and Venable launched their first lawsuit in February 1971, arguing that the black vote had been unconstitutionally diluted. Over the next five-and-a-half years, grounds for their attack would shift to the Voting Rights Act, which forbade election law changes aimed at reducing the impact of black votes.

At last on June 24, 1975, eight Supreme Court justices agreed that the city's Chesterfield County annexation had been racially motivated. A five-member majority saw the maneuver as having the "impermissible purpose of denying the right to vote . . . through perpetuating white majority power to exclude Negroes from office." A three-member minority, composed of Justices William Brennan, William Douglas, and Thurgood Marshall, used even harsher language in describing the racial goals. "The record is replete with statements by Richmond officials which prove beyond question that the predominant [if not sole] motive and desire of the 1969 settlement was to . . . avert a transfer of political control to what was fast becoming a black population majority," they said. The case was returned to district court for remedy, and a year later the long-sought agreement was reached. The city would retain the annexed area and its territory would be carved into nine wards for electing city council members. It was not what Holt, who preferred de-annexation, had wanted, but it was enough to bring black-majority rule to the city. Those drafting the ward plan drew four majority white, four majority black, and one swing district. When the elections were finally held, five of the winners were black and four were white. Curtis Holt, however, never won elective office.

The new council took office in March 1977 already saddled by a climate of wariness and distrust. Even so, the opening days of the new administration were relatively calm. In the first six months, only six votes followed strict racial lines. The bitterness in subsequent years more than compensated for that lull. At Marsh's installation, Vice-Mayor Henry Valentine, white Richmond's key emissary on the newly formed council, praised the mayor as a man with "a great deal of intelligence and integrity."

Valentine hailed the election as "a victory for the black electorate," even as he quipped: "It hasn't caused any jubilation in my
[white] area, though."[13] Within two years, Valentine was describing Marsh as a would-be emperor. And the editorial page of the
News Leader was routinely referring to the black majority with
such phrases as "monkey-see, monkey-do leaders of a banana
republic" or a "bunch of clowns in a Chinese fire drill."

At council meetings, dozens of votes followed racial and factional lines. "Even the normally routine matter of approving the
minutes of a previous meeting is beginning to cause problems for
Richmond City Council," a *News Leader* reporter wrote in September 1979. And the occasional sessions where there were no
fireworks commanded headlines. "Richmond City Council has
conducted a routine meeting—something out of the ordinary for
a group whose factional sessions have been dubbed 'The Monday
Night Soap Opera,' " the newspaper reported in October 1980.

"There is a race war being fought in this city, with some
powerful white residents determined to destroy Richmond if they
cannot restore white supremacy to City Hall," the *Afro-American*
concluded in September 1981. Valentine had outlined the opposing
view in equally graphic terms some months earlier. ". . . Black or
white, red or yellow, Democrat or Republican, liberal or conservative, the present majority on city council has compiled such a
dismal record that it borders on incompetence at worst and a
serious lack of good judgment at best," he wrote in a letter to the
editor of the *News Leader*.

Not the least of the members' problems, it soon emerged, was
the fact that many of the five blacks and four whites elected in 1977
were strangers, despite having grown up in the same city and
having acquired prominence on their individual turfs. The dispari-
ties in background and interests were as striking as the difference
in color. Among the departing seven-member white majority were
the president of a Main Street brokerage firm, a retired oil company executive, the president of one of the city's best-known realty
firms, the owner of a prosperous automobile dealership, a building
materials company executive, and the president of a major funeral
home. As had long been the case under at-large, citywide elections, Richmond's wealthy white neighborhoods were overrepre-
sented on the old council. Its poorer, black neighborhoods were

scarcely represented at all. In dramatic contrast, the new black majority included a civil rights lawyer, a postal workers' union official, two social workers, and a twenty-eight-year-old college student.

Henry Valentine and Claudette McDaniel exemplified the old and the new. Valentine, president in 1977 of Davenport & Company, a brokerage firm, was a member of one of Richmond's most established white families. The Valentine Museum, housed in an ancestor's home, is a notable center of the city's history and art. Valentine grew up in the posh West End. He won the city tennis championship in 1949 and, a few years later, shared the title at the Country Club of Virginia. At the University of Virginia, he was president of the student body. Conservative, bluntly honest, highly civic minded, Valentine is an example of white Richmond's best and brightest.

Claudette McDaniel, elected in 1977, might as well have come of age in another country. Her father was a chauffeur who was making fifty dollars a week when he retired; her mother, a housewife. She grew up with four brothers, ample love, boundless confidence, and little else in a poor black section of south Richmond. One of McDaniel's early memories was of the day she read that a children's fashion show was being held at a downtown department store. She hurried to arrive on time, only to be turned away at the door. The show, a woman told her, was for whites only. "A lady at the door, she was very nice, said everything is unfair and offered me a chair to stand on to watch. I came home in tears, and mother said, 'One day, all this will be changed.' "[14]

Seated in her office at the Medical College of Virginia one day in 1985, McDaniel was typically exuberant, even a tad outrageous. A medical therapy section chief, she was wearing a gold-knit tube dress, tan boots, loop earrings, nine rings, and grape polish on eight of her ten fingernails. Two were painted gold. "Communications were pretty poor," said McDaniel, recalling her early days on council. By 1985, McDaniel had become vice-mayor and had proved herself a capable, steel-edged politician. But in 1977, "whites didn't know the general black population. There'd always been a few 'acceptable' blacks that they dealt with. They didn't know a Claudette McDaniel. I came from the wrong side of the tracks."

What many whites felt they did know in 1977 was that the group of blacks just elected was incapable of running the city. Many said so privately. A few, like Valentine, acknowledged as much. Valentine recalls a meeting both he and McDaniel attended, not long after the black majority took office. "After it was over, she came up and said, 'You don't think we blacks can run the city, do you?' We sat and talked for a long time. And I said, 'The fact of the matter is, I don't. You haven't had the experience.' " The conversation was a measure of just how far white Richmond had to go.

At the center of the controversy was Marsh. Trim and slightly built with an understated air that masked both a sharp intelligence and a willful bent, Marsh grew up in an era when Richmond was strictly segregated. His evolution into a civil rights activist was a gradual one, however. As president of the Virginia Union student government in the 1950s, he was more consumed by controversy over dining hall chow and restrictions on co-ed dating than with racial injustice. Those who later viewed Marsh as an uncompromising black racist might be surprised to learn how little of a civil rights activist he initially considered himself. When he joined the law firm of Oliver Hill, the dean of Virginia's civil rights lawyers, the incentive was more his admiration for Hill than a burning quest to fight inequality. "I would have done whatever practice Mr. Hill wanted," he said. "In fact, I didn't realize the practice was as much civil rights as it was."

Over the next few years, Marsh would take part in some one hundred civil rights lawsuits, including almost every major school desegregation case in the state. Among them was the New Kent County school case, argued before the U.S. Supreme Court by law partner Samuel Tucker. In a landmark decision, the court said freedom-of-choice school desegregation plans must be abandoned if other plans would bring faster compliance with the law. By the time Marsh was elected Richmond's mayor, that and other cases had convinced him of the need for a reordered society. "I felt we had to move into the political arena if the struggle, the revolution, was to be successful," he said.

As mayor, Marsh moved quickly to change the job from one of ceremony to substance. A divided council approved his hiring of a $30,000 assistant. He was in and out of Washington, D.C., winning millions in federal grants. At home, he pushed for a revision in the state funding formula, for downtown redevelopment, and against federal highways circumventing the city. His view of Richmond's future could be at once bold and uncompromising, and its reception varied with the beholder. "Marsh just tried to run roughshod over the other members of council," complained former councilman Steve Kemp, who once spent $2,500 trying to block in court a majority-sponsored grant to a now-defunct theatre company. "Instead of having a white slave master, we had a black one," said Councilwoman Carolyn Wake, another white member. The counterview was expressed by Randolph Kendall, director of the Urban League. "Marsh was an NAACP lawyer. He saw a lot of things in those cases. He felt he had to do some things to make people realize he wasn't going to be pushed around. People couldn't deal with it," Kendall said.

By the fall of 1979, tensions were so high that Marsh would cancel an appearance at the city's annual Tobacco Festival parade. He had been persuaded by his wife that his safety was in jeopardy. A month later, he would be booed by an overwhelmingly white crowd attending a hockey game between the Richmond Rifles and the Soviet national team. No matter that Marsh had been instrumental in the return of hockey to the city. He had become the most controversial figure in a city where racial animosity no longer lay buried beneath a veneer of civility.

Throughout those years, whites insisted that their grievances against the black majority reflected concern over an abuse of power, not racism. They described Marsh as unpredictable and occasionally vindictive. Newspaper editorial writers branded him as an emperor and railed against his attempts to revamp the mayor's role. Others argued that he had failed to make the transition from civil rights activist to citywide official and that he was consumed with doing unto whites what had once been done unto him. Marsh's approach to governing was "decision by ambush," asserted Councilman William Leidinger, elected in 1980, two years after his explosive firing as city manager. A hefty man with a forceful presence, once a taxi-squad kicker for the Washington Redskins, Leidinger recalled as evidence an incident during his tenure as city manager. At about 5:00 P.M. on the very evening the council was slated to approve a key phase of a mammoth downtown development plan, Marsh telephoned Leidinger's office, insisting on an amendment. "He walked in at 6:00 P.M. and said he was going to introduce a resolution for a percentage of the work to go to minority firms. He said if the resolution wasn't adopted, we weren't going to go forward with the project. This agreement had been years in the making," Leidinger said. Less than an hour before the council session was to begin, Marsh, Leidinger, and the city attorney sat down and drafted the resolution.

Valentine was equally uncomplimentary in his recollections of the Marsh years. A slightly harried-looking man with deep-set eyes and boyishly trimmed gray hair, Valentine acknowledged that he is too much of a fighter to willingly hand over power to anyone, black or white. But Valentine insisted that he was initially willing to give Marsh the benefit of the doubt. "He screwed it up royally, right from the start. Three months after he was mayor, there was no communicating with anybody. As vice-mayor I got three calls a week from people who were infuriated because he had not made appointments," he said. Valentine still recalled his ire over Marsh's unexplained failure to show up at a U.S.-Russian track meet at the University of Richmond. Valentine had made the arrangements for Marsh's appearance and felt personally embarrassed by the absence. "You can say it's sour grapes, but if you're the vice-mayor and you're trying to run a business, it's not sour grapes. He just left a trail of infuriated people," Valentine said.

For Marsh and his allies, the black-white confrontation was defined in more cosmic, historic terms. The white Richmond establishment, they believed, simply could not stomach either its loss of power or Marsh's unwillingness to march to the corporate drumbeat. Confirming that view, they insisted, was a double standard by which the black majority was judged. Marsh, for instance, was chastised on newspaper editorial pages and elsewhere for autocratic, secretive leadership. And yet, his supporters asked, what could have been more high-handed or less open to public scrutiny than the annexation discussions that proceeded, largely unreported, for five years? If the black majority did not make the white minority privy to all its decisions, why was that different than when the former white majority failed to inform Marsh and two council allies of the specifics of the annexation agreement? In years past, white council majorities had moved to oust white city managers. So, if race was no issue, why was the Marsh majority acting "outrageously" when it decided to replace Leidinger with a more philosophically compatible manager?

As time passed, the animosity on council became as much personal as philosophical. Relations were epitomized by the mutual distrust of two members, Carolyn Wake and Henry Marsh. Wake is a white suburban housewife, the mother of four grown children, and an officer in a family-owned hardware store. Partial to red-plaid tartan suits and sedate, low-heeled shoes, Wake is conservative, patriotic, married to a self-made businessman, and a spokeswoman for middle America. On council, she represents much of the area that was annexed in 1970. Hers is a district of 1950s ranchers, small wooden bungalows, and apartment complexes. The stretch of Route 1 that passes through the area is known locally as "Jeff Davis Highway," honoring the Confederate president. A substantial portion of her constituency is lower middle-class whites. When she was appointed to fill a council vacancy in 1978, Wake said she viewed her selection as a calling to help resolve racial differences. Years earlier, Wake's husband had cast a deciding vote to hold an integrated church service in the small community in which they lived. Later, crosses were burned on the property of several members, including the Wakes. "I believed in civil rights. I thought I could make a difference. I thought I could work with Henry on the basis of issues. I was naive," she said. "I was totally not trusted and discounted because I was white."

Several appointments particularly angered Wake. The mother of a mentally retarded child, she was deeply interested in serving in a council slot on the city's mental health board. When a vacancy came up, Wake twice stressed her desire to Marsh. Based on his response, she expected to be appointed. One of the black members was named instead. Again, when a vacancy arose in one of the council seats held by a white member, Wake and others emphasized to Marsh that the person the black majority was planning to appoint was much too liberal to fairly represent the district's philosophy. Wake was among those thinking that Marsh had agreed to back a more conservative white man of their choosing. When the vote was taken, Marsh joined the other black members in electing the more liberal candidate, a white woman. "Finally,

I went to Henry," Wake recalled. "I said, 'You have told me blatant lies. You have not dealt with me honestly. From now on, I'm going to do everything I can to expose you.' "

Marsh's view of Wake became equally antagonistic. "That woman is filled with hatred. It spills out of her," he said. Wake and other whites refused to accept that he was not the slave master for the four other black council members and that he could not act alone, he said. While the five felt sufficiently embattled to present a united front to the community, usually through Marsh, the former mayor insisted that they were independent thinkers. Decisions about key matters like filling a council vacancy were discussed and decided on by more members than he, Marsh said. "She held me personally responsible for decisions that weren't really my decision," he said.

Marsh, meanwhile, harbored his own memories of personal slights at the hand of Wake. He was incensed by his treatment at a party held at Wake's home for a retiring white councilman, a former oil company executive. Even though they were frequently at political odds, Marsh said he had a great deal of respect for the retiring member. And so he and two other black councilmen went to the farewell party. As the hostess, Wake called on a couple dozen individuals to speak, Marsh said. The presence of Marsh and the other black council members was not even acknowledged. "Little things tell you a lot," he said.

If the Leidinger firing in 1978 was a step toward the breakdown of black-white political relations in Richmond, the second most explosive incident—and the one that may have sealed the fate of the Marsh majority—was the decision to block construction of a Hilton Hotel in downtown Richmond. At a wine and cheese party at the Bull & Bear Club in the summer of 1981, a Washington developer and his partner announced plans for a $24.5 million hotel. It would be located at the edge of the downtown financial district and would be the first major new center-city hotel in decades. Marsh had been invited to the announcement press conference, but—in what proved an ominous sign—did not appear. Three days earlier, it later emerged, Marsh had warned the developer that he was wary of the proposed construction.[15] His chief concern, he said, was what it would do to Project One.

Project One was the city's plan for the salvation of downtown

Richmond's shopping core, an area some blocks away from the financial district. The idea for a revamped shopping and convention complex had originated with the city's white establishment, before Marsh took office. The black majority, however, quickly recognized the importance of an economically viable downtown, particularly to thousands of black residents who worked there or lived nearby. The black council members not only embraced the development plans, but also quickly embellished them. A central part of their dream was to unite the north and south sides of Broad Street, a thoroughfare that had long been the city's unofficial racial dividing line. Richmond's major department stores had doors opening onto Broad Street, but few whites ever crossed over to the low-budget and discount shops on the street's north side.

In the summer of 1981, a major objective of Project One was to anchor the downtown redevelopment with a prestigious new hotel. Hopes for additional expansion might never materialize, Marsh and others feared, if the hotel plan fell through. Financing in that year's tight money market, however, was proving a difficult obstacle. When the Hilton Hotel plans were announced, the black majority was stunned at the thought that the hotel, located in a more affluent setting, might make the Broad Street project even less desirable to investors. A consultant's report supported that view. Marsh and the black majority decided to torpedo the Hilton Hotel. On a five to four, black-white split that November, the council denied city permission for the transfer of two parcels of surplus land to the Hilton developers. By an identical vote, the council refused to vacate a public easement and relocate sewer lines at the property. Without those adjustments, the hotel plan was dead. The Hilton developers went to court, eventually winning a multimillion-dollar settlement, but the project was not revived. Within six months, plans would be completed for construction of a Marriott Hotel at the Broad Street site.

Marsh was convinced that the move saved a downtown redevelopment project that by early 1986 had grown to include the Marriott, an office complex, refurbished department stores, and an urban shopping mall, designed by James Rouse. In Marsh's view, the Marriott Corporation would never have come to Richmond if the Hilton Hotel had been built. And without the Marriott Hotel, Rouse would never have launched the Sixth Street Festival

Marketplace. In 1981, however, Main Street was aghast at the Hilton Hotel developments. When the *Wall Street Journal* recorded the blockage of the hotel, many white executives were convinced the city had suffered a national black eye and that various businesses would locate elsewhere as a result. "A sort of shock wave went through the business community," recalled Buford Scott, a stockbroking executive prominent in civic affairs.

As a result, attacks on Marsh reached a fevered pitch in early 1982. Some blacks as well as whites began to question openly his leadership. More moderate black Richmonders spoke of growing embarrassment over the factionalism on the council and of a sense that the black majority must be held accountable for failure to calm the troubled waters. One of those dismayed by what he saw was Roy West, a black middle-school principal who—unlike Marsh—lived in a comfortable, middle-class section of north Richmond. Marsh, who undoubtedly could afford to move, maintained his family home only blocks from some of Richmond's most squalid slums. West's neighborhood, in contrast, was a collection of well-spaced houses and neatly trimmed lawns. Not unlike his surroundings, West was orderly and precise. He was a firm disciplinarian in the classroom and congenial, yet tightly controlled in his personal dealings.

In the spring of 1982, West was essentially unknown to Richmond's white leadership. Nor was he familiar with much of the town's black political establishment. He had never been active in civil rights organizations. While others were pursuing political causes, West had been bound to a more personal agenda. Intense and self-driven, he had displayed a work-ethic zeal in holding a series of school board jobs, completing a doctoral degree, and raising a family. West's first brush with political activism came in the late 1970s when a school board incident provided some notoriety and the makings of a political base. At the time, Richmond's black school superintendent—a close ally of the Marsh majority—was promoting a plan for consolidating city high schools into several complexes. Each three-school complex would be considered a single unit for administrative and athletic purposes. West openly opposed the move, and his forthrightness, many believed, resulted in his demotion from a high school to a middle school principal. West was also irritated by a two-year battle to keep a new school athletic center out of his neighborhood. He viewed his local councilwoman, one of the five black members, as unhelpful on the issue.

That unresponsiveness, coupled with the continued fighting on council, prompted West to challenge Councilwoman Willie Dell in the spring of 1982. "I saw the divisiveness as a manifestation of an abuse of power that was existing on that council. I felt it was time to end the bickering," he said. "Someone had to pay the price."

When the votes were tallied on May 4, West had won 3,858 votes to 3,361 for Dell. West's margin of victory came decisively in three white precincts in the 69 percent black district. West carried the white precincts by better than ten to one. Dell carried the black precincts by about two to one. West's election quickly set off a round of ecstatic telephone conversations and hopeful strategy huddles in white Richmond. Most Main Street executives had never met West, but they were determined not to let this opportunity pass. It was two months until the council would reorganize. If they could persuade the newcomer to run for mayor, the days of the Marsh majority were numbered. At one after-hours session at the Universal Leaf Company headquarters, about ten executives in various Richmond businesses urged West to join with the four whites on council to elect himself. West gave no commitment.

The final decision, West said, was not made until June 29, the night before the council was scheduled to vote. A group of about nine advisers, both black and white, met in the family room of West's home. The session was heated, lasting about three hours. "I was saying, 'No' to running, and the others were saying, 'Yes.' I didn't want to pay the price. I didn't want to deal with the agony." Then a question was asked that caused him to reassess, West said. "I was asked, 'If you don't vote for yourself, for whom are you going to vote?' That question was so provocative that it really awakened in me the realization that I had to take that leadership."

The next day, a hushed chamber listened as City Clerk E. A. Duffey polled the council members on their votes for mayor. Alphabetically, West came last. At his turn, the tally was dead-locked, four votes for Marsh, four for West. Duffey paused dramatically, then called West's name. Leaning into the microphone, West replied briskly, "Roy West." An era had ended; the controversy had not.

During the first six months of his tenure, there were thirty-nine votes in which West and the four white council members combined to defeat the four black members. Most such votes dealt with appointments to citizen boards or with council organization. West was clearly not inclined to stock city government with allies of Henry Marsh. Many of Marsh's appointees had been among the city's longtime black leaders, and the switches stirred predictable anger. Not long into West's term, the *Afro-American* ran an article headlined, "West Bats 0–17." As West's first anniversary in office approached, leaders of the Richmond Crusade for Voters—the city's most influential black political organization—issued a joint statement forecasting that "Richmond will not survive the bitterness, confusion, and strife being created" under West's leadership. "We are outraged at the tactics being used by Roy West to ignore and insult the black citizens of this community. We have attempted to exercise patience and fairness to Dr. West in spite of his blatant disregard for black people who have voted for him and whom he is supposed to represent," the statement said. An article in the *Times-Dispatch* on July 18 would underscore the continuing bitterness. "The City Council, just past the halfway point in the 1982–84 term, is as deeply divided as it has been at any time since ward elections brought blacks to power in Richmond," a reporter wrote.

Amid the furor, West was remarkably unshaken. Always something of a loner, sure of his own instincts and abilities, the mayor seemed to grow only more adamant about his course as controversy grew. He was, West acknowledged, taken aback by an attack from the city's black ministerial association—"I felt they would be about the business of healing"—but he was not deterred. Others might argue that West had sold out to whites, that years of black progress in the city were being destroyed. As for West, "I never had any second guesses about me at all," he said. "I knew me and I trusted me. I would never allow another person to mold my thinking about me."

The 1984 councilmanic elections, two years later, were viewed as a sort of political Armageddon within Richmond's black community. At stake was the city's leadership, as well as the aspirations of longtime black leaders who feared power was permanently slipping from their grasp. The rematch between West and Dell might be their final chance to reassert authority for years to come. Marsh allies minced no words in heaping venom on West. To blacks, West had become "an extension of the people that chastised and lambasted them over the years," said Norvell Robinson, board chairman of the Crusade for Voters. And Dr. Miles Jones, president of the predominantly black Baptist Ministers' Conference, complained: "Our political strength has been decimated under West's leadership."[16]

Such attacks could not compensate for West's immense popularity among his district's white voters or for the growing respect of his black middle-class neighbors. When the count was taken, Dell's 1984 tally was up five hundred votes from 1982, but West's total had increased by over one thousand votes. He had also narrowed the gap slightly in black precincts. The Marsh contingent had little alternative but to accept the inevitable. Marsh continued to hammer away at West initiatives, but his support— both on and off council—was seriously weakened.

By midpoint in West's second term, disappointment and even bitterness remained over the political coup, but resignation was becoming paramount among many Marsh allies. On council, controversy "is mellowing a lot because there is a recognition that Henry Marsh will not be mayor again," acknowledged Randolph Kendall of the Urban League. Even the antipathy of Miles Jones, one of Marsh's firmest defenders, had mellowed. When West was first elected, he said: "I reacted out of initial disgust and disappointment. For me, the man frustrated the process. I'd hoped we could create for the rest of the nation a model." Had Richmond's white establishment become convinced that there was no end run they could make around the Marsh-led majority, the bickering would have ended, Jones believed. "It was painful, but when you came out of it, there would have been some integrity to the operation. West provided an escape hatch." Still, Jones said a year after West's second election, "the process has evolved. Things change. Nobody has horns. . . ."

For blacks of every philosophical persuasion, problems more critical than political turf fights remained. In Richmond, as nationally, the primary obstacles to a truly integrated society seemed economic. A 1982 report by two Virginia Commonwealth University professors suggested how far black Richmonders had to go in penetrating the city's economic power structure. J. John Palen and Richard D. Morrison surveyed the 115 highest-profit corporations in the capital city. Of 1,547 officers, board members, and executives, 24—1.6 percent—were black. Moreover, all but 9 of the blacks identified in the survey were employed by a single black-owned bank. Among the city's fourteen largest law firms, including several of the biggest in the South, not a single one of the 167 partners was black. Six—or 2.2 percent—of the 267 associate partners were black. Despite "the considerable political changes of the 1970s," Palen and Morrison concluded, "Main Street remained a white street."[17]

Nor could black politicians dictate the integration of social institutions. White participation in Richmond public schools—relative to population—was the lowest in the state. Meanwhile, the number of blacks living in the city's most affluent neighborhoods remained minuscule. In the census block covering Richmond's prestigious Windsor Farms subdivision, where median family income was $53,993, versus $13,606 citywide, there were only 23 blacks among 2,234 residents. City housing authorities projected that most of those were servants, living in the homes of their white employers. Richmond's equal opportunity housing agency, HOME, estimated that about 30,000 Richmonders—14 percent of the population—lived in integrated neighborhoods in 1980. The figure was up from an estimated 6 percent a decade earlier. What remained unclear was whether those neighborhoods were truly integrated or simply in transition from white to black. "I don't like saying it," concluded Kent Willis, HOME's executive director, "but if a place in Richmond becomes 20 to 30 percent black, there may be an inexorable trend toward its becoming all black."

Unquestionably, the Voting Rights Act had vastly changed the Confederate capital. A ward system in council elections, imposed because of that act, had produced a far more democratic mix of local representatives. In board appointments, additions to the city payroll, and award of public contracts, a much larger and more diverse group of blacks shared the spoils of political power than might have been envisioned even a decade earlier.

At the lower end of the economic spectrum, however, blacks said that was not enough. "It's much worser [*sic*] now than twenty years ago," asserted Curtis Holt, the grass-roots organizer whose litigation produced Richmond's ward system. What Holt saw outside the front window of the public housing unit he shared in 1985 with his wife, a son, and a granddaughter, made him long for a gentler day. "The youth comes up useless," he said. "You have many persons without jobs that need to be on jobs."

A few miles away, Buford Scott sat in an upscale office in the hub of Richmond's financial district. A former Chamber of Commerce president, prominent in city politics, Scott had a different view. The Richmond of the mid-1980s is "one of the most exciting cities I know," he said. "We have moved through a very revolutionary day. Whites have learned that they can live with things that ten or fifteen years ago, they didn't think they could live with." Recently, Scott said, in historic Saint Paul's Episcopal Church, the child of a racially mixed couple was baptized. As he watched, Scott recalled the story—imprinted in Richmond folklore, if not in fact—of how Robert E. Lee took communion at the church one Sunday after the Civil War. So the story goes, an elderly black man in tattered clothes walked to the altar. As shocked parishioners watched in frozen silence, one white man walked forward to stand beside him. It was Lee. "I thought that's a big change in one church, one city in just over 100 years," said Scott.

So change that seemed painfully slow to the Curtis Holts of Richmond's black ghetto was dramatic, even startling to others. And in the 1980s, in Richmond, the question long central to southern politics remained—by whose timetable would change come? What the Richmond experience had shown was that it was unlikely to come by the agenda of the most doggedly assertive of black leaders. Power remained multifaceted. Coalition building appealed to a growing number of middle-class blacks, as well as to politically dethroned whites. And ultimately, in those communities where the emotional and economic investment of whites remained strong, the ballot alone could not mandate black power.

8. SUNFLOWER COUNTY
The Holdout

THE FACES at the courthouse in Sunflower County, a languid and historic spot in Mississippi's central Delta, seem largely untouched by time. On Mondays, Joe Baird, John Parker, Jim Corder, Edgar Donahoe, and Billy Cummins gather for supervisors' meetings. Like generations of local officeholders before them, they are mostly farmers, men whose fortunes spring from the dusky, alluvial soil swept here thousands of years ago on the floodwaters of the Mississippi and Yazoo rivers. In century-old tradition, as well, all five are white.

Across the hall is Sheriff C. O. Sessum's office. He too is white. So are Circuit Clerk Sam Ely and Chancery Clerk Jack Harper, the county's dominant political figure. They are not alone. The county tax assessor, the coroner, the two justice court judges, the five constables, the five election commissioners, the superintendent of education, and four of the five elected members of the school board are also white. As 1987 began, there was, in fact, one black elected official—school board member Lonnie Byrd—in all of county government. In the small Sunflower County towns of Indianola, Inverness, Ruleville, and Drew, the numbers were only somewhat less stark.

Two decades after the Voting Rights Act became law, blacks in Sunflower County held the upper hand in only one way, numerically. Three of every five residents of this once infamous county—birthplace of the white Citizens Council and home to civil rights heroine Fannie Lou Hamer and segregationist U.S. senator James O. Eastland—are black. Their continued political domination by a white minority is another of the ironies that abound in the Delta, a land so rich with natural resources, so cursed with poverty. In Sunflower County, two decades of federal surveillance over southern voting and an avalanche of regional change have not erased the mind-set of generations. Politics is still the domain of white folk.

That Sunflower and similar counties are destined to become political relics seems unquestioned. In the 1960s, there were across the South dozens of majority-black counties where no black person had held political office in the twentieth century. Complete political exclusion of blacks was, with rare exception, the rule. Two decades of black activism, registration drives, lawsuits, court orders and federally supervised redistricting plans have changed all that. With each election, the Sunflower counties move closer to extinction.

Still, in a dwindling number of places lawsuits and marches and federal registrars have not undone attitudes much longer than two decades in the making. Whites remain firmly in control. The fortunes of blacks, through intimidation or apathy or black acquiescence, still rest in white hands. Across the states first covered by the Voting Rights Act, there were fifteen majority-black counties, and more such towns, where in 1985 the governing board was totally white. By the start of 1987, the Delta had produced a smattering of black elected officials. But blacks ran the governing board in only two of twelve majority-black Delta counties. In six others, one black sat with four whites on the local board of supervisors. And in three counties—Sunflower, Tallahatchie, and Washington—the boards at the start of 1987, as in 1967, 1947, and 1927, were lily white. Sunflower County might well be the model for the rest.

"Our blacks is different," explained Billy Cummins, a lumbering and congenial white supervisor who farms 523 acres of Sunflower County's incredibly fertile soil. Born poor, raised in a house without running water, Cummins has—he believes—an innate understanding of the economic problems that face rural Mississippi blacks. That appreciation, he said, aids his continued election in a district that is about 49 percent black. Familiarity with local blacks has also helped white colleagues Baird, Parker, and Donahoe win in districts that are, respectively, 75 percent, 67 percent and 64 percent black, he said.

Such numbers are the dream of black political organizers across the nation, but in Sunflower County, they do not spell white defeat. Cummins has several explanations. One, he said, is the warm relationship he and other successful white politicians have with many black constituents. Cummins, for instance, appointed the first black among five county road commissioners. After the selection, he heard remarks like "I'm not gonna ask no nigger for nothin," Cummins said, but he was undeterred. Referring to the road supervisor, he openly boasted, "That Nigra, Silvester Williams, I think as much of him as of anyone, and he thinks as much of me." A second ingredient, Cummins said, is that many black voters simply trust the competence of whites who have run for political office in Sunflower County more than they trust that of black candidates. "They're not very well educated," he said of the county's black residents. "And they hadn't seen many blacks around here that they would really trust to put their faith in."

There are, of course, other theories, including several less complimentary to the county's white residents. Blacks insist that economic intimidation remains alive and well in a society where black farm workers are dependent on white landowners for survival. Across the Delta, political annals are rife with stories—albeit sketchily documented—of farm owners who directed their workers to stay in the fields past sundown on election day, forcing them to miss Mississippi's 6:00 P.M. poll closing. There are similar tales of catfish farms or pickling plants that "happened" to have pressing orders to fill on the date of a controversial election, of farm foremen who managed to increase their hires of day laborers just in time for an election, and of payoffs to poor blacks and other voting irregularities.

Even so, blacks as well as whites acknowledge that sheer numbers should give blacks a powerful voice in local politics. That volume alone has not, many say, is the product of a lingering human blight, "the plantation mentality," a mind-set grounded in illiteracy and limited education, in economic dependency and an unforgotten history of political violence. "People who come off the plantation have a certain mentality that white is all right. And it does not change," lamented Credell Calhoun, a black state legislator and former Democratic Party organizer in the Delta.

Johnnie Walls, Jr., a lawyer in nearby Greenville and a man regarded by many whites as a black radical, added: "What was done to blacks over the years was a masterful job. Our fight is now a mental fight more than anything else. If you would stop and think what terror has done to black people over the years, you would understand why it's hard to get people to flock to the polls. If they're not afraid to vote, they just don't know the value of it because they've been kept away."

All across Mississippi in the mid-1980s there were signs that this once scorned state had made quantum leaps since the race wars of the 1960s. Then, Mississippi was the symbol of American apartheid, the feverish, infectious core of a national ill. Its strategies to preserve separation of the races were the most ingenious; its tactics were the most ruthless; its resolve was the most complete of any southern state. In 1954, when state voters approved a constitutional amendment allowing the legislature to simply abolish public schools, rather than face integration, historian C. Vann Woodward exclaimed that the state had once again acted "in her historic role as leader of reaction in race policy, just as she had in 1875 to overthrow Reconstruction and in 1890 to disfranchise the Negro."[1]

To Martin Luther King, Jr., the Mississippi of the 1950s and 1960s was "a desert state sweltering with the heat of injustice and oppression."[2] And in 1963, when University of Mississippi professor James Silver described the magnolia state as "a closed society . . . as near to approximating a police state as anything we have yet seen in America,"[3] the epithet—the Closed Society—became a focus for surging national dismay.

By the 1980s, state leaders pointed with pride to a series of showcased advances. Everywhere, ordinary men and women anxiously asked a visitor, "What was your image of Mississippi? It's not what you expected, is it?" In 1968, there were 29 black elected officials in a state almost 40 percent black. By 1986, the figure was 521, the highest in the nation.[4] As late as 1975, there were only 4 blacks in the 174-member Mississippi legislature. By 1986, there were 20. In 1962, President John F. Kennedy sent thousands of state and national guardsmen to Oxford to dispel rioters as a lone

black man, James Meredith, integrated the University of Mississippi. The price of Meredith's admission was 160 injured marshals
and 2 deaths. In 1986, white students at the university still greatly
outnumbered blacks, but the black contingent among 9,053 undergraduate students had grown to 421.

In 1964 there were four black lawyers in the entire state of
Mississippi. By 1986, the first black law graduate of the University
of Mississippi was serving on the state supreme court. In 1964,
Fannie Lou Hamer, a Sunflower County sharecropper once
evicted from her plantation home for unsuccessfully trying to
register to vote, stunned the Democratic national convention in
Atlantic City with an account of her jail house beating in Winona
the previous year. Hamer's crime had been trying to use the lunch
counter at the local bus terminal. Her plea to the Democratic
delegates was to seat a delegation of black Mississippians at the
convention. Hamer failed, but by the 1980s, her long-range goal of
black inclusion in party politics had been realized. The Mississippi
Democratic Party had sixty white and thirty-two black local
chairmen and cochairmen. Governed by strict formulas, the state
party also boasted a racially mixed cast of officers.

Perhaps most significant of all, individual men and women
could report dozens of daily incidents that would have been unthinkable in 1965. The Reverend Harry Bowie told one such tale.
Bowie is an ebullient black Episcopal priest who in 1964 came
south to Mississippi, planning to spend a month as a civil rights
volunteer. Twenty years later, he was still there. Bowie recalled
a Democratic Party hearing in Laurel he was called on to chair
in 1985. The local party chairman, a white man, had in the view
of many, been violating state election laws. The executive director
of the state Democratic Party, who is white, attended the crowded
session. So did representatives of the white secretary of state and
attorney general. The audience was about 85 percent white. And
yet, it was Bowie, a black man, who led the meeting, answering
questions, and offering interpretations of state law. "They were
able to accept the fact that a black person would be more know-
ledgeable. Five to ten years ago, they would not have been able to
do that," Bowie said. "Then it would have been impossible that
I could have stood up in that situation."

As Harry Bowie and hundreds of other blacks would testify,

however, there were limits to this transformation. It was not, for them, as if some hellhole had suddenly been transformed to an Eden. Life in Mississippi was better; for many, not better enough. "This here new South," said Bowie, quoting a friend, "is nothin' but the old North, and that ain't good enough." The very numbers quoted by some to show change were used by others to show its limits. In a state 35 percent black, less than 5 percent of the undergraduate students at the major university, 11 percent of the legislators, and 2 of the 86 highest ranking state judges were black. In the updated Mississippi, Bowie said, "You don't have the hard, stomp-down drumbeat for segregation. You don't have the emotional intensity of people threatened to death about blacks in society. You have a whole lot of people who have made some honest and serious progress. But there is still that element of separation and difference. It is the result of some deep-seated prejudices and a lack of familiarity. Blacks and whites don't intermingle except in certain situations. It's endemic of the North and now the South."

By the 1980s, one had only to set foot in the Delta to recognize the gulf that still separated Mississippi blacks and whites. A great fertile crescent stretching down the state's northwest quarter from Memphis to Vicksburg, the Delta is a place where stunning beauty and natural richness coexist with shocking poverty and the scars of a violent past. Over thousands of years, black alluvial soil was swept there by the overflowing Mississippi River and its tributaries, forming deposits up to twenty-five-feet deep, producing the South's richest soil. Such assets gave birth in the 1800s to a thriving plantation economy, based on cotton production and the sweat of black slaves. There was little of the aura of graciousness that smoothed slavery's barbed edges in some other Old South sites, however. Farmhouses were more common than mansions. Labor demands were likely to be unyielding and harsh. When mechanization began to replace human toil in the 1940s, white landowners did little to soften the transition for thousands of black workers, other than to encourage migration north.

By the 1980s, the legacy of that bygone era was reflected in startling black-white gaps in education and income in the Delta's twelve majority-black counties. Statistics in Sunflower County were typical. In 1980 only one of five black Sunflower residents who were twenty-five or older had a high school education.[5] The percentage for whites was more than three times higher. Median family income for whites was $18,266. For blacks, the figure was less than half that amount, a paltry $7,640. With slight variations, the stories in Tunica, Quitman, Tallahatchie, LeFlore, Coahoma, and other Delta counties were the same. Everywhere, across soybean and cotton fields ribboned by highways flat and straight as an airport runway, stood shanties hammered together out of tar paper and ill-fitting planks, speaking more eloquently than words to the continuing plight of Mississippi blacks.

In the summer of 1985, the gateway to the Delta along Route 61 from Memphis was a garish assortment of steamy fruit stands, rusting junkyard autos, littered front yards, and ramshackled filling stations. There were boarded-up car washes, small, family-owned groceries, a "Power of Faith" revival tent, and a group of fluorescent-yellow trailers stocked with firecrackers and Fourth of July rockets. At roadside flea markets, local hucksters, half-clothed against the sweltering humidity, lounged under colorfully striped umbrellas and watched idly as customers sifted through stacks of straw hats and second-hand shirts.

Country music station WMC was crooning out "America's Coming Back Stronger" on the car radio. And as the urban clutter gave way to endless, level fields, to the distant sight of white farmhouses and rickety tenant shacks, to clusters of barefoot, dark-skinned children moving through the shimmering heat, there was indeed a sense that this road led back through time to another America. Scene after scene told a story of continued separation— economic, political, and social—between blacks and whites. Federal law and surveillance had gone far toward removing structural barriers to equality. Economics, tradition, and personal choice still exacted a mighty toll.

The span between blacks and whites was evident that hot Sunday afternoon in Tunica. Twenty-seven miles south of the Tennessee border, the town is the seat of government in one of the nation's poorest counties. Seventy-three percent of Tunica County's ninety-seven hundred residents are black. Welfare and social security checks are the largest single source of personal income in the county, and 45 percent of the local families live below the poverty line. The town of Tunica is a collection of quiet, tree-shaded streets, modest homes, and rigid boundaries. The most striking of those separates the town from North Tunica, a populous area that abuts Tunica but remains unincorporated. It is easy to see why. Annexation of North Tunica would send Tunica's black population soaring, and the depressing collection of overcrowded shanties and pockmarked streets would be an unwelcomed drain on town coffers.

At the Blue & White Restaurant, Tunica's nicest, the post-church crowd was gathered that August day to sample the cook's fare—plates piled high with fried chicken and three vegetables, pies lofty with meringue. The tables were crowded; the conversation was lively. There was talk of shopping sprees to Memphis and the exploits of grandchildren off at Ole Miss. In this homey scene, there was only one jarring note. Everyone in this most prosperous restaurant in a county 73 percent black was white. Decades earlier, the Blue & White Restaurant was segregated by the choice of its owners. By the 1980s, it remained so by the choice of potential patrons. "Blacks go to the black restaurants, and whites go to the white restaurants. That's just what the people want to do," explained state representative Clayton Henderson, whose 1979 election as the county's first black legislator was the product of court-ordered legislative reapportionment.

Across town and time was another Tunica. There, Mary Cox, four of her children, and one grandchild sat in their dilapidated home, constructed out of scrap lumber, tar paper, and bits of tin and screen. Cox, a widow living on $465 a month in social security payments, resided in what was ironically known as "New Subdivision." The cluttered all-black area, divided by a roadway from several white homes, was named in the early 1960s when black families began moving off the plantations and into town. Many of the families simply dismantled the shanties in which they had been living and brought the boards along. "New Subdivision" was the result.

In Mary Cox's home, there was no indoor toilet. Human waste was simply tossed into a mound of rushes and old boards a few yards from the house. Like many of its neighbors, the family got its water from an outdoor tap. Inside, Mary Cox gazed proudly at her sturdy, eleven-month-old grandson, asleep in one of the house's two bedrooms. In the other, two iron bed frames were

pushed against a wall, leaving a narrow walkway. Several children
bounced on the uncovered mattresses. Electrical cords dangled
from a single kitchen outlet, and the stench of urine competed
with the odor of beans cooking on a small stove. In winter months,
Cox said, the house was warmed with a gas heater, and she stuffed
rags into window cracks and nailed cardboard over doorways to
block the cold. "I'm making out 'til I can do a little better," she
said. Each month, Cox added, her money "runs out pretty regular." Just then, she was delaying a doctor's visit for her eight-year-
old son, who a few days earlier had stepped on a rusty nail. "His
foot's all swolled up," Cox said, "but there's no money for a
doctor."

A few miles away, several of Tunica's black families were
preparing to move into temporary quarters in trailer homes provided through the governor's office. Jesse Jackson had been in
town several days earlier, highlighting poverty in an area known
locally as "Sugar Ditch." There, as children played nearby, families dumped raw sewage into a ditch, which gave the area its name.
Embarrassed public officials had responded by ordering new trailers and laying plans to relocate the Sugar Ditch families. For
Mary Cox and dozens of others who had yet to feel the glow of
publicity, there was no such salvation.

Ongoing racial division was evident, too, in Greenville, to the
south. It was there that Hodding Carter, Jr., operated the *Delta
Democrat-Times,* winning a Pulitzer Prize in 1946 for editorials
urging racial moderation. The influence of Carter and others
helped set a community tone that has persisted. Washington
County, Greenville's home, is regarded by many as the most
liberal of the Delta counties on racial matters. Yet by 1987, a black
majority had still not cracked the local governing board. The
paternalism of local whites has helped make blacks complacent,
complained Johnnie Walls. "There've always been whites in this
county who made sure a little something happened for blacks," he
said.

Walls, who in 1984 frightened and angered white Mississippi
Democrats by threatening an independent race for the U.S. Senate, would fit easily into the flow of most northern cities. But in
Greenville, his brash and aggressive ways brand him as a somewhat dangerous outsider. As relatives and children bounded

through his living room on a summer evening, Walls protested that a veneer of cordiality does not mean blacks and whites are treated equally in the Delta. He described two personal incidents that for him underscored the lingering breaches in race relations. One day in 1983 Walls and his wife went jogging in a white subdivision not far from their home. A friend on the police force later told him that she had been directed to check out a report involving "two blacks in a white neighborhood." Upon investigation, the blacks turned out to be Walls and his wife. Two years later, in the summer of 1985, Walls and his brother stopped to look at a house for sale in the same neighborhood. They had been there only a few moments when a police officer pulled up behind them to ask if they needed help. "He assumed we had no business being there," Walls concluded.

Even more significant was the continuing economic gap between blacks and whites. Across the Delta, the disparity showed up not only in personal income. In almost any economic setting, the patterns of daily life underscored the inferiority of blacks. In county after county, if a black person wanted a job in banking, there would be no alternative but to approach someone white. If that same person wanted a teaching job, the employer, though not the majority of students, would invariably be white. If the interest was in farming or industry, almost without exception, the person to see was white.

Local bank boardrooms told the story as completely as any other setting. In Sunflower County, for instance, the Bank of the Delta, Planters Bank, and Peoples Bank of Indianola had, combined, thirty local directors. In a county 62 percent black, not a single bank director was black. Still, local whites took pride in the degree of change that had occurred. From the 1930s to the 1960s, for instance, the Planters Bank was reputed to be the most conservative and segregationist bank in the county. The men who ran the bank had strongly held views that did not include cutting blacks in for a share of the economic pie. In the mid-1970s, however, the bank was sold, and a decade later, there had been a notable change in bank policy. The deposits of blacks were welcomed, and the bank had even helped several local blacks finance a business.

"I've seen a lot of progress," said James B. Randall III, a

thirty-three-year-old county native who was president of the local
Planters Bank branch. "People of my generation look at people as
people." Even so, Randall admitted, "You don't change things
overnight. It takes decades." The idea of appointing a black director for the local bank board had been tossed around in conversation, he acknowledged. Should that occur, Randall had no doubt
that the decision would be a controversial one in Sunflower
County.

Eyebrows all across Sunflower County raised to mid-forehead
in 1983 when Jessie Lee, a local businesswoman, and several other
whites sponsored a mixed-race reception honoring jazz artist
B. B. King, a county native. Half of the 250-person guest list was
white, half black. Nothing of the sort had ever occurred in Sunflower County or the county seat of Indianola. The combination
was viewed with such amazement that the *New York Times* ran
a front-page story and CBS sent a film crew down to record
community reaction. Not everyone was taken with the idea of
blacks and whites rubbing shoulders at a social gathering. But the
sponsors were undeterred. For blacks who grew up in the county,
the day is remembered as simply remarkable. "Even the people
you knew were racist smiled at you," said one local black attorney.

In a setting where a mixed-race guest list made news, where
blacks were unrepresented in key financial circles, where overall
black income was half or less that of whites, where a morning jog
could produce a police complaint, it should have surprised no one
that blacks across the Delta also remained outside the political
power structure. In Sunflower County, two elections demonstrated the ongoing inability of blacks to gain a political foothold.
One was John Chance's 1979 bid for supervisor. A second was the
1982 city elections in which blacks made a major push to win office
in Indianola.

Chance, the assistant principal at Indianola Junior High
School and chairman of the Democratic Party in Sunflower
County, is young, educated, middle-class in values, noncontrover-
sial in style. He appears, in fact, to be the model of what local
whites describe when they speak of finding a "qualified" black for
whom to vote. Neither those credentials nor the racial makeup of
a district in which almost seven out of every ten voters is black
was enough to propel Chance into office, however. Campaigning

so hard in the summer heat that he even landed in the hospital for a week's stay, Chance lost to the longtime white incumbent, Joe Baird, by the lopsided vote of 733 to 474.

Six years later, Chance sat amid the chalk-and-sneakers smells of his junior high office and talked of that dispiriting loss. "I've asked myself a thousand times how I could have lost in that district," he said. Many blacks simply did not vote, he concluded. Others unquestionably backed Baird. Early in the campaign, Chance had gotten a foreshadowing of his defeat when he approached a couple of black men he had known since childhood. Chance was startled by their coolness when he asked for support. "Well," said one, "you're running against a good man." Chance had no firm evidence that whites manipulated the electoral process to create the results, but to his mind, there was little doubt that they did. "There were just a number of things that you couldn't really put your finger on, but you suspected a lot," he said.

Chance believed, for instance, that the failure of some day laborers to return to Inverness and other polling places at lunchtime on election day was as much by design as accident. Each morning during planting and harvesting months, black drivers scour the county with pickup trucks, transporting workers to farm sites. Usually, the laborers come back into town for lunch. "That day, they worked so far from the polling places that they didn't get back to vote," he said. Chance heard reports, too, of white landowners who suggested to their black employees that they vote for his white opponent. "They were told something like, 'You need to vote for Mr. Baird.' It was almost in the sense of a threat," he said. "But when you quote what you've heard to people, they're reluctant to talk."

Any reluctance, countered Joe Baird, stemmed from the fact that the charges simply were not true. Pausing in the courthouse after a day of budget hearings, Baird, a prominent farmer, insisted that his political success was the result of nothing more than hard work. "I've made a special effort to be aware of everybody's needs. . . . It never entered my mind as to black and white," he said.

County blacks were equally dismayed by their defeats in the 1982 Indianola elections in which they ran a full slate of candidates for mayor and aldermen. Indianola is a pleasant little town of eighty-two-hundred residents, just over 50 percent of whom are black. Typical of other Delta county seats, it is a focal point for the financial and commercial interests that support the county's shrinking agricultural and fledgling manufacturing base. There is a cluttered strip of fast-food and chain stores on the bypass and a more picturesque town center. There, a shaded bayou that feeds into the Sunflower River is a restful backdrop to the white-columned brick courthouse and a still active main street.

In 1982, despite the large black population, four of five town council members and almost every other elected official in Indianola were white. With an at-large electoral system, blacks had never been able to mount enough strength to defeat whites, who registered and voted in greater numbers. In Indianola, James Robinson, an elderly photographer, was the only black man who had mustered enough white support to win a seat on the town council. It was no secret that prominent whites had settled on Robinson as their choice for a black representative, nor that some blacks found Robinson too conciliatory.

Against that backdrop, blacks decided to mount a full-court press that would, they hoped, produce a breakthrough at last. On election night, black workers gathered at a local community center, ready to celebrate the long-awaited victory. The mood was upbeat and relaxed, full of high spirits and the certainty that at least one black member would be added to Indianola's council. As the moments passed, however, elation turned sour. When the tally was complete, one black man—James Robinson—had won. As word of the fiasco reached the community center, there was first disbelief, then fury. Emotions were running too high to accept calmly yet another defeat. Whites must have tampered with the ballot boxes, some said. There were angry shouts and a move to march on city hall. Finally, a few leaders succeeded in quieting the crowd. "I had been a poll worker. I had observed," said John Chance, who could view the council elections more dispassionately than his own race. "To me, nothing went wrong. Many of the blacks just voted for white candidates."

The outcome seemed to validate, once again, the argument of many whites that local blacks simply approved of their leadership. Certainly, there were in the county whites who had worked to give blacks some voice in the political process. Jack Harper, for instance, had long since given up the views that once made him a member of the white supremacist Citizens Council. In recent decades, as circuit clerk, he had worked quietly to better race relations, arguing for a racial mix in the Democratic Party, sharing his duties as a referee in youth court cases with a young black lawyer, and even cutting a television spot for the party's black congressional nominee in 1984. But it seemed far too simplistic to attribute all the political failings of Sunflower County blacks to the goodwill and superior performance of whites. What that scenario left out was the effects of continued poverty and economic dependence, as well as the scars of a recent and violent past.

Only twenty years earlier, Mississippi had been at the vanguard of southern opposition to racial integration. By the 1980s many blacks in Sunflower County and across the Delta had not forgotten. In that other day, Mississippi was the toughest state of them all. For its white elite, there was no dilemma between the American ideal of equality and the pervasive inequality in treatment of blacks. Whites were simply superior, and the commitment to maintaining that superiority was ordained by states' rights and a deep religious fundamentalism. If violence and intimidation were the price of continuity, then the end more than justified the means.

Briefly, in the post-Civil War era, blacks played a role in Mississippi state government. There were thirty black and seventy-seven white representatives in the 1870 state legislature. Blacks served as lieutenant governor, secretary of state, superintendent of education, Speaker of the House, and U.S. senator.[6] By 1875 that brief interlude ended. It fell victim to a violence that set the tone for Mississippi race relations during much of the next century. In Meridian, Vicksburg, and dozens of other sites, rifles and cannons cleared the path of black resistance. The task was completed in 1890 when Mississippi, setting a pattern for other southern states, adopted a new constitution that included stringent requirements for voting. Most black voters were wiped from the rolls.

During the next seventy-five years, Mississippi elected a series of race-baiting governors, unexcelled in their rhetorical venom. Governor James K. Vardaman (1904–8) described the Negro as "a lazy, lying, lustful animal which no conceivable amount of training can transform into a tolerable citizen."[7] Governor Theodore G. Bilbo, who followed him in 1916–20 and 1928–32 and was the state's dominant political figure for almost four decades, was equally unrestrained. "You and I know what's the best way to keep the nigger from voting," Bilbo smirked during his 1946 Senate reelection campaign. "You do it the night before the election. I don't have to tell you any more than that. Red-blooded men know what I mean."[8] Sanctioned by such leaders, white Mississippians responded with a degree of bloodshed unparalleled in the nation. Between 1883 and 1959 by one count, some 538 black people died by lynching in the state.[9]

As the sparks of black activism began to ignite in the late 1950s and early 1960s, violence became increasingly linked to political activity. In Amite County on the Louisiana border, Herbert Lee, a black voter registration worker, was shot to death by a white state legislator in 1961. An eyewitness to the murder later met a similar fate in the front yard of his home. The legislator, E. H. Hurst, was never prosecuted. In Lincoln County, just north of Amite, another voter registration worker was gunned down on the courthouse lawn before many eyewitnesses. No one came to trial. In May 1963, the home of the voter registration leader in Holmes County was firebombed with three Molotov cocktails while his family slept. Later, the victim and four other civil rights workers were charged with staging the fire in order to stir up racial tensions in the Delta. The charges were eventually dropped.[10]

Most such events prompted little attention outside Mississippi's borders, but four developments became etched on the nation's conscience. The beatings and jailings of Freedom Riders, an interracial group of civil rights activists who passed through the state in 1961, testing segregated public transportation, were reported with chilling detail. The bloody clash of students and federal marshals as James Meredith tried to integrate the University of Mississippi in 1962 stunned viewers. Next came the death of Medgar Evers, field secretary of the Mississippi NAACP, shot in the back outside his Jackson home in 1963. And in 1964, the "Mississippi Freedom Summer," which brought to the teeming state hundreds of clergymen, housewives, professors, and college students, produced a climactic horror. Across the state, twenty-four black churches burned and three young civil rights workers —one black, two white—found an early grave in an earthen dam in Neshoba County, near Philadelphia.

Not surprisingly, given that climate, only 6 percent of eligible blacks were registered to vote in Mississippi in 1964. Two years earlier, there were five Mississippi counties with black-majority populations and not a single registered voter.[11] The stories behind those appalling figures live in the oral histories of every Delta county. In Sunflower County, for instance, older blacks still talk of Dr. Clinton Battle, a black physician who tried to register to vote in Indianola in the early 1950s. White plantation owners, they say, warned farm workers against patronizing Battle, the bank called in his loans, and he was forced to abandon his practice and leave town.

A decade later, Fannie Lou Hamer, the daughter of Sunflower County sharecroppers, was similarly punished for her attempts to register. Hamer, who died in 1977, once recalled the 1962 episode in which she and seventeen other blacks went to the courthouse to register. The registrar "brought a big old book out there, and he gave me the sixteenth section of the Constitution of Mississippi, and that was dealing with de facto laws," she said. "He told me to give a reasonable interpretation. . . . Well, I flunked out."[12] Returning home, Hamer also found that she and her husband had been evicted as a result of her political foray.

It was Sunflower County, as well, that gave birth to the white Citizens Council. Launched in 1954 by Robert Patterson, a former Mississippi State football hero and farmer from nearby Itta Bena, the councils were a white-collar version of the Ku Klux Klan, dedicated to the preservation of a segregated state. At their peak in the 1950s and 1960s, local councils counted prominent judges, planters, and businessmen among their members. The Jackson office, by one account, had a card file detailing the racial views of almost every white person in the city, and the council's influence with the state legislature was legendary.[13]

Details might have faded with time, but two decades later that heritage still figured in the daily lives and the limited political participation of blacks. When Robert Clark, a legislator from nearby Holmes County, ran for Congress in the majority-black Second District in 1982 and 1984, he was at first shunned when he visited some rural black Delta homes. Only after he began to receive a bit of white support did those blacks, dependent on white landowners for their survival, begin to warm to his campaign.

"They live with those white folk; they depend on those white folk," explained Clark.

As violence waned in the late 1960s, civil rights activists believe local whites found more subtle forms of economic manipulation to keep black voting in check. Whites might, for instance, keep blacks working overtime in the fields and factories, or they might drop hints that support of black candidates would be viewed badly by their employers. By the mid-1980s, many prominent whites scoffed at those suggestions as absurd; many blacks were convinced of their truth. Often the evidence boiled down to the word of one man (white) against the word of another man (black).

On balance, the likelihood of white planters or businessmen actually threatening black employees who voted seemed remote. Intimidation might well have occurred, but there was not enough evidence to suggest that it happened in any systematic or large-scale way. Proof of misdeeds was hard to come by. Who was to say that an extra hour or two in the fields or at the factory on election day was not needed? If it rained the next day or an order went unfilled, it was the white manager, not the black worker, who was held accountable. However, despite white denials, claims of intimidation popped up as insistently as summer ironweed in court testimony and the conversations of black leaders. Whether by design or accident, some blacks clearly found it difficult to get to the polls because of work conditions. In a setting with the repressive history of the Delta, black political workers were not inclined to give white entrepreneurs the benefit of the doubt where voting rights were concerned. Nor in such a climate could black complaints be dismissed or ignored. The very perception that whites at times conspired to prevent voting no doubt had a chilling effect on black participation.

A typical black complaint was outlined in a Mississippi voting rights case by David Jordan, president of the Greenwood Voters League and for twenty years one of the Delta's most persistent advocates of black rights. "On voting days," said Jordan, "we have had it to the point where we have tried to bring people in from the county, actually picked them up, and for some strange reason, they have more work to do that day than any other day. There have been cases where they haven't had a job until election day, and there's a job found. Or [they] work late to keep them from going to the polls."[14]

In Greenwood, Indianola, and Greenville, black leaders described several incidents in which they believed plant workers had been kept late intentionally on election days during the early 1980s. The Baldwin Piano Company in Greenwood, the Delta Catfish Processing Plant in Indianola, and the Vlasic pickle bottlers outside Greenville were cited in the complaints. Officials of each company denied any design to prevent voting. The difficulty in sorting out reality and perception was demonstrated in the Vlasic incident. During the 1983 gubernatorial elections, said Johnnie Walls, there were numerous complaints at his office and at Democratic campaign headquarters about workers being required to stay overtime at the pickling plant. Normally, employees might punch out at 3:30 or 4:00 P.M. That day, the foreman insisted that they stay late, Walls said.

In response, Vlasic's plant manager said it is entirely possible that workers might have long hours on an election day. But then, he added, that is true of any day. Overtime work is a staple of the bottling operation. Cucumbers are shipped to the plant from out-of-state. When they arrive, the company has eight to sixteen hours to get them into containers before spoilage begins. The result, said the manager, Ray Oldach, is that employee hours are at the mercy of nature. A four-hour work plan one day can easily stretch to twelve hours the next. For the company to plan such overtime with an eye to controlling elections, he said, would be "absolutely ridiculous."

And so, the debate continued. On the one hand, white managers offered plausible explanations. On the other, black organizers grappled with the frustration of continued defeats and the certainty that votes were sometimes lost when minimum wage and farm laborers could not get to the polls. Most frustrating of all for blacks was the realization that population figures should have given them a hold on local politics. Whether or not intimidation existed, there were spots in the Delta where it was simply astounding that blacks could not win political office. Clearly in such places, blacks were staying home or voting for whites. To whites, there was no mystery in that performance. "The black activists want to manage the black voting population. The black voting population does not want to be managed," said Jack Harper, Sunflower County's pink-cheeked, longtime circuit clerk. "The inference that black people are being held down and not permitted to vote is an outright lie against the community." More likely, said black political workers, what the pattern showed was that decades of political and economic suppression, of ongoing dependence on whites for jobs and bank loans and store credit had left some blacks as convinced as whites of black inferiority. "Sometimes it seems that it's solely the fault of blacks that blacks are not elected, but I know that's not true," said John Chance. "It just seems it was placed in the minds of blacks years ago that there are certain things blacks can't do."

As the 1990s approached, several developments created optimism among Sunflower County blacks that they would enter the decade with black officials in place. Mike Espy's election to Congress in the fall of 1986 was chief among them. The Second District, which stretches down the Delta, was recarved prior to the 1982 elections with an eye toward maximizing black voter strength. Many observers expected Robert Clark, who carried the Democratic banner that year and again in 1984, to become Mississippi's first black congressman of the century. Clark, who had broken the color barrier in the state legislature in the late 1960s, had risen to chair the House Education Committee. Amiable, conciliatory, less strident than many of his fellow black Mississippians, Clark was a model of black moderation. "He was the annointed one. He had done all the things you are supposed to do," said Leslie McLemore, a political scientist and graduate school dean at Jackson State University.

In 1982, the Second District was slightly over 50 percent black and heavily Democratic. All that was needed for victory was a solid black turnout and a respectable show of support from white Democrats. In the end, Clark got neither—or, at least, not in sufficient measure. White voter turnout was heavy. Racial bloc voting was extreme. Webb Franklin, a former Democratic judge, backed by upper-crust white plantation and professional interests, became the Delta's first Republican congressman of the century. He was aided by tactics such as a television ad picturing Clark and asking, "Do you know who my opponent is?" Two years later, in 1984, Clark tried again. District lines had been revised once more, giving blacks even greater clout. Overall population was about 58 percent black. This time, Clark surely could not lose. Yet he did. The lingering curses of white racism and black subjugation remained too strong. Clark was far from alone in asserting, "It would not have been a race if I had been white."

In 1986, however, the tables turned. Espy, a black man and former consumer protection lawyer in the attorney general's office, decided to run a campaign that was strong on organization and weak in volume. The idea was to maximize black voter turn-out and minimize white fears. Espy obtained a list of licensed drivers from the Department of Motor Vehicles and matched it against the voter registration list for the Second District. Since driver records in Mississippi record race, while registration lists do not, Espy was able both to target black voters and to identify many unregistered blacks. He focused on improved black registra-tion and on an election day organization designed to make sure blacks got to the polls. Meanwhile, he tried to avoid any incidents —including even an appearance by Jesse Jackson—that might ignite Franklin's white supporters. The result was a 51–49 percent victory over Franklin and an injection of hope in spots like Sun-flower County.

All around them, blacks in Sunflower County could see evi-dence of political change. The 1985 municipal elections had been a time for black rejoicing all across Mississippi as blacks made breakthroughs in Jackson and Greenwood, Laurel, and Hatties-burg. From the Delta to the piney woods of south Mississippi, civil rights lawyers were pressing lawsuits expected further to erode at-large elections. Ward systems were becoming the order of the day. With them, election of blacks was sure to grow. In Indianola, a long-standing battle over creation of a ward plan had finally been resolved, and elections were expected to be held in the spring of 1987. Blacks and whites agreed that at least one additional black member would almost certainly join the majority-white council.

At the county level, however, predictions were more cautious. Producing a racial shift on the board of supervisors would not be so simple as changing from at-large to district elections. In Missis-sippi counties, supervisors are already elected by district. A re-vised Sunflower County district plan was being drawn up under court order, and proposals had been back and forth to the Justice Department for several years. No matter how the lines were even-tually drawn, three of the five districts were expected to have majority-black populations. But then, three of five already did.

Few residents—black or white—felt confident that a handful of additional black voters here, a few less there, would necessarily change age-old voting patterns.

"I'm not going to say Sunflower County will never have a black supervisor," noted James Corder, chairman of the county board and a white farmer. But he was also not willing to say that a slew of court orders or a much-negotiated redistricting plan held the magic solution for blacks. If numbers were all that mattered, he added, for Sunflower County blacks, "the opportunity's here now."

9. GREENE COUNTY
The Generations

A POLITICAL REVOLUTION, of sorts, came to Greene County, Alabama, in the fall of 1984. Similar change would soon sprout in more sophisticated settings across the South, sending pundits scurrying to record the advent of a new stage in the evolution of black politics. But for a time, before Sidney Barthelemy had broken with Dutch Morial to become mayor of New Orleans and John Lewis had embarrassed Atlanta's black political elite by defeating Julian Bond for Congress, tiny Greene County led the way.

A sparsely populated haven of vast natural spaces, of somber forests and hushed pastureland, Greene County seems an unlikely candidate for the vanguard of regional and national change. Drivers barreling through on their way from Meridian to Birmingham, ninety minutes to the northeast, seldom leave the interstate to sample the gravy-smothered hamburger steaks or garden-fresh collards on menus at the county's smattering of modest eating spots. Country backroads amble and twist past sylvan settings of glassy catfish ponds and lonely bungalows and empty into other roads that also seem to lead nowhere.

For outsiders, the major—and perhaps only—attraction is the greyhound racing park, Greenetrack, a fortress of gray-green aluminum, of floodlights and scoreboard rising out of the piney woods and bringing hundreds of Chevy pickups and dust-streaked sedans down from Tuscaloosa or over from Demopolis on a Satur-

169

day evening. For a few boisterous hours, the revelers can wager and drink, leaving behind sorely needed tax dollars before they disperse into the stillness of an Alabama night. Those few passersby with business in the county wend their way to Eutaw, a sturdy little town of towering magnolias and large frame houses that is home to one-fourth or so of the county's eleven thousand residents, 78 percent of whom are black. There, as likely as not, visitors congregate at the courthouse, a whitewashed stucco structure with wrought-iron balconies and deep-green shutters, resembling a fading antebellum mansion in both its beauty and disrepair. There, too, they will find the focal point of the 1984 revolution, a still unfolding political drama.

Surprisingly, this pastoral county is no stranger to political turmoil. Old cliques had been ousted, new ones installed before. But the 1984 coup was a cut apart. Some called it absolutely unthinkable, a treasonous, contemptible act, at odds with the forces of history. Those who planned and staged it said simply, "times change." Or, "no one in a democracy is safe from an election-by-election accounting." Greene County had heard some of the same arguments before, back in the 1960s. Then, the county reverberated with the voices of Martin Luther King, Jr., and others who led marches and spoke on the steps of Eutaw's First Baptist Church-Colored. In 1969, the people responded, sweeping into office black majorities on the county commission and school board. A year later, they won the offices of sheriff and probate judge, as well. Blacks reigned. Greene County, trailing Hancock County, Georgia, by a year, had become the second county in the South to be controlled by black voters and politicians. It would become a national model of what blacks could do, the victors said. For fifteen years, almost every facet of local government would rest in black hands.

In November 1984, that dynasty ended. A new group seized power. Once again, Greene County stood at the cutting edge of change. The difference was not in the color of the faces at the courthouse, however. Those were still black. What was different was that many of the new breed did not have the civil-rights-era roots of their predecessors. More startling, their election was directly attributable to white support. Not shying from arguments that once would have been heresy, the group insisted that Greene County was not being well run. Incumbents were tackling unemployment by putting everyone and his cousin on the county pay-roll, they said. The county was in financial jeopardy. Its infant mortality rate was the worst in the state; its unemployment rate —based on the 1980 census—was Alabama's highest. No other county had a higher ratio of individuals (47 percent) living in poverty. The new political activists were generally younger and better educated than their predecessors. And they openly pursued a strategy that, a few years earlier, even they might have labeled traitorous. Ignoring labels like "Uncle Tom" and "in-between nigger," they marched brazenly into white bastions like the Na-tional Guard Armory and said publicly and for all to hear, "Vote for me." Whites, elated at the prospect of retrieving some measure of influence, embraced them overwhelmingly.

In the months to follow, similar patterns would emerge in larger southern arenas. In the spring of 1986, Sidney Barthelemy, a black man, would depend on a black-white coalition to defeat the black mayoral candidate favored by New Orleans' traditional civil rights forces. In Atlanta, John Lewis would do the same. Political scientists forecast a new wave in black politics. And the questions formed. Did these biracial coalitions represent progress for blacks or a step backward? Were the blacks who joined them the forerunners of a more color-blind society, or were they the pawns of whites eager to reclaim power and to discredit more militant blacks? In Greene County, answers were already being written.

There, the saga was also a generational tale, that of an old war-horse and his young challenger. William McKinley Branch, the probate judge, and John Kennard, the tax assessor, were the leading characters. Branch, a honey-voiced raconteur with a warm, down-to-earth style, was for fifteen years the dominant political figure in Greene County. Fired from his schoolteaching job when he founded the local NAACP chapter in the early 1960s, Branch helped orchestrate the 1969 election victories, and as pro-bate judge beginning in 1970, guided the county commission and its policies. Part homey philanthropist, part skilled manipulator, Branch commanded widespread personal loyalty. He remained in office after the 1984 coup, operating out of quarters a few hundred yards from the main courthouse. There, he held court, answering dozens of phone calls daily with a cheery "Hello, Senator," a "Good morning, Deacon," or a "How are you, Mr. Representative?" Clearly, as commission chairman and the father confessor of county politics, he remained an institution. But he had been stripped of the council majority that produced much of his clout. Leading the opposition was Kennard, half Branch's age, a dean's list graduate of the University of Alabama who, as a boy, had sat in Branch's classroom. His maverick ways and unbowed confidence were reflected in a booming baritone and in the cowboy garb, complete with hat, boots, and leather jacket, in which he strode the courthouse square. Unintimidated by his elders or by the clamp of tradition, Kennard began to move early in 1984 after a county surplus eroded into a half-million-dollar debt. He helped recruit candidates to run against the incumbent commissioners. He made no secret of his belief that ruling blacks no longer merited the public trust. On election day, all four incumbent commissioners were defeated. Six of seven people on the Kennard slate —Kennard as tax assessor, a school board member, the tax collector, and three commissioners—were elected. Judge Branch, who acted as a fifth commission member, was left in a two-person minority.

In a series of interviews, beginning not long after the November 1984 election and concluding in the fall of 1986, Branch and Kennard spoke of history, of their conflicting visions, and of the path of black political progress in a small, struggling county each man cherished as home.

BRANCH:

"My name is Judge William McKinley Branch, and I was born in Forkland, Alabama. I've lived here all my days. My grandparents on my mother's side was sold as slaves from Virginia, and my grandparents on my daddy's side was sold as slaves from, I believe, Kentucky. They lived a very fruitful life because they had seven children of their own, plus my father had to rear two of his brothers and one sister. When he and mamma got married, he was eighteen and she was fourteen. And, of course, they gave us all a high school education and three went to college. I had a liberal arts course and a bachelor of science course, and I got a couple of honorary degrees. I started in the ministry at eleven, and got married, and we have seven children.

"Growing up here, at the time I was coming up, there was no type of social relationship between white and black. You were just only a servant-master relationship. I remember what really set me out for political achievement was that my father borrowed $150 from a merchant, and he paid that merchant three to four bales of cotton a year for six years. At the end of the six years, that merchant repossessed what we had, with this exception. My brothers and I told daddy, 'Now, daddy, we've worked here all summer, and we're not going to let this man take all our corn and our cows.' So, when daddy'd leave, we'd hook up the wagon and we hauled about four loads of corn down in the swamp. We carried us about two milk cows and three oxen. What we was going to do was plow the oxen and the cows was going to give the milk, and we's going to have milk and bread. And so, that's what we did. It was quite humiliating for us to walk from here about eight miles on the other side of Demopolis to the swamp, right down through the town, driving the cows.

"What I couldn't understand, how could it take my father six years, paying three and four bales of cotton a year, to have everything repossessed for $150? And another thing, why is it that we're out here in the fields working hard all day, and at the end of the year, we was able to get maybe a couple of pair of overalls and a pair of shoes, and that had to do us that whole winter? I said to myself, there's something wrong with this system.

"And I noticed that the whites lived in nice houses. We did the work, and the houses we lived in, you could see up through the ceiling and cracks in the floor. My mother and daddy, when I first could recollect, had one big single room and a kitchen. We had one bed, and we had to sleep on pallets on the floor. We didn't have lamps, no electricity whatsoever, and my mamma, she would take one of these Nehi bottles—big as an R.C. bottle—and she would put kerosene in the bottle, and take old union underwears and make a wick, and you could see through the night. At that time, we were pestered by bedbugs. She would go from pallet to pallet, seeing a kid if it would rustle the least bit. So, I can't ever forget her for that."

KENNARD:

"I grew up here in rural southwest Alabama. We had an extremely large family, six boys and six girls. I was born and reared in Forkland. We still go to church there. Every Sunday, about fourteen or fifteen of us eat dinner at my parent's house. Mom cooks.

That's the kind of life that I never want to get away from. It's the kind of setting where we get together and discuss family problems and progress, the county's problems and progress. I was the eighth child, born in 1952. My parents were sharecroppers. They lived on the land of an extremely large landowner on the south side of the county. Basically, tenants were given housing, in return for which, we raised the cotton. The landowner was not a ruthless individual, but my parents did not get what was due them. At the end of the year, he would always say, 'If you'd picked one more bale of cotton, you'd have come out even.'

"My family got their land in 1959, some heir property from my father's father. What happened was my older brother went off to Stillman College [a black college in Tuscaloosa], and the landlord got mad about that. And they got put off the place. He said it was the loss of a field hand he should have had. But the basic thing was that he didn't want my brother to go to school. My family was told that they had to move, and they moved near Demopolis. I remember the Whites Only signs there, the beginning of the movement."

In 1962, a Justice Department probe into Greene County politics found that fewer than three hundred black people in a county then 81 percent black were registered to vote. The white minority easily dominated local politics. In response, Branch and others mobilized the Greene County Civic Organization, and in 1965—when the Voting Rights Act took effect—the county was one of the first in the South to be assigned federal registrars. By the early spring of 1966, black registration had shot upward to almost thirty-eight hundred. Frustrated in their early tries at political office, blacks mobilized for the 1968 elections.[1] On September 10, the Alabama secretary of state ruled that black candidates, who were running under the label of the National Democratic Party of Alabama, had not met the state's onerous filing requirements. They were declared ineligible for the ballot. The U.S. Supreme Court, acting swiftly, ruled otherwise, and the matter seemed resolved. On election day, however, blacks were astounded to find that their names still were not on the local ballot. The white probate judge, James Dennis Herndon, had decided that blacks had sidestepped a legal technicality in nominating their candidates. Again, the case wound up in Supreme Court chambers in Washington, and a special election was ordered for July 29, 1969. Victory became a regional cause as civil rights workers invaded the county, holding daily rallies and organizing a fleet of forty cars to take citizens to the polls.

BRANCH:

"I taught school for about fifteen years, and then when I organized the NAACP, they kicked me out of the school system. The then superintendent told me that I had organized something subversive, the NAACP. He called me in one day and said, 'I'm going to have to let you go.' Said, 'because you're engaged in something that is not so healthy for the community.' And he said, 'I tell you what I'll do. You just go on and offer your resignation, and I'll give you an A-1 recommendation anywhere outside the state of Alabama.' I said to him, 'Now, I appreciate that, but I'm going to stay right here.' I said, 'The problem is that we don't hardly have the right to vote. We need civil rights and human rights. I cannot run away from the problem, and I'm going to stay right here if I have to eat corn bread and drink water.'

"From 1965 to 1968, there was a mass eviction in this county. People wanted to register to vote, and the landlords kicked them off. We had about eighty families that were evicted because they registered to vote. But we were able to retain 95 percent of them in Greene County. And how we did that was, we put on a campaign of going around, talking to black folks who had land. We told them, 'Now listen, if you don't let them have but a half-acre of land, let's try to keep these folks here.' I had some land, a little ol' ten-acre block right up the road. And the first thing, I laid an example. I think we got about thirteen families on that place. Sometimes, we'd help them build a log cabin, or find an old house somewhere. We'd go and tear it down, pull the nails out, and then help build without any cost to them. And at first, some of the blacks who registered got mad with us. They said, 'You caused us to be out of homes.' But about a year after, when they were in their new homes, they came back and begged our pardon.

"About 1967, prior to the election, I led a delegation to a white group in the courthouse, and I asked them, 'Why don't we run an integrated slate, four commissioners, two white, two black? Same thing on the board of education.' And these fellows, evidently they were KKers [Ku Klux Klan members], they said to me, 'We've drawn a hard line against you damn niggers, and we're going to keep it.' I said, 'Here, we're going to take it.' And two years later, we took it.

"In 1968, the county election officials left the black candidates names off the ballot for county commission and the board of education. They didn't know their names were not on the ballot 'til election day. I was so excited about my own race [Branch was running for Congress], I didn't notice too much until way up in the day. Then, we said, 'Something's wrong with this thing.' And they were talking about, 'Well, y'all didn't file right. Y'all didn't file right.' And I said to them, 'Gentlemen, if there's any justice in the United States, our names have got to go back on the ballot.' So, on Christmas Eve, 1968, me and those black officers went to Atlanta, Georgia, to see a fellow named Chuck Morgan who was head of the civil liberties thing [the American Civil Liberties Union] at the time. We were giving deposition on Christmas Eve, and we took it to the United States Supreme Court. I believe it was February of 1969, the night when [television commentator] Walter Cronkite announced that black candidates in Greene County, Alabama, have been ordered back on the ballot. And that order set the date of the election, July 29, 1969. And of course, we won it, almost by a landslide.

"The day after the election, we had one to shoot himself. He died later. Just a white citizen. He was a businessman, lived in Eutaw. I don't recall his name. His cook said he woke up that morning: 'Well, the damn niggers done took over.' And sometime later in the day, he shot himself. . . . The day of our inauguration, some of the black fellows from the SCLC [Southern Christian Leadership Conference] went down and swam in the swimming pool. And that made them [whites] sick too."

KENNARD:

"My parents were very liberal. They allowed us to march. From 1960 to 1969, there was a great deal of work in this county. I doubt if twenty black people were registered in the early part of the 1960s. The good thing in Greene County was that the masses of people did get registered to vote. Landowners sent word to us, if anyone registered to vote, they would be put off the plantations. Black people with land would sell somebody a half-acre, and then nobody could tell you what to do.

"I remember in 1969, when a special election was ordered by the Supreme Court. Everybody just experienced euphoria. It was July 29, 1969. I was in high school. When they won, it was one of the best feelings some of our elderly people had ever had. I remember gathering to wait for the election returns at the First Baptist Church in Eutaw. Martin King had gotten killed in 1968. Everybody was more and doubly determined to make his dreams come true. People were just shouting and having a hallelujah good time."

A year later, Branch was elected probate judge, and Tom Gilmore, a lanky, black preacher, ousted the incumbent sheriff.

BRANCH:

"So, when I ran for judge and Gilmore ran for sheriff, they sent some black fellows to us, some of their Toms. They offered Gilmore and myself $10,000 and enough black angus cows to go into the cattle business. We said, 'No, we can't take it.' They came again with $20,000. And the last time, they came with $25,000 apiece. And I said, 'You go back and tell those fellows, not only are we going to run, but we're going to win.' He say, 'You won't live three months.' I said, 'You also tell them, what happen to me will happen to the incumbent probate judge. And what happen to Gilmore will happen to the incumbent sheriff, Bill Lee.' Evidently, he told them.

[After the election, Branch went to visit the white probate judge whom he had defeated.] "I said, 'Listen, I'd like to keep your entire staff on.' All white. He said, 'Don't you say nothing to them. I'm going to give you the damn key on that day, and that's all I'm going to do.' The only cooperation I got was from a probate judge over in Choctaw County. He would slip in at night through the back door, he and his deputy clerk, and we'd slip him out. He was scared. He was the man who really helped orientate us to a lot of things."

KENNARD:

"When I came back from college, blacks held the majority of offices in this county. . . . I was elected [in 1978], and all of the white workers just left. There were three workers in the tax assessor's office. I took office November 16, and on the night of the fifteenth, the whites just left. I didn't get any help at all from the old tax assessor. All this was Greek to me. There wasn't a black person around who knew anything about this. But we learned. The state association of tax assessors lent a lot of help. Slowly, but surely, we started doing things for ourselves.

"In the early days, what we were trying to do was elect black people to office, any black person who had the courage to run. We did as best we could, but we were not as resourceful as we should have been in recruiting really qualified people. From 1980 on, people were beginning to look at the record and say, 'What have you done?' When I was elected the first time around, no question about it, I was elected by and large by the black community. Everybody felt good to have a black person for the first time in the tax assessor's office. But in the final analysis, after the warm feeling is gone, the taxes still have to be assessed. Sooner or later, you will be judged, not on what color you are, but on the amount of services that you're able to provide for the average person.

"Greene County is different from most other counties. Black people have had unquestioned control of this county, I mean absolute control for the past fifteen years. Now, when you look around Greene County and see the unemployment rate exactly as it has been or higher, and Branch has been the person in charge, when you look at the fact that we don't have the jobs, when you look at the fact that the county is broke, then you have to say to yourself that just getting a black person in office is not the solution.

"There is a new generation of people here now. I was the first in my family to graduate from the University of Alabama. But now, I have a younger brother and two younger sisters who've gone there. And there are a lot of other families who have the same thing. . . . The younger generation is saying, 'I didn't march because I wasn't born then. But I want a job.' The younger people don't care if you're white or black; they want an opportunity to work."

BRANCH:
"You never reach all your goals. But the major goals we set out, we've reached some and made progress on the others. When we came in, we didn't even have an industrial board. So now we have a biracial

industrial board, and we have developed an industrial park called the Crossroads of America. We've built some low-rent houses. We've got what they call the William McKinley Branch Heights, just outside the city limits of Eutaw. Then, there's Martin Luther King Village, just above Branch Heights. When we got Branch Heights, we had to secure water and a sewage disposal system. Whites are still in control of the city of Eutaw, and they wouldn't let us have the water, gas, or sewer. So we had to go back to HUD [the Department of Housing and Urban Development] and get enough money to build an independent sewage disposal system.

"We were lucky enough to get grants to rehabilitate houses. People didn't have any kitchen cabinets, or refrigerators, or heat. And another little grant we've got is for housing weatherization. Then another thing, we have four major nutrition sites in this county. We've established what is known as the West Alabama Health Service, and although it cost us money from our general fund, it's gratifying to know that these poor folk can get health care.

"I just got federal funds every time I could. I believe we've gotten at least $90- to $100 million, and that's conservative."

KENNARD:

"More could have been done. Greene County is the second smallest county in the state, and we get more money per capita than any other county. In Greene County, you have two major railroads, you have the Tennessee Tombigbee being completed, two interstate highways converging. We're sitting in the best position for industrial development, and there's been little effort to go out and sell the county. The educational level has not skyrocketed as it should have. We have one of the best preschools in the country, but by the time children reach the fourth or fifth grades, the scores are really low.

"They [the Branch faction] did do one fantastic thing. On September 30, 1977, the Greenetrack opened. It was a tremendous boost."

BRANCH:

"Back in 1973 was when the idea first got started. I went to Mobile. I was invited down on a community service program, and they gave us free passes to the Mobile track. I talked to one of the commissioners there, and he gave me a brochure and showed me how lucrative of income it was. I came back to Greene County and asked the commissioners to authorize the passing of a bill that would allow us to have one. And they laughed at me at first, the people around here. The commissioners laughed. My attorney laughed at me, so I told him to go down and study it, and when he came back, he said, 'Man, that's a lucrative thing.' Then we had our legislator to introduce it.

"The minister of the First Baptist Church-White in Eutaw came to my office one day. I said, 'Have a seat, Doctor.' 'Naw Judge, I just came by to let you know, I'm gonna fight you on that dog track.' I said, 'I don't blame you. If you think we're wrong, you fight us. And I'll tell you two other things I want you to fight, fight that whiskey store down there across from the jail house and fight racism.' When I said those, baby, he ain't said no more to me since from that day until this one about the dog track. And the next time he did say anything, he wasn't saying it to me. He was over in city hall trying to determine which way the money from the track was given to charity.

"Of course now, it's the greatest thing that could ever happen. We're in a lot better shape than most of the counties because we've got a real good source of income, and that's Greenetrack."

KENNARD:

"The track brings in $3 million or more a year. Four percent of the take goes to the county government, the rest to the owners, trainers, and betters. Of the 4 percent that is earmarked for county government, 30 percent goes for education. The track tripled the amount of money we were getting. Then, voters began to look for some positive changes. But the revenues from Greenetrack were basically unaccounted for in terms of what we were getting."

In the summer of 1984, the *Greene County Democrat* published an audit showing a $424,000 shortfall in the county's general fund. By December, in an article in the *Tuscaloosa News,* Branch acknowledged that overall debts totaled about $700,000.[2] Nor did he deny that four years earlier, Greene County had had a $600,000 surplus. Branch described the financial problems as "temporary." He attributed much of the gap to unrecovered money invested in an industrial park and to an almost $400,000 outlay for a water and sewer project. Federal reimbursement was pending, and Greenetrack revenues would soon cover any lag, he said. But Kennard saw those troubles as continued evidence of mismanagement. The county payroll was bloated, he said. A summer youth program had hired lavishly, spending about $300,000, more than three times the budgeted amount. Citizens—black and white—were outraged at the prospect of covering debts with a tax hike. The combination, he said, produced Greene County's historic political confrontation in the fall of 1984.

KENNARD:

"In the summer of 1984, when the audit hit the paper and we were half-a-million dollars in debt, everybody was up in arms. I decided as an individual that I was not going to go behind anyone's back. I was going to go public. The county government had tried to put everybody on the payroll. There were 137 county employees, and most areas around here don't have nowhere near that number.

"What brought this thing to a head in Greene County was that in February [1984], the county commission wanted to raise the taxes. Right now, we pay 23 1/2 mills, or $23.50 per $1,000 of appraised value. What they wanted to do was add a 47 percent increase to the 23 1/2 mills. They had not used the money properly, and now they wanted to go back to the people and raise taxes just to cover up their own ineptness. Well, I opposed that.

"From where I sit, I know who the delinquent taxpayers of this county are. It's not the white community. It's the poor black person who can hardly afford the taxes at this point. And then, you're going to go and raise his taxes by 47 percent. That was where we drew the line. Well, an amazing thing happened. For the first time, the white community and the black community came together. We got a petition. There were over fourteen hundred signatures that were gathered against the property tax proposal. When the county commission was presented with that many signatures—black and white, rich and poor—they knew they'd better not put that thing to a referendum. They knew it would never pass. That was the beginning of black and white working together against something that neither wanted."

BRANCH:

"There was no legitimate basis [for the black-white political coalition that formed in 1984]. The people who were defeated did the best they could under the circumstances. John Kennard didn't know. We've got a lot of money tied up in industrial property that came from our general fund. We've got almost $1 million that we can't get back until somebody comes in and buys the property for industry. And I know that's wise spending because you're spending for the future. When industry used to come to us, they'd sort of have us up and thinking we were going to get it, and then [snaps fingers] up and gone to a white government. We have an ideal location and everything, but our skins are black. Most of the industry looked at the complexion of the governmental officials. Skin deep.

[As for the county payroll and the summer jobs program], "I didn't come into office only to develop roads. I came into office to develop people. I feel gratified by trying to put as many people to work as I possibly could. That's one of the bright stars in my administration. I love it and I don't regret it. . . . I don't think we waste a dime in humanity."

As the 1984 election approached, Kennard began to sense the possibilities for a coalition of black and white voters. Among whites, a local Methodist minister, an assistant district attorney, a Eutaw attorney and others shared his vision. The interest was not in fielding white candidates, but in finding black candidates willing to buck the black establishment. Four men, including one incumbent county commissioner, agreed to seek commission spots running on the Kennard team.

KENNARD:

"After 1976, you had had some [political] competition among blacks in the county. But a black wouldn't dare solicit white votes in the open. I was, in 1984, the very first black politician to go to the National Guard Armory. I was determined to go to the whites, and the new guys running with me went too. I felt I was running for public office, and it was necessary to go to where the people traditionally are. This was the traditional white setting. Since 1969, the white community in Greene County had not really been addressed. A whole generation had grown up and not had the privilege of local candidates coming to visit them.

"At the first meeting at the National Guard Armory, I addressed a small crowd. I was very warmly received. Then, there was a second meeting and more than five hundred people showed up. The other candidates [on his team] were there too. After that, I had a kickoff rally at the Eutaw Activity Center, a traditional black setting, and I invited the white community to come there. They showed up in record numbers.

"Over 90 percent of the black people said it was time for somebody to break the ice. All this stuff about "We Shall Overcome" was in the sixties. There's a philosophy among the old-line black leadership that there's something evil and demonic and a master plan in the white community to enslave blacks. I just don't believe that."

BRANCH:

"Kennard and the other blacks were nothing but puppets. It was just a group that the whites could corral. They were just craving for power. That's all. Now, I'll tell you what the whites tried to do. What they really wanted to do was run a campaign against me. See, any man that the whites cannot control as a "boy," they'll do any tactic they want to defeat. The whites, they don't want to come together on a sure 'nuf brotherly basis like I tried to get them to do. What they want to do is to show that they can outdo so and so.

"Can't no white walk up to me and say with the truth that I've ever slighted or had any ill will toward whites. Now, when I was in charge of the phase of the court here that dealt with traffic violations, violations of misdemeanors, I have found some blacks guilty and some whites guilty and have turned around and helped them pay their fine.

"I don't hate them [the Kennard faction] for it. I feel sorry for them. You see, the thing was so obvious, people who could barely read and write could tell it. They offered them money. I've got some reliable information from some reliable people. They were offered money to do that. You know what? I have been offered all kinds of money to, you know, sell out. But I can't do that. I've got to live with myself. People who forget their history are doomed to repeat it."

KENNARD:

"If anyone has benefited from the white community, it's Branch. Branch is a stockholder in Greenetrack. He is one of two black stockholders. Here again, I get blamed for being the Uncle Tom. But Greenetrack is in Greene County because there was no way they [the owners] could put it anywhere else. Before a track can be located in any political subdivision, it requires a referendum of the people of the county. This is the one county where Branch had the absolute control of the majority of the people. In return for Branch getting a majority of the people in this county to vote, he was given some stock in it. He was in a position of leverage. He could have demanded more things for the people of this county, as opposed to more things for himself personally. And he chose the personal route, and that is why we only have two black stockholders."

BRANCH:

"He doesn't know. He does not know. I never thought of becoming a board member. But the people who had money to invest, they knew I was instrumental in getting it here, and they offered me an opportunity to buy stock, me and one more person. And that's how it happened. It was up to them. It's a private enterprise. I was surprised at them letting me get in on it."

In the September 1984 primary, all four members of Kennard's team led in the county commission races. The contest brought about 3,800 voters to the polls and attracted 680 absentee ballots. The absentee ballots—about 18 percent of the total—favored those aligned with traditional black leaders by margins of up to three to one. In the runoff a few weeks later, three of the newcomers were elected, despite major defeats in the absentee-ballot box. The fourth commission candidate aligned with Kennard, Dr. Warren Burke, led by 237 votes until the absentee ballots were counted.

With those ballots included, he lost the election by 72 votes. In protest, Kennard and others contacted federal law enforcement officials and demanded an investigation. More than any previous action, Kennard's promotion of and cooperation with the absentee-ballot probe—which became part of a larger Black Belt investigation—infuriated traditional black leaders.

KENNARD:

"There is no secret about the fact that I'm cooperating with the FBI to try to bring an end to the vote stealing in Greene County. We have got to learn that we have to play the game by the same set of rules that everybody else plays by. People were voting who've been gone from this county for ten to fifteen years, and I'm saying this was condoned by the top of the government down. They knew they could holler FBI conspiracy, and they felt they could get away with it. What we did to our people was absolutely ridiculous. It was pathetic.

"You'll hear a lot about the conspiracy of the Reagan administration. I know in Greene County what happened, and it was not a conspiracy on the part of the Reagan administration. What happened in Greene County was that black people who had been in office and had not done that much were afraid and conspired to defraud the voters of this county. This is the second smallest county, and it had more absentee voters than the largest."

BRANCH:

"It [heavy use of absentee ballots] had been done all the while. I didn't see anything different in that election. In the old days, they [whites] would vote dead folks. They just magnified it to make us look like gangsters in this area to keep people from voting absentee.

"The information I received was that it was a one-sided investigation. The evidences I saw were where people on the other side had done the same thing it was alleged the [defendants] had done. For example, some of the leaders on the other side helped these old folks vote. They came there, filled out the ballots, and had them to sign it. That was brought to the attention of the Justice Department, and they didn't do anything about it.

"In Reconstruction we had one black representative in the legislature from this area, and by hook or crook, he was disenfranchised and the election set aside. It's a systematic elimination of black people in government, and this voter investigation thing is just another phase of it."

KENNARD:

"I really was not after a conviction. My single purpose was to stop vote stealing. The black leaders were saying that the white community did it back then and, hell, I'm not going to argue that. But because they did it doesn't make it right for us to do it. We wanted to make a statement to the public officials. Be in office, do your job, and if not, the people are going to get you out. That was the objective."

Did the Reagan administration have a more political objective in pursuing the vote fraud investigation?

KENNARD:

"That is something that has been said, and Reagan has denied it. I don't know. Ronald Reagan could well have benefited from the investigation, but he did not perpetuate it. Black people did, and it was against black people. Reagan may have benefited, or Ed Meese may have enjoyed himself, but it never would have started if black people hadn't complained."

Fifteen months after the coalition candidates took office, Branch and Kennard offered individual assessments of the impact on Greene County. Seated under a picture of Martin Luther King, Jr., his cowboy boots propped on a wooden desk, Kennard seemed assured and optimistic, a man whose reach had extended beyond the cramped confines of the tax assessor's office. Primary elections were a few months away, and Kennard was running for the state legislature against a black incumbent in a three-county district. His strategy was to shape the same black-white coalition that had carried Greene County in 1984. But Branch was also upbeat, sensing a possible comeback for traditional civil rights forces. The vote fraud investigation had been denounced by black leaders nationwide, and Kennard's role in it had helped focus opposition to him.

Countywide elections for the county commission were also being replaced by district elections and allies of Branch had drawn the district lines.

KENNARD:

"The new commission has done some marvelous things. They were installed in January 1985. The unemployment rate was about 17 percent. It's still high, but they have been instrumental in getting two new industries to locate in Greene County. The Scott Paper Company in Boligee is a direct tribute to the new council. Scott Paper Company was almost committed to go to the port of Epps in Sumter County. Our new commissioners met with the officials of Scott and convinced them that we simply had a better location. Then, there's United Roofing Company. They make the felt that goes between your roof and your shingles. [Their coming] is a direct result of my personal effort and the efforts of the incumbent commissioners. The gentleman that owns United Roofing is from here. He has wanted to come back to Greene County, but he wanted the basic assurance from the county commissioners that they would be an asset rather than a liability.

"Now there are still some problems, even with the new commissioners. The old commissioners had gotten the county in such a rut that they had to borrow something to the tune of $300,000 to run the government in 1984. Well, they didn't pay it back. The bill is now over $340,000 and [the bank] has turned it over to a collection agency. Those guys are out of office and the new commissioners are in, and this is a problem that they have inherited.

"The coalition today is much stronger. The additional strength came because, for the first time in a long time, people started seeing each other. The coalition came about basically because of politics. But after the politics left, last summer there was a white person at my church. This was unheard of. Last night, I was over at a church in the white community. This had nothing to do with politics. The Christmas program at the Episcopal church here in Eutaw was completely integrated. These were things that were unheard of. Politics was the catalyst, but people are looking at people as human beings, rather than as black or white. They started not seeing a black tax assessor, but a tax assessor."

BRANCH:

"I think that [coalition] movement is dead. I don't think it's going to survive long. We've been redistricted. The commissioners are going to be elected by district this time, and I think it's going to be different. Whether in Greene County or anywhere in the nation, you're going to have political factions. I think that's a sign of political progress, when people decide they'll go with their convictions. I love that. [But Kennard], to me he was just a puppet on those white folk's string. Now that's my connotation. Yeah! [As for the new commissioners], I don't see any marked improvement. I do not. Most of all this getting money in here was during the previous administration. They hadn't done too much yet.

"Race relations in Greene County have changed superficially. But every now and then, it'll surface that the racial hatred thing is still there. Sometimes they take a group of blacks and try to pay them, and that'll let you know. Plus, they really don't want us to come to their churches. They don't want to go to school with us. If there's any whites that go to school with us, it's the poor kind who can't financially sustain going to the private school.

"Some little white boys'll come to my office when they want to do some research. And they'll tell me quite often, 'I wanted to go to the public school, but my daddy won't let me.' The adult white'll threaten them with disinheritance, see. And they'll become an outcast. And so, [the coalition] was just a matter of [whites] feeling their way and seeing can they get themselves back in power."

KENNARD:

"The misconception of the coalition was this. People expected, the black leadership club of Alabama expected, that the white community wanted to dominate. That was not the purpose of the alliance. The only thing they wanted was what I wanted, responsible people in government. So there've been no appointments of whites to any board. There's been no change, say, in the county attorney. They've not asked for it.

"The problem with black leaders in this state and nation is that they automatically assume that when the white community gets involved and supports a candidate, that they're going to control that individual. I don't understand the automatic assumption that we're going to be used if we form a coalition. If somebody has to be used, why does it have to be John Kennard? Why can't it be the white community?"

BRANCH:

"I taught John Kennard. He and I, we're never going to change our attitudes. No. That shows you're an amateur. I don't agree with him, but I'll never fall out with him. In everybody's life is some wrongs they have done, and he's no exception. If God would say everybody's going to hell because you done sinned once in your life. . . . You've got to be able to forgive. It's not easy sometimes, but you've got to get hold of yourself and do what you feel is morally and spiritually right."

KENNARD:

"Branch taught me when I was a kid. He was my principal. I respect the man as a human being. He did some courageous things as far as transforming Greene County from a white-controlled government to a black controlled, and no one can ever take that away from him. The failure he had was that he really did not deal with the problems that affected everybody. And that problem is unemployment. That problem is poor education. You're in charge of a county. You're in charge of a $5-million budget. There are times that you have to say, 'No,' and I've never heard him say that yet."

In the aftermath of the 1986 elections, both factions in Greene County claimed victory. Kennard was defeated for the legislature with surprising ease, and traditional political forces heralded that loss as a repudiation of the black-white coalition he had formed. Allies of Kennard argued that three of five county commission seats had been won by individuals they favored, despite the disadvantage of the new district lines. Clearly, Greene County voters were unwilling to abandon their political roots. But, just as clearly, the concept of a biracial coalition had become imbedded in local political thought.

BRANCH:

"The coalition fell through. The original civil rights folks came out victorious. They were more representative of the mass of the people. They were more concerned about the poor and about giving them a chance to participate in government. It's just as fictitious as Humpty Dumpty Sat on a Wall that that was a true black-white coalition. In reality, it was just to get power for themselves.

"All over these United States, unless black and white, Jew and Gentile can get together, this country is going from bad to worse. But I think it's going to be generations to come before people recognize each other as brothers and sisters. I don't see that in the near future."

KENNARD:

"Greene County, most counties in the Black Belt, are going to go backward and forward trying one thing and another politically. We will not get stability until we find some way to solve the economic problems. Whoever has the majority will be under fire.

"Beyond a doubt, the possibility the coalition offers is one that is real. People, really blacks, in the Black Belt of Alabama cannot lift themselves up by their own bootstraps. They have to work with whites. I think there will inevitably be some kind of coalition because I just don't think blacks can do it by themselves. . . . We've suffered for so long. It's fifteen years between now and the twenty-first century, and we in Greene County have got to find some medium to work."

10. HARVEY GANTT
Against the Odds

THE PHOTOGRAPHS SHOW a sturdy young man, round-cheeked and wide-eyed. His hair is closely cropped, and the bit of fuzz that passes for a mustache is trimmed. His suit appears to be an understated gray, and with his white shirt and narrow tie, his plaid overcoat and matching hat, he looks a shade too proper, too correct for the setting—the campus of South Carolina's Clemson University. The youth's name is Harvey Gantt, and on that cold, bright day in January 1963, he had just become the first black student to integrate a white state school in one of the most elitist and aristocratic of southern states. At precisely 1:33 P.M., a black sedan deposited Gantt and his father in front of Clemson's aging, brick administration building. As cameras clicked like the sound of popping corn and a cluster of wary onlookers eyed the historic scene, Gantt disappeared into the building, emerging minutes later as a student, formally enrolled in the School of Architecture.

Only four months earlier, the similar admission of James Meredith to the University of Mississippi had sent rolls of thunder across southern skies. Two people were killed—one shot in the back, one in the head—and another fifty injured in the rioting that accompanied Meredith's arrival. Some twenty thousand federal and state troops quelled the uprising. Now, a brief span later, the cameras were recording Gantt's campus debut. What they captured was a horde of newsmen surrounding Gantt, who was smiling into a row of microphones. His look in a series of shots is amused, friendly, unconcerned. It is almost as if he were posing

for the campus yearbook or accepting some coveted award. From
the vantage point of the 1980s, the most striking thing about those
pictures of Gantt is this: there is not a hint of fear about him.

Two decades later in 1983, Harvey Gantt once again invaded
a white man's world. He did so with the same aplomb, the same
unassuming, indisputable confidence that marked his youthful
foray into Clemson's segregated halls. This time, the hurdle he
crossed was a political one. He became the first black mayor of
Charlotte, North Carolina, a conservative, corporate town in the
south-central section of the Tar Heel State. The distinction of
winning office was not the most remarkable part of Gantt's accomplishment, however. What made his victory of almost singular
interest was the makeup of those who elected him. About four out
of every five voters in Charlotte were white, and two out of every
five whites who voted cast their ballots for Gantt. Local blacks
supported Gantt overwhelmingly, but their ballots alone could not
have come close to putting him in office. Two years later in 1985,
running against another respected white businessman, Gantt captured even more white votes.

By the 1980s, black officials elected by black voters were no
longer a novelty. But blacks elected on the balloting of southern
whites remained as rare as a June bug on a November day, or as
a black student at Clemson University in the early 1960s. In many
settings, it would not have mattered that Gantt, as smooth and
buttoned-down as any banking executive or insurance salesman in
town, had graduated with honors at Clemson. Or that he had a
master's degree in urban planning from the Massachusetts Institute of Technology. Or that he had served the prerequisite terms
on council and was a successful architect in a city where planned
growth and urban design were the topics of the day. What would
have counted, pure and simple, was that Gantt is black and that
he lived in a town where almost 70 percent of the residents are
white. That Gantt—in Charlotte, as at Clemson—remained unbowed by fear and tradition, said much about the man. That
Charlotte accepted him with similar independence labeled the city
as one of a handful that might offer the nation a new perspective
on the unimportance of race.

Rufus Carson, mayor in the little hamlet of Franklin, Alabama, is one example. Councilman Lemon Coleman, Jr., a long-

time educator in Pineville, Louisiana, just outside Alexandria, also fits the bill. So do Noel Taylor, a black minister who is mayor of Roanoke, Virginia, and Bobby Scott, a Harvard-educated state senator from the shipbuilding city of Newport News. They—and not many more—are members of an elite group of southern black elected officials whose towns or districts are mostly white. The list grows a bit longer if black legislators and councilmen elected in multimember, majority-white districts are counted. But often, in such cases, tokenism is involved. One or two blacks may be included on a citywide slate in which they are substantially outnumbered by whites. "With at-large districts, we have black councilmen off and on, but that's exactly what it is, off and on," complained Adell Adams, who oversees political action for the South Carolina NAACP. "It's a very iffy situation. If there are seven seats, they'll give the blacks one. 'That's yours, but don't ask me for more.' " Those blacks, like Gantt, Carson, Coleman, Taylor, and Scott, who win in white districts without the buffer of white running mates are a rare breed, indeed. At a time when racial block voting remains the norm, these politicians somehow have managed to escape racial stigma.

Political scientists and the small cadre of blacks who have won in white districts suggest several ingredients for success. First, the black candidate must have better than average qualifications and almost always must be demonstrably superior to any white opponents. Mediocrity is not allowed. When Bobby Scott ran for the Virginia Senate in a 70 percent white district, he coupled the prestige of a top-notch education with experience gleaned from several terms in the Virginia House of Delegates. His white opponent, who was less sophisticated intellectually and knew little about the workings of state government, was no match for him in face-to-face encounters. Similarly, when Lemon Coleman ran for the council in a Pineville district that is 90 percent white, he could point to a master's degree from Southern University and an additional thirty hours of work toward a doctorate. No white opponent's educational pedigree came close. "I was just more qualified than those in the races with me," said Coleman, matter-of-factly. Links to both black and white organizations and voters are also essential. A black candidate whose entire civic experience is in the NAACP and the local black Baptist church is unlikely to attract substantial white support. Whites must have had an opportunity to see past their prejudices and to know the black candidate as an individual. "You need to demonstrate a broad-based civic background," said Virginia's Scott. "If the community knows the candidate, then race becomes less of a factor, if any."

Often, the initial step to higher office is election to a nonthreatening post in which the black official is outnumbered by whites. Once whites become familiar with his skills, stereotypical fears abate. For instance, Carson, a federal employee with undergraduate and master's degrees from Tuskegee Institute, first became recognized among whites in Franklin when he helped spearhead the town's drive for incorporation. After he was elected as the only black councilman in the 55-percent-white town, Carson occasionally presided at council meetings. He was simply more skilled at conducting a meeting than his white colleagues, and when a vacancy occurred in the mayor's office, other council members acknowledged that fact by appointing him mayor. By the time an election rolled around, white voters were already comfortable enough with his stewardship to look past color. Leonard Cole, in an extensive 1976 comparison of black and white officials in New Jersey, recorded the same phenomenon. "Incumbent blacks not only win reelection but often receive more votes than at their first election," he found. "As whites are exposed to black officials, the importance of a candidate's race as an electoral determinant appears to diminish."[1]

Still another trait frequently accompanying success is a mild manner. The black candidate does not need to be an Uncle Tom sort, but he does need to be much more adept at calming tempers than at inflaming passions. "He's a very gentle man, good-natured, not abrasive or too pointed," said a local editorial writer in describing Lawrence A. Davies, the black mayor of Fredericksburg, Virginia, an 80 percent white town just south of Washington. And a political reporter in Roanoke, where the population is 78 percent white, described Mayor Taylor similarly. "He doesn't make any enemies. He never says anything bad about anyone. He's not a militant," the reporter said. The refrain regularly repeated in describing such politicians is that they did not run as "black candidates," but as candidates who happened to be black. "You can't run as a black candidate, trying to attract only black votes," said Coleman. "You've got to attract both."

The white communities that elect black candidates often fit one of two categories. At times, the black population is so small as to be nonthreatening. "Where there's a very small black population, people feel no competition. Where there's a more even population, there's more concern on both sides," said Edward Bishop, a retired school principal and black alderman in Corinth, Mississippi, a town 82 percent white. Also open to minority officials are communities that have already come to grips with racial hostility and survived.

Many of those ingredients were at play in 1983 when Harvey Gantt was elected mayor of Charlotte and became the most prominent example of a southern black politician who has succeeded with local whites.

The town where Gantt decided to hang out his architectural shingle in 1971 was in many ways a traditional southern city, conservative in its voting patterns, controlled by a group of staid businessmen, opposed to violence, but uncomfortable with pushing the idea of integration too far, too fast. In other ways, Charlotte's personality was its own. Neither cosmopolitan nor provincial, the city was often seen as a nondescript sprawl of garden apartments, single-story homes, Holiday Inns, discount department stores, and fast-food franchises. There were pockets of elegance in the upper-crust, white neighborhoods of the southeast, and some ramshackle slums amid the mostly black enclaves to the northwest. But in many ways, the city resembled nothing so much as one giant, unbroken stretch of suburbia, a sort of medium-flavored concoction in which the army of regional representatives and traveling salesmen who emptied out the subdivisions each Monday morning, returning in time for happy hour each Friday afternoon, set the tone.

The city came honestly by its identity crisis. Indeed, there was no natural reason—no river, no mountain, no early transportation artery—for its existence. Since shortly after the turn of the century, Charlotte had been the largest city in North Carolina. But its personality, not unlike its geographic location, seemed off-center to much of the rest of the state. What Charlotte did serve as was a commercial center for a tobacco- and textile-producing region that stretched from western North Carolina to eastern South Carolina. That function began to emerge in the late nineteenth century as Mecklenburg County, where Charlotte is

located, became the state's largest producer of cotton. Charlotte
was tapped as the urban support center for the county and the
surrounding area. At one point, about one-third of the cotton mills
operating across the South were located within a hundred-mile
radius of Charlotte, and the city's calling as a financial, trade, and
service center grew.[2]

By the 1980s, Charlotte's population had soared to about
340,000, and the city had become the largest metropolitan center
between Washington, D.C., and Atlanta. There were sleek, new
office towers downtown and a smattering of high-tech companies
to complement the city's growing reputation as a white-collar
haven in a blue-collar state. More than 300 of the Fortune 500
companies had offices in the urban area. Five of the nation's 150
largest banks operated in Charlotte, compared with 3 in Atlanta.
And the city's $26 million in banking resources gave it greater
banking capital than any city between Philadelphia and Dallas.
In the decade from 1974 to 1984, more than 1,200 new firms
opened shop, bringing in 27,000 jobs and more than $1 billion in
investments.[3]

The racial climate that accompanied that growth was generally characterized by attempts to get along. In 1957, three years
after *Brown v. Board of Education,* Mecklenburg County began
voluntarily integrating public schools without a court order. Time
was to prove that integration far from complete, but many communities were ignoring the Supreme Court's mandate altogether.
Again, in the early 1960s, a group of prominent businessmen decided quietly and peacefully to integrate uptown restaurants. At
the suggestion of a restaurateur by the name of James "Slug"
Claiborne, they simply invited various local blacks out to lunch
at white restaurants, and over the course of chicken salad or roast
beef sandwiches and iced tea, settled the issue without protests or
sit-ins. A far more formidable challenge to racial harmony was
lurking on the horizon, however.

In 1964, a black Presbyterian minister named Darius Swann
filed a lawsuit, protesting that the integration of Charlotte-Mecklenburg schools was proceeding too slowly. Swann had spent
much of the 1950s as a missionary to India and had returned to
Charlotte determined to spread a bit of political salvation on the
home front. In 1970, his quest reached fruition. U.S. District Judge

James McMillan, who until then had enjoyed the anonymity of a typically upstanding local jurist, agreed with Swann's assessment of the school situation. In what was to become a national test case for one of the most divisive social issues of the 1970s, McMillan ordered that all available means, including busing, be used to eliminate single-race public schools. The next year, in a unanimous decision, the Supreme Court stunned local parents by upholding that opinion. The rulings were greeted by a tempest of protest. Angry, placard-waving crowds descended on the courthouse. McMillan was burned in effigy. Thousands of No Forced Busing bumper stickers cropped up across the city. The offices of Julius Chambers, the black attorney who represented Swann, were leveled by an arsonist one dark night. And before the fury subsided, every high school in the city had shut its doors at least once to protect against racial violence. In the fall of 1971, in one of the most unexpected and disappointing incidents, twenty-two people were injured and sixty-eight windows smashed at Myers Park High, a prestigious public school located in the city's wealthy southeast.[4] It seemed that an endless nightmare had befallen a once sane city.

Then, gradually, change came. Haltingly, grudgingly, parents began to accept—not welcome, not prefer, but accept—that busing and school integration had become facts of life in Charlotte. Their choices were to abandon the public schools, to continue a senseless guerrilla warfare, or to cope with an unwanted, but unalterable situation. They chose the latter course. In so doing, they forged a spirit that would redefine what Charlotte was about. The city had faced a crisis of conscience, and decency had prevailed, not because of the dictates of an elite establishment, but because ordinary men and women of incompatible persuasions had managed to find common ground.

The impetus for the resolution came in the fall of 1973 when the school board appointed leaders of various civic organizations to a Citizens Advisory Committee.[5] Few expected much to come out of the group. The appointments seemed a typical ploy, designed to provide a rubber stamp for school board decisions. However, various members of the new group had already recognized a disturbing fact. The busing plan then in effect was disproportionately aimed at the neighborhoods of blacks and working-class whites. The children of the affluent southeast, where a majority of the school board members happened to live, were not being forced to share the burden of boarding school buses and traveling across town. As the citizens' committee began to meet, a focus emerged that had less to do with abandoning busing than with developing a plan that was fair. It was a goal that could be shared by blacks and both liberal and blue-collar whites. Suddenly, individuals who had been at opposite extremes of the busing controversy were sitting side by side around kitchen tables and backyard barbecue pits, calculating distances and computing percentages. By the time they finished, more had been developed than an equitable plan. There was also a consensus that busing had come to Charlotte to stay. In 1975, Judge McMillan accepted a compromise busing plan that touched every area of the city. He also ordered the busing case closed.

By the mid-1980s, no one pretended that busing was a popular feature of public school education in Charlotte. But there was a deep pride in the way the community had dealt with an issue that elsewhere had decimated harmony. By 1985, 39 percent of the children in the Charlotte-Mecklenburg system were black, compared with 32 percent in the year busing was instigated. An estimated 17 percent of the system's 72,400 students were being bused for desegregation purposes. The percentage of whites had slipped some, but there was none of the wholesale abandonment of public education by whites that had occurred in other cities. The best evidence of the city's attitude toward busing was offered in the fall of 1984 when President Ronald Reagan misstepped by attacking the institution during a campaign appearance in Charlotte. Democrats, he said, "favor busing that takes innocent children out of the neighborhood school and makes them pawns in a social experiment that nobody wants." The crowd—overwhelmingly white, enthusiastically loyal to Reagan—greeted the remark with silence. The next day, The Charlotte Observer chastised Reagan. "You were wrong, Mr. President," an editorial writer admonished. "If you had set out deliberately to upset the people of this community, you couldn't have come up with a more disturbing statement." The city's proudest achievement, the newspaper said, was its integrated schools. That forward thrust in race relations, as much as anything else, paved the way for the city to overlook color in electing a black mayor in 1983.

If the climate fostered by Charlotte's busing episode figured mightily in Gantt's election, other factors aided him as well. It helped that the city is not dominated by a wealthy, ruling clique of pedigreed blue bloods. Founded by immigrants of sturdy, Scotch-Irish stock, developed with a steady influx of new corporate faces, the town has long seemed more impressed by accomplishment than breeding. Managers of big corporations, not members of lofty, old families, are paramount in the upper class. To be sure, local government in the mid-twentieth century was controlled by a predictably conservative, business-oriented group that was white, Anglo-Saxon, Protestant, and male. But, for the most part, those men were not so entrenched—either by ancestry or fortune—that they were immune to shifts within the electorate. And Charlotte's was an electorate that was regularly shifting.

Hundreds of companies produced a regular turnover of white-collar employees, men and women imported from other areas of the country for training or a few years' employment before being transferred out again. Frequently, they brought with them new ideas, moderate views on race and an openness to change that escaped less transient settings. "There's a great influx of diversity of people," explained Minette Trosch, an influential Republican councilwoman. That mix aided in 1977 when the same coalition that had resolved the busing controversy—blacks, liberals, and low-to-middle-income whites—combined to push through a new form of local government. By an eighty-vote margin, district representation replaced at-large elections. The business interests that had dominated city politics suddenly found themselves playing second fiddle to neighborhood groups. The eleven-member council elected when Gantt won his second term in 1985 reflected the shift. Its members included six white women and five men, of whom two were black; of the three white men, one was Jewish. There was not a single representative of the old, monied establishment that had once dominated public affairs. The white-Protestant-male political syndrome had become a relic.

Also paving Gantt's way was the presence of the *Charlotte Observer,* a newspaper whose progressive editorial page consistently urged calm and reason in responding to racial pressures. And the decision of Julius Chambers to locate in the city contributed to relatively forward-thinking racial attitudes. Chambers, who left Charlotte for New York in 1984 to become the third director in the NAACP Legal Defense Fund's history, arrived in the city twenty years earlier with degrees from Columbia University and the University of North Carolina Law School. He quickly set about challenging North Carolina's segregated institutions and shortly had lawsuits pending against about half of the state's school systems. A bespectacled man with magnetic energy, Chambers took three landmark cases to the Supreme Court within a short span and won each of them. One dealt with job qualifications. Another banned dual seniority systems for blacks and whites. And the third was *Swann v. Charlotte-Mecklenburg Board of Education,* the case that legitimized busing as a school desegregation tool.

Not the least of Chambers' accomplishments was to attract dozens of bright, young black professionals to Charlotte, including Gantt. Among them were college professors, doctors, dentists, social workers, lawyers, and others who would create a black leadership pool for the community. They found in Charlotte a white establishment open to dialogue. "It's not an oasis here," Gantt cautioned as he sat in a spacious office decorated with oriental carpets, upholstered arm chairs, and wood paneling. "If there's anything I want to say, it's that. I think if you had a vote on busing tomorrow, a majority of people would say, 'Let's go back to neighborhood schools.' But this city does have a unique blend of people who ultimately care." Charlotte, Gantt said, is a town where the chairman of the biggest bank will sit down with the head of a community group and work out details for building a library, including a donation of land. It is a city where a variety of groups—not just social workers and ministers—feel a vested interest in dealing with a problem such as teenage pregnancy. And, despite a basic conservatism, it is a locale where business managers are willing to look creatively at community concerns. "A corporation that comes to Charlotte and doesn't get involved in civic affairs isn't very highly thought of," Gantt said. "Eventually, they become an outsider."

One other item was essential to the election of a black mayor, and that was the makeup of Gantt himself. He seemed the quintessential politician for an upwardly mobile, professionally oriented town of the 1980s. With his early morning jobs, his gentrified inner-city neighborhood, his backyard tennis court, his glossy résumé, and facility for debating growth management and land-use issues, Gantt defied traditional racial stereotypes. His identity was that of a successful architect and city planner; race was secondary. And yet, the commitment that had taken him to Clemson University on a winter day in 1963 was part of his makeup too. Mel Watt, a state senator from Charlotte and Gantt's closest friend, noted that the experience had left its mark in subtle and not-so-subtle ways. Like most members of Chambers' old law firm, including Watt, Gantt instinctively will not sit with his back to the door or in front of an open window, Watt said. The trait is a holdover from the days when a bullet might be waiting around any corner. "Everybody in our law firm's like that. You should see us scrambling for a table in the back when we all go out to lunch together," he quipped. By the 1980s, Watt and Gantt could laugh at the habit. But, like the history it represented, the reflex was ingrained in their natures.

Gantt's earliest memories are set in the public housing project in Charleston, South Carolina, where his parents lived during the first few years of his life. His father was a mechanic at the Charleston Naval Shipyard, a man who personified a puritanical work ethic and eventually rose to the status of supervisor. Gantt's mother was a strong, matriarchal figure, who raised four daughters and a son with a firm hand. Gantt would later attribute much of his success to two circumstances of his childhood—the personal strength that came from a loving home life and the economic security born of his father's federal employment. His description of life in the Gantt household sounds idealized, but the story is typical of those told by many successful southern blacks who came of age in the 1940s and 1950s. "Growing up, we were poor, but not really poor. My father had no great amount of education, but he was quite a wise man. My mother did not read Dr. Spock, but she had a great sense of understanding on how to teach the important values of responsibility, accountability, love, and fairness," Gantt once said. "We had no TV and only one radio, so we learned how to talk to each other and to share joys and sorrows, victories and defeat. We had rituals and traditions to observe, lest we were severely punished—rituals such as eating meals together, doing homework at specified times, going to church on Sunday, being polite to elders, and respecting those in authority."[6] His parents,

Gantt said, became his personal heroes because of their steadfast faith in the vision of America proclaimed by Martin Luther King, Jr., and Roy Wilkins. "They were essentially poor people, but they believed so much in America. . . . They taught me what perseverance was all about."

Equally central to Gantt's developing interest in civil rights was the freedom that came from his father's shipyard job. At a time when economic intimidation was often the price of black political activism, Gantt enjoyed the luxury of knowing the family would not suffer economically for any political activity. When, as a teenager, he began to join in sit-ins and protest marches, his parents fully supported the involvement. And when the notion of applying to Clemson surfaced, the fact that his father encouraged the quest was central to his decision to go forward, Gantt said.

When the time came to apply for college, like other black youths of the day, Gantt automatically looked north or west. Few black schools were equipped to provide the architectural training he wanted, and southern white colleges were out of the question. He enrolled at Iowa State University. After a year, however, he had grown weary of the cold weather and more certain that he eventually wanted to go home to the South. He was aware of the mounting pressure to integrate state colleges across the region, and his sights turned to Clemson.

In January 1961, Gantt applied for admission. His initial request for an application form was answered promptly. Secretaries in the admissions office had no way of knowing that the material was being forwarded to a black student. But when Gantt's transcript was submitted, listing his grades at a black Charleston high school, his race was no longer a secret. The request for admission was denied. Gantt received a letter complimenting his performing at Iowa State and suggesting that he complete his education there. A year later, in January 1962, Gantt again sought admission to Clemson. By the summer, the request had not been formally acted upon, and in July, he filed suit in federal court.

Unbeknown to Gantt, key figures in the South Carolina power structure, including Governor Ernest F. Hollings, had already recognized that it was only a matter of time until federal judges ordered state colleges desegregated. Aghast at the turmoil that had swept Oxford, Mississippi, with Meredith's admission, they were determined to avoid a similar conflagration in South Carolina. During the fall of 1962, Clemson administrators quietly drafted statements shunning violence in the event of an admission order for Gantt. Prominent businessmen were secretly polled, and they too pledged to use their influence in support of law and order. Governor Hollings, who would later move to the U.S. Senate, urged the legislature to respond with dignity in an address on January 9. "As we meet, South Carolina is running out of courts," he warned. When the expected order came through a few days later, the strategy was in place for the peaceful desegregation of Clemson.[7]

While Gantt knew nothing of the particulars of the preparations, he had guessed that integration might proceed more peacefully in South Carolina. "Instinctively, there was something that said to me that South Carolina has always been a kind of classy racist state," said Gantt when asked as mayor about the courage his action had required. "My feeling was that, while we might not morally be able to appeal to South Carolinians about the fairness of my going to school, once admitted, their manners would take over. That's precisely what happened."

Over the years, Gantt has downplayed the difficulty of his action. The marshals who protected him were unobtrusive, he said, and within about six weeks, guards disappeared altogether. Unlike Meredith at Ole Miss, he did not call press conferences or try to become a cause célèbre. Serious about earning a degree in architecture, he quickly buckled down to studies and largely ignored the controversy swirling around him. Others, however, recall that the climate at Clemson was considerably more adversarial than Gantt generally allows. This was, after all, the era of men like longtime football coach Frank Howard, a countrified, tobacco-spitting native Alabamian who personified southern opposition to integration. Two decades after Gantt's arrival, Howard would remain so insensitive on racial matters that he would publicly equate the Heisman Trophy won by a black running back at the University of South Carolina with a watermelon on display at the state fair. When Atlantic Coast Conference basketball was integrated in the mid-1960s, Clemson—which trailed most conference schools in adopting the change—was one stop where black athletes could count on taunts from the crowd. There also are stories about students who dribbled basketballs in the hallway outside Gantt's dorm room and devised other distractions to hamper his studies. Their efforts could not penetrate Gantt's calm. "There was, of course, some danger," recalled Gantt. "I don't sit in front of open windows. I didn't while I was there for fear of some fool doing something irrational. But I never went around worrying about my life. It just didn't seem to be the thing to do when you're nineteen years old."

Diploma finally in hand, Gantt arrived in Charlotte, becoming the city's first black architect. Three years later, he moved his growing family to Boston. There, he earned a master's degree in urban planning at MIT before returning to North Carolina to become planning director for Soul City. Located in rural Warren County, the ill-fated project was a vision of civil rights organizer Floyd McKissick of CORE, who wanted to design a model biracial city. With the dream fizzling, Gantt moved back to Charlotte in 1971 and helped launch an architectural firm. His first political break came three years later. A black councilman had just won a North Carolina Senate seat, and the remaining white council members were charged with finding a replacement. At first, it seemed that a better-known local black leader would get the seat, but then, someone suggested Gantt. It is generally agreed that the local black establishment would have preferred another candidate, but Mayor John Belk, the towering, husky-voiced chairman of a chain of prosperous department stores, took a liking to Gantt. When the council split evenly on the appointment, Belk broke the tie in favor of Gantt.

In 1979, Gantt decided to bid for higher office. Eddie Knox, a fast-climbing local lawyer and former state senator known to have his eye on the governorship, was the heir apparent to Belk. Gantt's entry to the mayoral contest was generally dismissed as a stab at greater visibility for the young councilman. "Only two people in Charlotte expected us to win that race, me and Harvey," recalled Watt, who lived next door to Gantt in a downtown gaslight district, known as the Fourth Ward. Watt, a Yale graduate raised by a mother who was a domestic and factory worker, became Gantt's campaign manager. The two calculated turnout percentages and decided that, with a solid black vote, Gantt actually had a shot at defeating Knox. Few commentators predicted anything other than a cakewalk for the white mayoral candidate. A few days before the election, however, Knox supporters began to detect that general apathy over the election was working to Gantt's advantage. A defeat in the mayoral race would derail their candidate's substantial political ambitions. And so, many Gantt supporters believe, Knox—or at least some important backers—abandoned their traditional moderation on race and began to quietly warn against the repercussions of electing a black mayor. Knox, who turned Republican after losing the Democratic primary for governor in 1984, denies that he was part of any plan to defame Gantt because of race. But, from whatever source, flyers did surface in the closing days of the campaign that questioned Gantt's ability to be mayor of "all the people." "When people saw that the race was neck and neck, it sort of brought back the Old South kind of thing," said Gantt.

While Knox denies the charge, Watt believes that racial overtones were also injected into a series of last-minute telephone calls that helped turn the tide against Gantt. "It got to the point where Knox was really running scared," said Watt. "His political life was on the line. He began behind-the-scenes to inject race into it. He got on the phone, he and his workers, and said, 'Hey, a black man is about to take over this city if you don't get out and vote.'"

Regardless of the truth of the specific charges aimed at Knox, there is little doubt that even in a relatively progressive city like Charlotte, Gantt's campaign prompted sidewalk whispers about the city's becoming "another Atlanta." For years, complained Gantt, Charlotte was a city that dreamed of copying Atlanta in growth and image. "Suddenly it was bad to be like Atlanta," he said. "What that meant was that Atlanta had elected black mayors, and there were some feelings that we would become a city of a black majority, or that the mayor would only be interested in black issues. We had to contend with that."

Gantt lost the 1979 race, but the margin was only twelve hundred votes out of nearly fifty-one thousand cast. He recalls the moment when he had to face supporters and admit defeat as the most difficult of his public career, more taxing even that his first day at Clemson University. But most observers saw in the unexpectedly slim defeat only the seeds of the victory that would be Gantt's four years later.

By 1983, when Gantt staged his comeback, most political strategists had accepted that race would not work as a campaign issue in Charlotte. Republican mayoral candidate Ed Peacock seemed to go out of his way to avoid racial innuendo. The year's bitter and racially tinged contest for mayor of Chicago, pitting Harold Washington against Bernard Epton, had served as a powerful example of the liabilities of turning elections into a black-white confrontation, and Charlotte profited from the lesson. "If anybody compared Harvey Gantt to Harold Washington, Harvey ought to sue them for slander, and I will sue 'em if they compare me to Bernard Epton," Peacock told a local newspaper reporter.[8] Only once, according to Gantt, did Peacock lapse from his promise to keep race out of the campaign. As election day approached and polls showed Gantt in command of the electorate, Peacock gave a speech that arguably tried to link Gantt to controversy surrounding the Reverend Jesse Jackson and some voter-registration irregularities. "He was so soundly repudiated by me and by the press and everybody else," that the incident was not repeated, Gantt said. When the vote was tallied, Gantt won 41 percent of the white vote, almost unanimous black support, and a two-year term as mayor.

By 1985, when Gantt faced a Republican realtor and former councilman named Dave Berryhill, race had diminished even further as a campaign issue. Some Gantt supporters saw the suggestion of a racial theme in Berryhill's slogan, A Return to Leadership. The implication, they said, was that a black man could not lead. But Berryhill heatedly retorted that they were grabbing at straws, and his claim was supported by the absence of other racial comments. Gantt won 61 percent of the vote citywide that year.

With the start of his second term as mayor a few weeks away, Gantt—a striking, broad-featured man with deep-set eyes and graying hair—sat one day on a speakers' platform at the front of a meeting room in an uptown Charlotte motel. As several hundred Rotarians, about 99 percent of them white, forked their way through a baked-chicken luncheon, Gantt flashed his gleaming smile at various acquaintances and joined the laughter as the master of ceremonies pitted the North Carolina State grads against the Duke crowd and the UNC group in the sports-conscious audience. Aware of complaints that he is too distant, not folksy enough, the mayor grinned conspicuously as the ribbing turned to Clemson. Gantt, of course, is a Clemson man, a dyed-in-the-wool backer of the orange and white, and so there were a few Tiger paw quips just to keep the record even. It was a memorable scene. The onetime iconoclast now rooted for the team. The onetime opposition welcomed his support. The evolution seemed complete. As Gantt rose to speak, gliding his way through complex issues with extemporaneous ease, the same nonracial tenor permeated his message. Here, he talked about changing Charlotte's downtown core from "simply a place of employment to an active mixed-use area." There was a reference to a "strategy of balanced growth," and here again, an admonition that "a good thoroughfare plan makes no sense without a good land-use plan."

When Gantt first appeared on Charlotte's political scene in the early 1970s, he was already using such terms. His lexicon was that of an urban planner, not a civil rights activist. In his first race for mayor, one council member recalled, voters were not yet used to hearing talk about controlled growth, an issue that would become a staple of local politics as Charlotte stretched. "People were asking, 'What's he talking about?' " the councilwoman said. By the mid-1980s, they had adopted the same vocabulary. "Now, southeast Charlotte residents are saying, 'Who's going to have a disincentive to stop the growth?' " That Gantt was ahead of his time in identifying the central theme of local government and that the issues he most often addressed were perceived as nonracial, citywide concerns had much to do with his success.

As mayor, Gantt did not ignore minority interests. He pushed, for instance, for increased black involvement in awarding city contracts. But in most minds, he seemed more identified with growth issues. The 1985 campaign reflected that fact. Three of the four points stressed in Gantt's campaign literature, "economic development, balanced growth, and paying for growth fairly," had to do with expansion. Throughout the race, the debate focused on Gantt's ideas about growth. Supporters proclaimed him a visionary; detractors portrayed him as an impractical dreamer. Talk centered on his risky, election-year proposal for higher taxes to meet road needs and on whether his attempts to stem the growth southeast of the city had worked or simply left residents with inadequate services. There was discussion of inner-versus-outer beltways and of saddling developers with impact fees for water, sewers, parks, and schools. Gantt was given to comments such as, "I don't see a road just as something to carry traffic, but I look at what a road will do," or, "We are not going to solve all of our problems in transportation without a program of public transportation and without an absolutely tough-minded land-use policy." The issues of which he spoke, observers said time and again, were not primarily black concerns.

Gantt, not unlike a growing number of other successful black politicians, saw the matter in a slightly different light. The key as mayor, he believed, was to address citywide interests without losing sight of the needs of poorer residents, many of whom are black. Often, Gantt found, the two strains ran parallel, but it was important to couch arguments in terms that appealed to more than a disadvantaged minority. Although he did not routinely say so, many of the causes he chose to champion—downtown redevelopment, public transportation, managed growth, a local income tax instead of a sales tax—had racial implications. If downtown became a vibrant spot with an entertainment and shopping capacity, not just an employment center that emptied out at 5:00 P.M., who would benefit more than the black families that lived nearby? An expanded system of public transportation might be sold to middle-class whites as an alternative to the auto-congested highways that threatened to strangle southeast Charlotte, or more altruistically, as an alternative for the handicapped and the elderly. But the inner-city blacks who might find work if they could manage transportation to the suburbs were perhaps the greatest beneficiaries of all. When Gantt talked, as he regularly did, about "disincentives" designed to retard or shift the rapid expansion of southeast Charlotte, he appealed to the concerns of upper-middle-class whites who limped to work on traffic-clogged arteries. But if, in limiting water and sewer expansion in the southeast, growth went elsewhere, black areas of town might benefit. Resources such as shopping centers or new subdivisions theoretically could locate in the heavily black northwest or in east Charlotte, where the number of black residences was expanding. When Gantt suggested meeting local revenue needs, first with a local gas tax and then with an income tax, he was selecting taxing methods that considered the financial conditions of various taxpayers. Some other alternatives, such as a sales tax, might have taken a higher percentage of income from the poor. "One of the things I decided when I came into this office was that I would address areas of inequity where they occurred. But at the same time, I would broaden the issues," said Gantt. "And so, my issues often didn't deal with any specific race. They were in terms of quality of life." An intellectual might look at various positions and see the importance for black residents. But most people would see the value only in nonracial terms.

Just as Gantt had attempted to avoid doctrinaire solutions in Charlotte, so he believed that black leaders nationwide must expand and alter their vision in the years ahead. If Gantt was an example, the willingness to bypass dated formulas and rhetoric would determine the extent to which black politicians could appeal across racial lines. They must be prepared to talk about urban growth, revenue shortages, and resource allocation—the issues of the 1980s—in ways that made sense for white interests, as well as black. They needed also to look at continuing racial problems with an honesty that admitted complexities and recognized the successes, as well as the failures, of past decades. As an example of the need for new thinking, Gantt believed black politicians should lead in developing a revised social welfare policy that was grounded neither in New Deal benevolence nor benign neglect. In that vein, Gantt copied traditional black politicians by continuing to speak out about the black underclass. But the targets of his criticism were both conservatives and liberals. In a 1982 speech dealing with racial issues, for instance, he spoke of "paternalistic, often ill-conceived social programs of the sixties and seventies" and warned that "too often the public has felt that our problems could be solved by government." But he also chided whites who concluded that "the price of busing their children, or missing a promotion because of affirmative action, or accepting scattered-site housing in the neighborhood was too great." Again, the successful tack for Gantt, a black politician in a white world, was an evenhanded one that finally focused more on solution than blame.

Across the South, most black activists expected that it would be several generations before blacks—even those who excelled, as did Gantt—could routinely expect to receive significant white support when they ran for office. A 1975 study in the *American*

Journal of Political Science, focusing on a broad group of black mayors, found that only 7 percent had majority-white constituencies.[9] A few years later, Albert Karnig and Susan Welch, in their study, *Black Representation and Urban Policy,* agreed that with notable exceptions, such as Los Angeles Mayor Tom Bradley, "blacks win mayoral elections only when blacks constitute a near majority of the population."[10] In contrast, Tom Cavanagh, long-time research associate at the Joint Center for Political Studies, suggested in an interview that the late 1980s and 1990s would see growing numbers of blacks elected in heavily white districts. Progress, he said, is evolutionary, and as blacks gain credibility through experience at the lower levels of government, white resistance will evaporate. "The reason is generational replacement," said Cavanagh.

In settings like Jackson, Mississippi, and Montgomery, Alabama, men and women who had worked for years in the trenches of black politics were less sure. Jerome Gray, director of field operations for the predominantly black Alabama Democratic Conference, for instance, thought long before coming up with any black Alabamians elected in majority-white, single-member districts. There were in 1985 about sixty-two black municipal council members from Alabama cities that were mostly white. But those were elected at-large from slates dominated by whites. Meanwhile, all of Alabama's black legislators, county commissioners, and probate judges were elected from majority-black districts, Gray said. In some few places where the populace is more educated than average, where income levels are higher, and racial polarization is muted, whites may be more willing to give minority candidates a chance. But in most settings, "it's not getting any easier," he said. A state away in Jackson, Credell Calhoun, a state legislator and former Democratic Party organizer, agreed. "In Mississippi, whites vote for whites," he said. "It seems to be changing a little, but if you get 20 percent out of any white precinct, you're doing real good."

In a first-floor suite in Charlotte's largest black-owned office building, a racially mixed group of campaign workers stuffed envelopes and answered telephones. Don Baker, the black half of Gantt's campaign management team, watched the scene through an open doorway. Racism exists in Charlotte, he said, but it is not evident among policymakers or in broad public sentiment. In addition, Gantt's personality and credentials are such that he transcends whatever racial barriers exist, Baker said. Across town, Don Carroll, a tall, balding white lawyer who completed the management duo, agreed. What produced Gantt's success, he said, was the rare blend of a candidate with exceptional abilities and a community in which circumstances had combined to dismantle racial fears. Neither man is certain that it is a formula that can be marketed elsewhere. "I get to feeling so positive here in Charlotte," said Baker, who grew up in rural Arkansas. "But then you go back home, back to the rural South, even just outside Charlotte, and black people are still looking in the window saying, 'When am I going to get a share?' "

11. DOUG WILDER
The Future

As a college student in Richmond in the late 1940s, Doug Wilder would sometimes walk uptown to a posh gathering at the favorite political watering hole of blue-blooded Virginians, the John Marshall Hotel. He'd bypass the polished brass doors where uniformed guards tipped their hats to senators and congressmen and the festive lobby where knots of cigar-puffing moguls traded a ribald joke or the latest in stock tips. Instead, Wilder would enter the bustling hotel through a passage specially designated for him and his friends—the kitchen. Once there, he would don white coat, black trousers, bow tie, and the faceless, anonymous mask of a black waiter in a white man's world. In the stately ballrooms, he would move from table to table, filling crystal water glasses, deftly balancing trays of soiled dishes, catching talk of Virginia's road problems or the coming election or, most often, the state's great and revered heritage, a legacy that to his fertile, young mind did not yet seem particularly great or revered.

Two decades later, Wilder was again at a political gathering at the John Marshall Hotel when, to his astonishment, a roomful of businessmen and lawmakers burst into a lusty round of Stephen Foster's "Carry Me Back To Ol' Virginny." By that time, Wilder was no longer waiting tables. He had just become the first black man elected to the Virginia Senate in the twentieth century, a milestone he had somehow reached without hearing the official state song sung publicly. As the guests at the Virginia Food Dealers Association's legislative luncheon progressed through the references to "ol' massah" and "this ol' darkey's heart," Wilder began to boil with a private rage. He stormed out of the room, and the next day on the Senate floor unleashed a diatribe that did not produce the song's repeal but did drastically curtail its performance.

Through the years, other events—state central committee meetings, Democratic conventions, political strategy huddles—brought Wilder to the John Marshall. And so, it was only fitting that on a November night in 1985, the aging, but proud hotel should be the scene of its onetime employee's brightest hour. In the same fancy ballroom where Wilder had once waited tables, a raucous, upbeat crowd sipped bourbon and awaited election night returns. From early evening, it had been clear that the Democratic candidates for governor and attorney general were winners. The only question was the outcome of the race for lieutenant governor, and the lingering doubts had as much to do with history as with the tallies being posted on huge screens around the room. Not since Reconstruction had a black person been elected to statewide executive office anywhere in the South. Never had anyone black been elected to state office in Virginia. Yet, in 1985, the Democratic nominee for lieutenant governor was none other than Doug Wilder.

At last, party officials began to file onto a crowded stage. There were shouts of jubilation as the newly elected governor and attorney general followed. And then, near pandemonium erupted as a slight, caramel-skinned man, arms held high in a victory sign, strode into the room with a peacock's flash and a smile that said as surely as any television commentator could who had won the race for Virginia's second highest office. In that victors' circle, there was no question about who was the politician of the hour. "He has spent the last year having all of the so-called experts say he would be a drag on the ticket," said Attorney-General elect Mary Sue Terry in tribute. "Tonight, the people of Virginia voted for the future," added Governor-elect Gerald Baliles. The crowd spoke, too, delaying Wilder's departure to well past midnight. Baliles and Terry had long since left for their private celebrations, but still the throng of men and women, white and black, young and old, pressed forward for a touch of Wilder's hand.

"Hey, Doug. Hey, Doug," they shouted, as sweat streamed down Wilder's glowing face.

"I brought you Hampton. I want you to know," called out a white legislator.

"God bless you; we prayed for you," an elderly black woman said softly, clutching Wilder's palm.

A child was lifted above the crowd for a kiss. A woman hugged Wilder and then, speechless, erupted in laughter. Signs, brochures, newspapers, even an "I'm just wild about Wilder" T-shirt, were thrust upward for autographs. An ex-Marine clutched a just-snapped Polaroid photo of the scene, destined, he said, for the family album. A college friend spoke of Wilder's unshakable optimism. Reporters tugged at the sleeve of Wilder's gray, pin-striped suit and pressed him for interpretations of the night's events. A prominent white businessman, long active in Democratic circles, stood watching the scene in awe. Recalling Wilder's odyssey from a waiter's segregated world to the realm of a legislative outsider to this moment of acclaim, he shook his head. "It is," he said, "part of the magic and miracle of America."

Wilder's election on that November night was a fitting climax to two decades of black voter involvement that began regionally in 1965 when the Voting Rights Act took effect. His win—the sort of unexpected, seminal event that forever changes political thought—forecast new horizons for southern blacks in the late 1980s and 1990s. Almost a century of experience had said that a black man simply could not be elected to major statewide office in a former Confederate state. Across the region, election after election had proven that that was so. Charles Evers in Mississippi, Maynard Jackson in Georgia, Howard Lee in North Carolina, Jim Clyburn in South Carolina, and other brave, if foolhardy, souls had demonstrated the principle. Doug Wilder, a suave, yet street-wise Richmond lawyer, a fifteen-year Senate veteran, the grandson of a slave, was slated by almost everyone but himself to provide additional proof of the ironclad rule. That he defied it instead said simply that southern politics would never again be quite the same. Wilder had won 51.8 percent of the vote against a clean-cut, conservative white Republican. He had done so without a particularly heavy black turnout and by winning support from a startling 44 percent of white voters.[1] Campaign handbooks had just been rewritten.

The election did not say that southern racism is dead. Far too much proof of racial division, some of it in Wilder's own contest, remained. But the Virginia results did say, unequivocally, that skin tone was no longer the only, or even the predominant, criterion on which many white southerners based their votes. The results offered a measure of vindication to those southerners who had long insisted that the once-scorned region would eventually set the national pace in race relations. It strengthened the resolve of other black politicians eyeing statewide races, and it forced white party officials to reassess those candidates' chances. It also provided a telling rebuttal to a chorus of Democrats, calling in the wake of the 1984 presidential elections for a diminished—or, at least, less visible—role for blacks in the southern Democratic Party. At a turbulent moment in southern black politics, it injected a powerful, new ingredient into a debate over future directions. Clashing voices were calling for blacks to become more active in Republican circles, to abandon two-party politics, to demand more control over Democratic Party policies, or to quietly accept an influential, but behind-the-scenes role in Democratic affairs. Wilder's election suggested that blacks need not give up hope on the Democratic Party and that whites—both Democrat and Republican—might have less to fear than they had imagined by embracing black candidates.

No one was predicting that a new generation of Wilder clones was on the brink of seizing statewide offices across the South. What his election had proved, Wilder said, was that "ordinary people of ordinary stripe and ordinary beginnings can be elected everywhere if it can take place in Virginia. . . . There is light at the end of the tunnel." His victory did not mean that the end of the tunnel had been reached. History could not be so suddenly and totally discounted. With rare exception, the twentieth-century history of black candidacies for executive or federal office in the states first covered by the Voting Rights Act was a tale of defeat.

Nor could many of the particulars of the Wilder race be automatically duplicated elsewhere. Virginia's population, for instance, was only 18 percent black in 1985, lower than in Alabama, Georgia, Louisiana, Mississippi, North Carolina, or South Carolina. While the smaller figure might seem a disadvantage, studies have shown that white voters often are less threatened and more likely to support black candidates when the electorate is not heavily black.[2] Second, the entire 1985 Republican ticket in Virginia was remarkably lackluster. When Wilder and his opponent, state senator John Chichester, were matched side by side on experience, performance, and acuity, the only thing to be said for Chichester was that he was the more conservative of the pair. Third, the unusual popularity of departing governor Chuck Robb lent a mantle of respectability and good feeling to all the Democratic candidates, including Wilder. Fourth, Wilder benefited from a series of Republican mistakes, including overconfidence and an unwillingness by Chichester to attack him on personal, but legitimate political grounds. Chichester apparently feared that such an assault would brand him a racist, and to that extent Wilder was aided in the campaign by being black. And fifth, Wilder's nomination was by a convention, not a primary. It is easier for a minority candidate to dominate in a controlled, convention setting. "The Virginia mix and circumstances were peculiar," concluded Don Fowler, national Democratic committeeman and a former state party chairman in South Carolina. "Just because it happened in Virginia in 1985 doesn't mean it can happen in Alabama in 1986 or Georgia in 1987."

Before Wilder, the last time someone black held statewide executive office in the South was in the late 1800s. In 1870, Alonzo J. Ransier of South Carolina became the region's first black lieutenant governor. A year later, Pickney B. S. Pinchback, a Louisiana mulatto who had been elected president pro tempore of the state Senate, proceeded to become lieutenant governor in that state when the incumbent died. Pinchback was named acting governor for a month in December 1872 during impeachment proceedings against the white carpetbagger governor. In 1874 in Mississippi, Blanche K. Bruce became the first black man elected to a full term in the U.S. Senate. Earlier, Hiram Rhoades Revels, another black Mississippian, had served a partial term. And from 1870 to 1901, twenty black southerners—eight from South Carolina, four from North Carolina, three from Alabama, and one each from Louisiana, Georgia, Florida, Mississippi, and Virginia—served in the House of Representatives.[3]

Such involvement halted abruptly with the advent of the twentieth century, and by the 1970s the experience of Charles Evers was typical. Evers is a large, emotional man who took over as Mississippi field secretary for the NAACP after his brother, Medgar, was murdered in 1963. Self-described in his 1971 autobiography as "a reformed hustler . . . more vocal, sassy" than his brother, Charles Evers was determined through-out the 1970s that blacks gain a voice in statewide Mississippi politics. "You've got to keep trying 'til white people start voting for blacks, as well as blacks for whites," said Evers in a 1985 interview. Over more than a decade, Evers waged a series of campaigns for congressman, senator, and governor. In 1969, he was elected mayor of tiny Fayette, but attempts at higher office were routinely rewarded with defeat. During a special congres-sional election in 1968, Evers initially ran first against a field of six whites, but he lost two to one in the runoff. In 1971, despite the formation of a national support committee, including the likes of former vice-president Hubert H. Humphrey and Massa-chussetts senator Edward M. Kennedy, he was swamped by bet-ter than three to one in an independent gubernatorial bid. And in 1978, an Evers race as an independent for the U.S. Senate split Democratic votes and resulted in the election of Mississippi's first Republican senator of the century, Thad Cochran.

Elsewhere, across the South, the faces differed, but the stories were the same. In Georgia in 1968, Maynard Jackson's bid for the U.S. Senate produced a trouncing by Senator Herman Talmadge. In 1976, Howard Lee, the black mayor of the predominantly white university town of Chapel Hill, North Carolina, tried to parlay his success in that cloistered setting into a statewide bid for lieutenant governor. He ran first in a field of eight in the initial primary. In the runoff, however, he could not withstand such subtle racial tactics as his opponent's ads, "Vote for Jimmy Green. He's One of Us," or an eleventh-hour whisper campaign alleging that blacks would hire an assassin to kill the governor if Lee became the state's second-in-command.

In 1978 in South Carolina, Jim Clyburn also came close to winning, but not close enough. Clyburn, who was later appointed state human affairs commissioner, placed first in a three-man primary for secretary of state but lost the runoff by twenty-eight thousand votes. Like other early black candidates, Clyburn be-lieves race was central to his defeat. "It was used in a very sophis-ticated way," he said, recalling an incident involving a joint television appearance. His opponent, Clyburn said, gave a speech along these lines. "He said, 'My opponent has vowed not to make race an issue, and I must congratulate him. But the newspapers have made a big point of the fact that he will be the first black elected statewide since Reconstruction.' He was making the race thing very pronounced but not taking the blame himself," Clyburn said.

Against that backdrop, Wilder's announcement that he was running for lieutenant governor of Virginia was greeted by white Democrats with emotions ranging from skepticism to dismay. Those who later dissected the race for clues about how to elect black southerners would have found little to reassure them in the early days of the campaign. Throughout the fall of 1984 and winter of 1985, opposition to Wilder's candidacy festered within Democratic circles. A prominent University of Virginia political scientist, acknowledging what others were saying privately, gave Wilder ninety-nine-to-one odds of winning the general election, and—based on 1984 presidential election trends in the South—suggested that he might even pull down Democratic running mates for governor and attorney general. Robb's press secretary, asked about Wilder's prospects, lamented in the *Washington Post:* "This is still Virginia." Wilder was slipped private assurances that the state party chairmanship would be his if he would only step aside. And in a final blow, eleven prominent legislators, including the state Democratic Party chairman and the Speaker of the House, were caught in a secret meeting aimed at discussing their fears of the "Wilder problem."

Even Wilder, who maintained a perpetual optimism throughout the race, seemed taken aback. "I didn't know how difficult it would be until I announced," said Wilder on a wintry day ten months before his election. As he gazed through a frosted legislative office window, overlooking the Capitol Square statues of George Washington and former senator Harry Byrd, Sr., Wilder mused: "I never would have expected a secret meeting. I never would have expected the comment from the governor's press secretary. I thought the governor would have been more embracive. . . . Fortunately, the acceptability with the people is far more open."

Certainly, Wilder was no stranger to racial innuendo or to long odds. In 1969, he had become the first black elected to the Virginia

Senate in modern times. Not long afterward, Virginia's monied establishment made clear its indignation over his defeat of a prominent white conservative. Wilder was the only senator who did not receive an engraved invitation to a traditional assembly opening party hosted by a wealthy Charlottesville executive. As late as 1983, the social stigma had not been fully erased. That year, Wilder had been giving Democratic Party officials fits by threatening an independent race for the U.S. Senate seat being vacated by Harry Byrd, Jr. Al Smith, the chairman of the House Democratic Caucus and a conservative fundraiser for Governor Robb, and two other prominent Democrats had been asked to take Wilder to lunch to try to sort out some of the problems. When Wilder suggested that they dine at the Commonwealth Club, a downtown Richmond bastion of white male conservatism, Smith—a member —refused. One of those attending the luncheon described this scenario. As the four drove away from the capitol grounds, Smith, a folksy fast-food magnate, who was picking his teeth with a paper clip, asked Wilder, "Paps, where're we gonna eat?"

Wilder suggested the Commonwealth Club, which was nearby.

"I called. They're all filled up," replied Smith.

"I know all the waiters," quipped Wilder.

There was an uncomfortable pause, and then Smith, apparently unaware that black guests if not black members were allowed at the club, said: "Life's too short for me to be embarrassed by taking you to the Commonwealth Club."

A few minutes later, Wilder, who was driving, stopped his car in the middle of the street, and turned to Smith. "You don't need a reservation for the grill," he said. When Smith did not reply, Wilder added, "In other words, you're not going to take me to the club."

Jerking the gear shift down, Wilder headed the car toward his own integrated club. "Then I'll take you to mine," he said.

The world in which Doug Wilder came of age, not unlike that of many first-generation black politicians, was at once segregated and tightly knit, rife with poverty, yet defined by a moral code that encouraged strong family values, discipline, and hard work. Exclusion from the larger society was a handicap, but it was offset at least partially by the confidence and security born of excelling within one's own arena. By the time Doug Wilder as a young adult ran headlong into racial barriers, his family and his community had already instilled in him a sense of personal worth. It was a belief that would not be shaken by denied invitations or other slights. During his campaign for lieutenant governor, more than one commentator noted the ease and assurance with which Wilder seemed to move in white circles. He had become, some said, the ultimate insider. More nearly, he had become the ultimate politician, able to use his race when it worked to advantage, comfortable in operating without racial identity when the need arose.

Wilder grew up in depression-era Richmond, the second and youngest son in a family of ten children. His father was a proud and formal man, who sold insurance and made ends meet by raising chickens and cows. Wilder's paternal grandfather, James, had built a home in Richmond's Church Hill section after being freed from slavery, and he was respected and sought after in the black community. His grandchildren were regularly admonished to remember that they were Wilders and had an honorable family name to uphold. Their father, who rarely appeared before his children without wearing a coat and tie, took note even if a child was reported to have passed a neighbor without saying hello. If one child misbehaved, the entire lot was at times disciplined, occasionally with a belt. The theory, said Wilder's youngest sister, Jean Miller, was that "if one did it, others were probably thinking about doing it."

While money was often a family problem, hunger and true deprivation never were. Indeed, there is a Norman Rockwell quality to the memories of Wilder entertaining at the local barber shop with an account of his first professional baseball game, encountering his father's wrath by staying too late at the local pool hall, or salvaging a school program by filling an unexpected gap with an extemporaneous speech.

As Wilder reached young adulthood, his personal thoughts on race became increasingly militant. Growing up, he had been aware of, but not consumed by his family's racial history and by the unbreachable lines between black and white Richmond. Family folklore included the story of how his slave grandfather would walk to nearby Hanover County to visit his wife and children, who had been sold to a white owner there. If he was accidentally late returning home, the sympathetic overseer would beat on a saddle, and James Wilder would yell as if he were being struck. Like others of his generation, Wilder had encountered the discomforts of growing up in a world with segregated public facilities. It was not until his graduation from all-black Virginia Union College, with a degree in chemistry, that he fully realized how crippling that system might be. Applying for a job with the Virginia Employment Commission, Wilder was told that the only state work open to him would be as a cook. Not long afterward he joined the army, discovering there some black comrades who—like he— were toying with the idea that armed revolution might be the only way to cure America's social ills. He was fascinated by the terrorist Mau Mau uprising against British colonial rule in Kenya. Adopting the symbol of the Kikuyu tribesmen, he and an Army buddy exchanged letters signed, "The Burning Spear." In later years, Wilder dismissed those sentiments as the misguided notions of youth.

Decorated for bravery after he and two other Americans captured nineteen Chinese soldiers in Korea, Wilder returned to Richmond. He eventually made his way to Howard University Law School, a private law practice, and the state Senate. Early Senate photos show Wilder with a stiff-jawed, unsmiling face, dwarfed by a massive halo of dark hair. By 1985, the Afro had been clipped, and his hair was sprinkled with enough gray to look white in newspaper photographs. Lawmakers who once stole into the Senate clerk's office to shake their heads in dismay over Wilder's rising seniority had either retired or long since resigned themselves to his increasingly powerful role. Tiny laugh lines crinkled the skin at the edges of his toothy grin, and he moved with an easy confidence, his 5-foot-9-inch frame adorned in well-cut suits and expensive jewelry. Financially and politically, he was at the peak of his game. As his white Mercedes and stately home in an integrated Richmond neighborhood testified, Wilder had come far from the childhood days when chickens scratched in the backyard. A successful law practice and an impressive real estate portfolio qualified him as a self-made millionaire. In the Senate, he had become a Democratic fixture, skillfully alternating between theatrical outrage on some matters, particularly racially tinged ones, and quiet accommodation on others. His oratory was flowery and stylized, always commanding an appreciative audience, but he could also inject a jiving, good humor—as well as a snappish retort —into private dealings. Wilder had become part of the club, but never so much a part as to sidestep his origins. His underlying commitment was reflected in three items—busts of Abraham Lincoln and Martin Luther King and a portrait of Frederick Douglass, the fiery nineteenth-century abolitionist—which decorated his private law office.

It was a gutsy power play in 1982 that finally cemented Wilder's hold as a statewide power broker and set the stage for his later nomination as lieutenant governor. That year, Democrats stood ready to nominate a moderate suburban legislator from Virginia Beach for the U.S. Senate seat being vacated by Harry Byrd, Jr. Blacks, meanwhile, had been angered and embarrassed by the indifference of the white Democratic power structure in the 1982 legislative session. Even though blacks had provided a critical margin of votes in the Democrats' 1981 sweep of statewide offices, their legislative agenda had been largely ignored. When the prospective Senate nominee, Owen B. Pickett, appealed to conservative former Byrdites in his opening campaign speech, blacks led by Wilder decided to show their clout. Wilder threatened to run as an independent, throwing Democrats into disarray. The case that Pickett was a conservative on racial matters was unconvincing, but he had made a mistake at a critical time. Wilder and other blacks did not hesitate to exploit it. Meanwhile, a series of episodes seemed to play into their hands. The speaker of the House of Delegates, an old-school, white Democrat, referred in an interview to black legislators as "those boys." No matter that A.L. Philpott at times called whites "boys" as well. The idea that an influential Democrat would be so insensitive to the historical use of the word, as a slur against blacks, prompted calls for a public apology. Smith's refusal to take Wilder to the Commonwealth Club also made headlines. Governor Robb, dismayed at the escalating rhetoric and the potency of Wilder's threat, finally advised Pickett to drop the Senate bid. Even though he had won enough delegates to ensure nomination, the lawmaker did. Seldom, if ever, had a southern black politician so successfully manipulated political power. Doug Wilder had challenged the governor and the Democratic Party hierarchy to a showdown, and he had won.

By 1985, the lesson had not been forgotten. White Democrats grumbled about Wilder's bid for lieutenant governor, but none was willing to tackle him head-on. The party in 1982 had already come to grips with the futility of waging a statewide campaign without black support. If Wilder and other blacks went away from the 1985 nominating convention miffed, the party's prospects in the fall elections were worth less than a handful of used paper ballots. A sense of inevitability began to attach itself to the Wilder campaign. At the convention, to the delight of watching Republicans, Wilder's selection was assured. To oppose him, the GOP picked John Chichester, a Fredericksburg insurance salesman whose seven-year Senate record was highlighted by predictability and an engaging smile. His chief break with obscurity came in 1980 when he scuttled Senate approval of the Equal Rights Amendment with a procedural ploy.

After his nomination, Wilder's campaign was a shoestring classic, fueled by the candidate's personal blend of sophistication and backroom savvy. Wilder locked his Mercedes in the garage and set off on a statewide tour in a borrowed station wagon. The four-thousand-mile trek might have been dismissed as grandstanding had Wilder been white, but the curiosity about this precedent-setting campaign and Wilder's willingness to show up in hundreds of majority-white settings commanded headlines. Along the way, Wilder and a small group of Senate advisers pushed the right pressure points whenever Democratic support seemed lukewarm. For instance, House Speaker A.L. Philpott (who had stopped calling blacks "boys" in public, but—friends said—still on occasion referred to them as "niggers" in private) was reminded of the tactical advantage if ten black members of the House suddenly owed him an immense debt of gratitude. Philpott, who had from time to time been plagued by rumors of an impending coup in the legislature, decided to host a breakfast for Wilder. He was the first of the old guard power brokers to take the plunge, and the breakfast was viewed as a turning point. Ever after, Democratic officeholders were reminded that they could do no less than A.L. Philpott.

As his campaign manager, Wilder hired Paul Goldman, a former VISTA worker and transplanted New Yorker, who brought a quirky and largely unproven brilliance to the campaign.

Through the years, Goldman had been involved with other Virginia candidates; few of them turned out winners. In 1985, however, his offbeat intelligence, personal zealotry, and willingness to scrap political convention were precisely what was needed to showcase Wilder's historic bid. A physical fitness devotee, Goldman gave up his six-miles-a-day jogs, stocked the office with wheat germ and granola, and immersed himself in every facet of day-to-day operations and overall strategy. By election day, his office was a thicket of empty Diet Pepsi cans, bags of orange peels, and dried-fruit wrappers. Boxes of videotapes and Federal Express envelopes littered the floor. One stem of Goldman's glasses had been missing throughout the campaign, a lens occasionally popped out, and his shirts looked as if they had been slept in for days. But Goldman had on his hands a winner of national magnitude, and he was in no small measure responsible.

From the beginning, Wilder and Goldman adopted an unlikely campaign strategy. They decided to limit their paid staff to two, plus a driver and a part-time computer operator. The bulk of their resources would be poured into television. Across town, Chichester was assembling a traditional coterie of workers, including a manager, six department heads, and several other paid staff members. Goldman and Michael Brown, a former director of field operations for the state NAACP, filled all those functions for Wilder. Pleading poverty throughout the summer, Wilder and Goldman hinted broadly that they would be unable to afford any television advertising. Actually, campaign resources were being squirreled away for that very purpose. In late September, when Wilder announced that he was going on the air with a major television buy, the Chichester campaign was shocked. Chichester's manager, Dennis Peterson, fumed that Wilder had misled the public, but what mattered most was that Chichester was caught shorthanded.

By the end of October, Wilder had invested almost $400,000 in television, compared with about $135,000 spent by Chichester. The Wilder media total would eventually reach $500,000 out of a $700,000 budget. That advertising showed sharp contrasts between the two candidates and seemed critical in shaping public impressions of them. Wilder, for instance, stressed his selling points: that he had more Senate experience than the last five lieutenant governors combined, that he had chaired three major Senate committees, that he had placed fifth in Senate effectiveness in a recent newspaper poll, that he had won a bronze star in Korea, and that he was the author of legislation controlling drug paraphernalia and setting tough penalties for prison escapees. The primary message of Chichester's ads—except for a series aired in the last panic-stricken days of the campaign—seemed to be that the candidate was a nice guy.

Media budgets were not the GOP's only frustration as the campaign unfolded. Wilder had long been viewed as one of the most liberal members of the Virginia Senate, and Republicans entered the campaign expecting that all they need do in conservative Virginia was hammer home the label. Their strategy did not take into account Wilder's glibness in debate, nor Chichester's relative inarticulateness. Neither did it plan for a strategy in which Wilder would capitalize on race to defuse the issue early in the campaign. "Part of our strategy was to force them to deal with the liberal issue early on," acknowledged Goldman. Two approaches were planned; both worked. One was to portray "liberalism" as a code word for "black." A second goal was to link Wyatt Durrette, the GOP nominee for governor, to any haggling over liberal-conservative credentials. Unlike Chichester, whose voting pattern was predictably conservative, Durrette at times had vacillated on litmus-test issues like collective bargaining for public employees.

When Durrette, soon after the Democratic nominating convention, said Republicans had a good chance of winning because the Democratic ticket included one of the most liberal men ever to run for office in Virginia, Wilder was ready to pounce. The claim, he said, was a subtle form of racism. Republicans ridiculed the charge, but Wilder had clearly struck a sensitive chord. Thereafter in the campaign, Chichester seemed studiously to avoid using the word "liberal" to describe Wilder. Wilder was also ready with a list of forty-nine public-policy positions, which—he said—showed that he was not a liberal. After each item, he chose to compare his position, not with that of Chichester, but with that of Durrette. His challenge to Durrette to back up the charge of liberalism went unanswered.

In other ways, Wilder charted new and sometimes unexpected territory in dealing with race in the campaign. He decided neither to hide nor accentuate his color. On the day when he announced his candidacy, for instance, Wilder could not resist the delicious irony of posing in front of a portrait of Harry Byrd, Sr., the architect of massive resistance to public school integration. It was precisely the sort of detail to appeal to the brassy side of his nature. At the same time, Wilder rejected offers from Jesse Jackson and other prominent blacks to come to the state to campaign. In 1984, Jackson had turned out more Virginians at Democratic mass meetings than any other presidential contender, and his presence might well have fired black enthusiasm for Wilder. But Wilder was not about to issue a rallying cry that could be heard and feared by whites. Throughout the contest, his appeals to black voters were made quietly, and he consciously distanced himself from Jackson. Asked about campaign lessons for blacks nationally, Wilder in a postelection analysis cited first and foremost the virtues of running as a political moderate.

In other ways, as well, Wilder worked to avoid racial stereotyping. He consciously moderated his image and tone, insisting that the media cared more than voters about racial matters, and softening the sort of rhetoric that might have disproved that premise. Wilder, who had once publicly exploded over racial connotations in a Stephen Foster song, began telling jokes about "CPT" (colored people's time) and "WPT" (white people's time). Refusing to be controlled by his racial identity, he also rejected advice that he keep his face off television and out of the newspapers.

The masterpiece of Wilder's ad campaign was an unplanned segment featuring a burly, white policeman from a small southside community. Joe Alder happened onto a filming session in his rural county one day and readily agreed to help Wilder. An elated Goldman picked up a pen and, impromptu, wrote the words for a television spot that became the most talked-about performance of the 1985 campaign. When Alder rested one beefy arm on the top of his patrol car and stated his support of Wilder for "loo-tin-yant guv-ner," he delivered a body blow to racial prejudice. Boss Hogg and Archie Bunker might just as well have sent their blessing. Redneck Virginia liked Wilder.

If Wilder seemed confident in his treatment of the racial issue, the Chichester campaign proved unexpectedly confused by it. Within the Republican's inner circle, there was never any plan to exploit race. For one thing, to have done so would have been personally distasteful to Chichester, who had no stomach for bigotry and who valued his clean-cut image. For another, the GOP recognized that it was not necessary to emphasize the obvious. "Doug Wilder has nothing to worry about our appealing to race," said Peterson during the fall campaign. "The press would be on it like a frog on a lily pad." And he added, "even if we wanted to, which we don't, we wouldn't have to because the press never makes reference to him without saying he's black."

There was also a sense that any overt appeal to racial prejudice might have devastating effects. Republican and Democratic strategists agreed that many voters still had racial biases, but that those same Virginians would react negatively to being openly confronted with their feelings. The view seemed confirmed when a former governor and onetime segregationist, Mills E. Godwin, Jr., ridiculed Wilder for opposing "Carry Me Back to Ol' Virginny" as the state song. According to Republican pollsters, the impact was felt immediately. Tracking showed a five-to-six-point drop for the GOP gubernatorial nominee, Durrette, in urban centers like Tidewater and the Washington, D.C., suburbs. Plagued by such concerns, Chichester's campaign sometimes found itself floundering over fears that any attack would appear racist. In one instance, Peterson spent about $400 redoing a radio spot made by a former GOP governor because of such concerns. In the commercial, former governor John N. Dalton, a racial moderate who died in 1986, said it was important to vote for a candidate for lieutenant governor with whom Virginians were "comfortable politically." An ad production worker suggested that the word "comfortable" might be interpreted as a racial slur. Peterson, afraid that the worker was correct, spent almost $400 having the line edited out.

Republicans also avoided controversy because they felt no need to do otherwise. During the summer and early fall, Chichester was regarded as a shoo-in who stood to gain little by actively campaigning. As Wilder was piling up headlines, largely due to curiosity about his unprecedented campaign, Chichester was enjoying a steady, but unhurried campaign pace. Contrary to public perception, however, private campaign polls never showed Chichester with the comfortable lead he was widely presumed to hold. An August 6–8 survey, conducted by national GOP pollster

Richard Wirthlin, reported a nip-and-tuck battle with Wilder slightly ahead. In a five-hundred-person sample, Wirthlin found 35 percent backing Wilder, 33 percent for Chichester and 32 percent undecided. The tally matched the tracking of in-state, GOP consultant Ed DeBolt, who was concentrating on the race for governor. DeBolt and other Republicans credited the early showing to a quick cementing of Wilder's Democratic support. They fully expected that the large pool of undecided voters would break heavily to Chichester. "Unless John blows it," DeBolt said in late September, Chichester should win 58 to 60 percent of the final tally. "It's not a race we've done a lot of worrying about," he added.

At Chichester's Richmond headquarters, however, the bravado of the summer months was fading rapidly. Workers were becoming increasingly worried about Chichester's inability to gain ground. The ongoing, behind-the-scenes debate in the Chichester campaign was over exploitation of three Wilder shortcomings, described by one campaign official as "golden issues." The GOP campaign staff knew of the three from the outset, but it was not until the frantic, closing days of the campaign that the candidate agreed to go public. At issue were late payment of taxes, slum property, and a judicial reprimand. City tax records showed that Wilder had a pattern, extending over several years, of late tax payments on several properties. In mid-campaign, for instance, news sources reported that Wilder owed about $1,316 in delinquent personal property taxes and penalties. A second issue involved a 1978 disciplinary reprimand in which a circuit court judge berated Wilder for "inexcusable procrastination" in his handling of a legal case. The reprimand was upheld by the Virginia Supreme Court. The third issue dealt with repeated complaints by neighbors and city officials about allegedly unsafe conditions at a vacant row house owned by Wilder. In each instance, Wilder offered a rebuttal. The late tax payments, he said, were merely an oversight. He believed he had acted appropriately in the legal case, and repairs were gradually being made at the row house. Still, key Republicans argued that the trio of charges were grist for a devastating assault on Wilder. Chichester refused.

The turning point did not come until mid-October. From October 14 to 17, V. Lance Tarrance & Associates in Houston con-

ducted a voter survey for the GOP camp. The results, with the
election less than three weeks away, confirmed that Chichester
was not making progress. Just under 35 percent of those polled
favored Wilder, 31 percent preferred Chichester and 34 percent
were undecided. More alarming, 31 percent of the male Republicans and 26 percent of the female Republicans polled were voting
for Wilder.

With time evaporating, worried Chichester supporters scheduled a finance committee meeting at the Farmington County Club
in Charlottesville. About thirty people, including former governor
Godwin and Terry Dolan of the National Conservative Political
Action Committee, attended. The stated aim was to find ways of
financing a last-minute media campaign, but the meeting rapidly
evolved into discussion of what those ads should say. The message,
strong and clear, was that Chichester was not being hard enough
on Wilder and that his only hope of winning was to change course.
Reluctantly, Chichester agreed. A camera crew was on hand, and
before the day ended, filming had begun. One ad would focus on
Wilder's unkempt property; another, on the Supreme Court reprimand. Before the ads were ready, however, some of Chichester's
doubts resurfaced, and there would be another delay before the
television spots aired. Meanwhile, Wilder's television ads were
running at full steam, virtually unanswered.

During the week of October 22, another GOP survey was
taken, and this time there was no mistaking the results. Wilder
had moved up to 40.5 percent of the vote, while Chichester's tally
was dropping. The undecideds were shrinking, and they were
breaking heavily to Wilder. Among male Republicans, 39 percent
favored Wilder, and among male ticket splitters—usually a
stronghold for Republicans—almost half were in the Wilder
camp. For the GOP, the problem was no longer a matter of
winning converts. Their traditional base was evaporating as well.
Decorum had become an unaffordable luxury. On October 28,
with the election eight days away, an ad picturing Wilder and
charging, "He's been publicly reprimanded by the state supreme
court. He's been hauled before the general court of Richmond for
maintaining hazardous properties," finally debuted on television
stations across the state.

Over the next seventy-two hours, a campaign that had scarcely dared hope for victory was consumed with frantic debate about how best to preserve its fragile and miraculous lead. Pollsters, who saw Wilder's margin slipping, advised a counterassault. So did Robert Squier, a Washington, D.C., political consultant who had become an informal, behind-the-scenes adviser. So did a group of nine men, among them a Wilder law partner, the campaign treasurer, and the clerk of the Virginia Senate, who gathered at Wilder's office four nights before the election. Their mission was to watch two hastily filmed ads, one accusing Chichester of legislative conflict of interest, another talking about mudslinging. The group agreed that the ads should be used. Goldman, still unsure, distributed the spots to television stations across the Commonwealth and readied for an eleventh-hour, weekend assault. "If I go with the ads and he loses, that'll be the reason, and if I don't go with the ads and he loses, that'll be the reason," George Stoddart, press secretary to Governor Robb, recalled Goldman saying.

In the end, Wilder said, "No," it was better to leave voters with a positive last impression. Wilder's media finale would be, instead, an ad in which Governor Robb cited Wilder for "a clear edge in terms of experience, a clear edge in terms of effectiveness, a clear edge in terms of leadership." By election night, the ten-point Wilder lead that had shown up in Democratic polls before the ads started running, and the even wider gap in GOP polls, had shrunk dramatically. Wilder carried 51.8 percent of the vote in the closest of the three statewide races. For jubilant Democrats, any fraction of a percent was enough.

In the election aftermath, most analysts agreed that Wilder had skillfully avoided racial pitfalls. Among the decisions Republicans praised was his unwillingness to respond to Chichester's final advertising attack. The reason, as with most analysis in the precedent-setting campaign, had racial overtones. "It would have played right into John's hands," said DeBolt. "The first neat thing that Doug did was realizing he could never attack a white man and get away with it. As it was, he was a nonthreatening, harmless black. It was the only strategy that would have worked, and he pulled it off beautifully."

Spectacular as Wilder's victory was, it must be viewed essentially as a milestone, not the climax of an evolutionary shift. It would take more than one such triumph to spell the end of race as a factor in regional politics. Nationally, as well, black political progress cannot be charted in a steady upward line. As 1987 began, blacks held five statewide executive positions, lieutenant governor of Virginia, treasurers of New Mexico and Connecticut, comptroller of Illinois, and secretary of state in Michigan. However, nine years earlier in 1978, the list of statewide black officeholders was longer. It included lieutenant governors in California and Colorado, secretary of state in Michigan, treasurer in Connecticut, U.S. senator in Massachusetts, superintendent of education in California, and comptroller in Illinois. Wilder's win was noteworthy because it reaffirmed hope and suggested that progress would continue, however erratically. The unthinkable had become possible, and a new plateau of expectation had been reached. Other southern states might not yet be ready to follow Virginia's lead. A black candidate might still need superior qualifications to have an even shot at defeating a white candidate among a majority-white electorate. But a threshold had been crossed. Wilder's victory would make it easier for black candidates to decide to run for major office and for political parties to feel comfortable with their running.

Few observers in the weeks and months following Wilder's victory expected that subtle shift to produce immediate or dramatic results. For instance, in Mississippi, Democratic Party chairman Steve Patterson, a Jackson investment banker, hailed the Virginia experience as proof that biracial coalitions are possible in the South. But he saw little immediate prospect for electing a black official statewide. "I don't know that lingering racism is any stronger here than in Virginia," mused Patterson, "but it would be very difficult at this point."

Across the South, this message was echoed by dozens of other political activists. "Racism isn't dead anywhere—not in Louisiana or any of the other forty-nine states," said former judge Israel Augustine of New Orleans. Augustine, who is black, ran against incumbent Congresswoman Lindy Boggs in Louisiana's Second Congressional District in 1984. In a district 52 percent black, Augustine could muster only 39 percent of the vote against the popular Mrs. Boggs, who is white. In South Carolina, Adell Adams, political action chair for the state NAACP, lamented the unwillingness of whites to vote for blacks in statewide contests.

"At no time can we get more than 10 percent of the white vote," she said. The difficulty was reinforced in 1986 when Jim Clyburn was again defeated in a race for secretary of state. Even Judge Robert Benham, of the Georgia Appeals Court, the first black man elected to a statewide post there, had few illusions about the limits of black power. Benham, a north Georgia lawyer, said he believes many white Georgians were delighted at the chance to vote for a black judicial candidate when he ran in 1984. But the judge added just as readily that a black candidate running for governor, attorney general, or U.S. senator would not be elected. "I'm sure he would pick up tremendous support but not enough to prevail. I'm sure race would rear its ugly head," Benham said.

As the end of the 1980s approached, competing voices speculated about the role southern blacks should play in regional and national politics in the years ahead. Polls showed a loyalty by the region's blacks to the Democratic Party that was unsurpassed in any other section of the country.[4] Yet southern blacks were not unaffected by a biracial national trend toward greater political independence. And mounting economic divisions between an increasingly healthy black middle class and an increasingly vulnerable black underclass posed questions about continued racial unity. Once the most outrageous examples of segregation were gone and time had eased their memory, how much really bound a welfare mother living in poverty in southeast Atlanta and a rising, young stockbroker with a degree in economics and a BMW parked outside his mid-city townhouse, even if both were black? And if blacks did not remain a monolithic force within the Democratic Party, where would they turn? To independent politics? To a Republican Party whose leader—Ronald Reagan—had backed policies undercutting major civil rights gains? And what of southern whites? Could one sensational victory in Virginia dispel the fear that the region's white voters were abandoning a political party increasingly viewed as the haven of blacks?

Democrats at mid-decade suggested two divergent approaches to the party's racial dilemma. If blacks were the most loyal party members, one group said, then the party should begin to nominate some blacks for major offices. Patterson advocated that course in a letter circulated to his fellow southern chairmen after the 1984 presidential campaign. First, he said, the party must appeal to young, upwardly mobile baby-boomers by avoiding economic policies that focus on a redistribution of wealth. Second, Democrats must motivate their constituencies—blacks, women, Hispanics—by nominating members of those groups for office. Thad Beyle, a University of North Carolina political scientist, agreed. "If Democrats are going to have to rely on blacks, they're going to have to turn to having a visible black on the ticket so that blacks can turn out," he said.

Wilder's Virginia victory did far more than any position paper or philosophical argument to add credence to that view. His nomination alone was enough to cement liberal and black support for the 1985 Virginia Democratic ticket. His presence also freed Democratic running mates to spend their time focusing on moderate and conservative voters. Still, there were risks. Wilder's campaign was remarkably free of direct appeals to black voters. On the strength of his past performance for blacks and his muted campaign rhetoric, he succeeded in treading the delicate tightrope between motivating blacks and arousing the fears of whites. In the process, he sacrificed a large black turnout, but any loss was more than offset by the retention of white support. In other times and places, black candidates might not be so skilled or so fortunate.

A second alternative was suggested by white Democrats who were worried about the prospect of highlighting black party involvement. In their view, blacks needed to accept the political reality that many white voters still regarded them with alarm. There was little to be gained from winning a nomination, they said, if the result was a lost election. If blacks became a majority of the Democratic Party, then Democrats would become a minority, and blacks would be the inevitable losers. The greater wisdom, they argued, would be for blacks to accept a behind-the-scenes role in which they could influence the officials they had helped to elect.

Particularly in the wake of the Wilder election, it was not a game plan that held great appeal for southern blacks. The days of patiently biding one's time belonged to another era. Risky as the course might be, it seemed much more likely that the region's black voters would play an aggressive role in political campaigns within their states during the remainder of the century and beyond.

Precisely what form that activism would take was uncertain.

One school of black activists has long held that pursuit of independent politics is the only avenue to real influence. The grass-roots swell embracing Jesse Jackson's presidential bid again fueled hopes that blacks might emerge as a truly independent force, committed to their own agenda, not any political party's. Nowhere is the tradition of independent black politics stronger than in Mississippi, and talk of abandoning the Democratic Party was predictably at its peak in that state. The Mississippi Freedom Democratic Party, founded in the early 1960s as an alternative to the white-dominated establishment party, operated there until blacks began to be given a voice in regular party politics. Even after the FDP stopped fielding candidates, the split between loyalist Democrats (mostly blacks and liberal whites) and regular Democrats (more conservative whites) resulted in frequent independent campaigns in the state. In 1985, prominent blacks, including Democratic national committeeman Bennie Thompson and Greenville lawyer Johnnie Walls, insisted that blacks should keep open the option of independent races. They were willing to work with Democrats, but their greater allegiance was to black causes. "If I have to give up my principles, then I say to hell with the Democratic Party," said Thompson.

The Rev. Jackson also forecast an increasingly independent role for southern black voters. "Blacks vote for whoever appeals to their interests; they are becoming more independent and intelligent," said Jackson, as he sat in his Chicago office following a regular Saturday morning radio broadcast. In Jackson's view, black voters in the remainder of the 1980s and the 1990s would move to the left of both the Republican and Democratic parties, increasingly unaligned with either. If America's most prominent black politician had concerns about disintegrating cohesion between middle class and poor blacks, he did not admit to them. "Middle-class blacks are still one bad cold away from the projects," he insisted. Their interests remained wedded to those of poor blacks, he said.

Jackson himself, however, was proof of the mounting schisms in the political thought of southern blacks. He had made a strong regional showing during his bid for the presidency. Yet most prominent black leaders had stuck with the Democratic Party's mainstream candidate, Walter Mondale. Wilder's middle-of-the-road campaign strategy, plus the growing success of black candidates like Mayor Sidney Barthelemy in New Orleans or Mayor Roy West in Richmond, both of whom owed their elections to white voters, also argued against the sort of separatism envisioned by Jackson. From the quarters of Mayor Andrew Young of Atlanta to the cramped tax assessor's office in tiny Greene County, Alabama, blacks were becoming increasingly adept at manipulating mainstream politics. That they would abandon such progress in droves seemed unlikely.

Nor, despite growing economic and philosophical differences, did it seem probable that southern blacks were on the verge of any substantial defection to the Republican Party. Many blacks did seem increasingly open to a more conservative economic policy. Theoretically that attitude, plus a growing black middle class, bode well for Republicans. Yet the GOP had provided few regional candidates with whom blacks identified, and the Reagan record on civil rights enforcement argued against massive black involvement. Many blacks were appalled by Justice Department efforts under Reagan to rewrite consent decrees in which fifty-one cities had agreed to hire more black employees. Items of complaint included the makeup of the U.S. Civil Rights Commission, the Black Belt vote fraud investigation, and such matters as the administration's interpretation of the amended Section 2 of the Voting Rights Act. Under Reagan, the Justice Department had applied a much tougher standard than many civil rights advocates thought fair in deciding when the section had been violated. In mid-1986, the Supreme Court agreed with the critics.

The outgrowth of those and other differences, many said, was that black southerners would remain primarily within the Democratic Party, occasionally dipping into Republican and independent politics. Undoubtedly, as the years passed and such concerns diminished, the GOP would pick up additional strength among blacks. But to some extent, that was because the number of black Republicans had nowhere to go but up. Nothing in the southern landscape in the mid-1980s foretold a large-scale political realignment.

Still, for southern Democrats to take black support for granted seemed risky. Black Democrats appeared bent on demanding a larger, not smaller share of party spoils. As Doug Wilder had demonstrated in 1982, the threat of withdrawal from the party was a potent force when carefully used. As blacks became increasingly assertive, they would undoubtedly form tactical alliances with Republicans in some individual races. But those instances promised to remain the exception, not the rule.

For blacks, the challenge in their third decade of political power would be to accommodate growing diversity without losing sight of common moorings. It would not be an easy task. Already, mounting internal dissension over political tactics signaled danger, as well as progress. When delegates committed to Jackson booed Andrew Young at the 1984 Democratic convention, white Americans glimpsed the depth of emotion capable of dividing the haves and have-nots of black politics. What they saw, too, was a black political force no longer bound to hide its fissures from public view. Painful as the convention experience was for some, it was a milestone on the path of black political progress. True assimilation into the political mainstream would be marked by the freedom to disagree openly not only with whites, but also with each other. As a second and third generation of black public officials took office, there were increased signs of such independence. Black voters had long dealt with internal differences as acute as any experienced by whites. But in the days when the only hope of progress was to confront the common enemy united, those frictions were routinely submerged. By the mid-1980s, southern blacks had become confident enough of their clout in some communities to war publicly. In such places, coalitions with whites were no longer anathema. Understandably, black victims of such biracial strategies saw shades of past sellouts to whites in their own defeats. But to others, the new freedom to draw on both black and white support was a sign of having arrived.

For southern blacks, success in the third decade of their political emancipation would be measured also by tangible economic and social gains. In the years after the Voting Rights Act took effect, numbers were the test. Each new face on the roster of black elected officials signaled victory. What those sheriffs, commissioners, and registrars achieved was less important than that they existed. The early years were consumed, too, by fighting a rearguard action against whites. As dozens of court cases proved, power was not easily yielded. If an election law could be manipulated to preserve the status quo, it frequently was. Only Congress and the federal courts, interpreting a law heralded as the salvation of southern blacks, could derail the attempted subversion. By the mid-1980s, communities remained where blacks had yet to travel the road to political freedom. Yet the number of such places was ever dwindling. In time, it seemed, with the guarantees of the Voting Rights Act, they too would change. The broader question as a new decade began was one of performance—whether black officials could help shape a fairer, more successful social welfare policy, whether the economic gulf dividing poor blacks from other southerners might somehow be bridged, whether the inner cities and isolated counties where many blacks held office might be blended into the whole of southern life. "Blacks aren't just wanting a black face in city hall. They want results," said Harvey Gantt. "The time when you could blame the system is gone," added Wilder. "It's not the easy old game of finger pointing."

In truth, little in the way of southern black political power had come easily. Those who welcomed the Voting Rights Act in 1965 might have been shocked to realize that, twenty years later, blacks in Mobile, or Jackson, or Edgefield County would have progressed no further than the threshold of political influence. Many would be distressed to realize how ineffective politics had been at removing economic shackles. They might grieve that some spots in the Mississippi Delta or south Georgia remained politically unchanged. Achieving concrete gains from voting, and even from electing black officials, was proving to be a slower, more evolutionary process than many had hoped. Yet few could help but be impressed by the altered conditions that could propel a Harvey Gantt or a Doug Wilder to office. By the standards of 1965, a region and its people had been transformed. The number of places where blacks had attained real political power, and where whites acknowledged that power and lived with it, was striking, even while other places remained unchanged.

Oliver Hill, a longtime civil rights lawyer who is a regal-looking man with a white goatee and mustache and a pear-shaped frame, viewed southern politics from the perspective of a half-century of voting rights activism. His first petition seeking to open a primary election to black voters was filed in 1939 in Greenville

County, Virginia. Toying with a silver and wood pipe as he sat in his law office in the heart of what was once Richmond's most vibrant black neighborhood, Hill spoke of achievement and failure and of his growing understanding that major shifts in society do not come quickly. "It's unrealistic to think in any evolutionary fashion that there would be any substantial change in control in such a short period of time," he said. "The only way for that to happen is violent revolution."

The changes in southern politics had been a matter of law, not revolution. As time passed, the law had been revised and reinterpreted, and communities that once rejected its authority had been forced to bow to its weight. No law, however, could dictate economic and social equality, define the competence of elected officials, or make political power the major determinant in shaping the quality of life. And so, as blacks embarked on a third decade of involvement in the southern political scene, much remained to be done. Some places still waited for old formulas to be applied. In others, the time for new remedies had arrived. The metamorphosis, still incomplete, continued.

NOTES

---

2. Selma

1. John Lewis. Interview by author. Selma, Alabama, 3 March 1985.

2. "Black Elected Officials in 1985," *Focus,* 13 (May 1985): 4, 5.

3. This figure was derived by the author from figures provided by the Joint Center for Political Studies and from interviews with public officials representing offices of secretaries of state, associations of county commissioners, state municipal leagues, and others, in each of the seven states.

4. This data came from telephone interviews, conducted by the author in April 1985 with officials in offices of the county commission or circuit clerk in each of the eighty-two counties.

5. Steven Lawson, *Black Ballots, Voting Rights in the South, 1944–1969* (New York: Columbia University Press, 1976), 93, 146.

6. Steven Lawson, *In Pursuit of Power: Southern Blacks and Electoral Politics, 1965–1982* (New York: Columbia University Press, 1985), 296. See also U.S. Bureau of the Census, *Voting and Registration in the Election of 1984,* Series P-20, No. 397, January 1985, 7–9.

7. U.S. Census, *Voting and Registration in the Election of November 1984,* 7–9. See also Pat Watters and Reese Cleghorn, *Climbing Jacob's Ladder: The Arrival of Negroes in Southern Politics* (New York: Harcourt, Brace & World, 1967), 245.

8. John Wilson, information officer for the U.S. Justice Department. Telephone interview by author. June 1986.

9. *United States v. Marengo County Commission,* Civil Action No. 78-474-H in U.S. District Court for the Southern District of Alabama, *Proposed Findings of Fact & Conclusions of Law for the United States,* 20 June 1985, 15.

10. *Jordan v. Winter,* No. GC 82-80-WK-0 in U.S. District Court for the Northern District of Mississippi, *Deposition Testimony of Jake Bertram Ayers,* 18 November 1983, 11.

11. Rodney Strong, acting director of Atlanta's office of contract compliance. Interview by author. Atlanta, 26 February 1985; and Norma Duarte, assistant in that office. Telephone interview by author. June 1986.

12. This information was derived by the author using 1980 Census Bureau data found in publications on the "General Social and Economic Characteristics" of individual states.

13. Leonard Cole, *Blacks in Power: A Comparative Study of Black and White Elected Officials* (Princeton: Princeton University Press, 1976), 28.

14. Richard Kluger, *Simple Justice* (New York: Vintage Books, 1975), 67–68.

15. Gunnar Myrdal, *An American Dilemma: The Negro Problem and Modern Democracy* (New York: Harper & Bros., 1944; New York: Pantheon Books, 1972), 475.

16. Michael Namorato, ed., *Have We Overcome? Race Relations Since Brown* (Jackson: University of Mississippi Press, 1979), 126.

17. Data provided by the Voting Section of the Civil Rights Division of the U.S. Justice Department.

18. Watters and Cleghorn, *Climbing Jacob's Ladder,* 245.

19. Lawson, *In Pursuit of Power,* 159.

20. Data on hundreds of Voting Rights Act objections can be found in the files of the Civil Rights Division of the U.S. Justice Department. Many key objections are also described in 1982 testimony on the extension of the Voting Rights Act. See Subcommittee on the Constitution of the Senate Committee on the Judiciary, *Bills to Amend the Voting Rights Act of 1965,* 97th Cong., 2nd sess., 1 January—1 March 1982. See also Subcommittee on Civil and Constitutional Rights of the House Committee on the Judiciary, *Extension of the Voting Rights Act,* 97th Cong., 1st sess., 6 May—13 July, 1981.

21. Robert Mundt and Peggy Heilig, "District Representation: Demands and Effects in the Urban South," *Journal of Politics* 44 (November 1982): 1035. Mundt and Heilig describe a wide body of research reaching this conclusion. See also Thomas Cavanagh and Denise Stockton, "Black Elected Officials and Their Constituencies" (Washington: Joint Center for Political Studies, 1983): 20–21. For a somewhat different view, see Cole, *Blacks in Power,* 62.

3. Edgefield County

1. Laughlin McDonald, "Voting Rights on the Chopping Block," *Southern Exposure* 9 (Spring 1981): 90.

2. Myrdal, *An American Dilemma,* 45.

3. Hancock County's story is told in John Rozier, *Black Boss: Political Revolution in a Georgia County* (Athens: University of Georgia Press, 1982), 1–196.

4. U.S. Bureau of the Census, *1980 Census of the Population: South Carolina, General Social and Economic Characteristics,* PC80-1-C48.

5. Donald R. Matthews and James W. Prothro, *Negroes and the New Southern Politics* (New York: Harcourt, Brace & World, 1966), 286.

6. *The Charlotte Observer,* 30 August 1981.

7. McDonald, "Voting Rights on the Chopping Block," 89.

8. Ibid., 90.

9. For McCain's full testimony, see Subcommittee on the Constitution, Senate Judiciary Committee, *Bills to Amend the Voting Rights Act of 1965,* 1130–1143.

10. *McCain v. Lybrand,* Civil Action No. 74-281 in U.S. District Court for the District of South Carolina, *Final Order,* 17 April 1980, 4–15.

11. Ibid., 18.

12. Statistics from the Edgefield County Board of Registration.

4. Atlanta

1. Rodney Strong. Interview by author. Atlanta, Georgia. 26 February 1985.

2. U.S. Bureau of the Census, *1980 Census of the Population: Georgia, General Social and Economic Characteristics, PC80-1-C12.* See also comparable reports for Alabama, North Carolina, Louisiana, South Carolina, and Mississippi.

3. Ibid.

4. Karl Taeuber, "Racial Residential Segregation, 28 Cities, 1970–1980," a working paper of the Center for Demography and Ecology, University of Wisconsin, March 1983, 8. The four were Chicago, Illinois; Philadelphia, Pennsylvania; Cleveland, Ohio; and St. Louis, Missouri.

5. Community Relations Commission, "Blacks and Women on Corporation Boards in Atlanta," January 1979, 3.

6. Charles Jaret, "Is Atlanta a 'Black Mecca?': Black Migration and Living Conditions in the Urban South," a paper presented at the 1985 annual meeting of the Southern Sociological Society, 10—13 April 1985, 21.

7. Celestine Sibley, *Peachtree Street, USA* (New York: Doubleday, 1963), 89.

8. Ivan Allen, Jr., and Paul Hemphill, *Mayor: Notes on the Sixties* (New York: Simon and Schuster, 1971), 34ff.

9. Ibid., 110.

10. "A British Journal Also Takes a Look at Atlanta," reprinted from the *Economist,* London, in the *Atlanta Constitution,* 3 April 1975.

11. Dave Miller, manager of airport planning for Atlanta under former mayor Maynard Jackson. Telephone interview with author. 25 April 1986.

12. Cooks maintains, for instance, that Young's widely publicized description of the Ayatollah Khomeini as a saint was misrepresented. Young, responding to a reporter's questions, was trying to show that the frame of reference of Iranians in viewing Khomeini was different from that of Americans. It was in the Iranian context that Young described Khomeini as a saint, Cooks said.

13. Paul Lieberman of the *Atlanta Constitution* reported extensively on Young's business dealings during the mayor's first term in office. Helpful articles include: "The Andrew Young Years: Mayor Plays Chief Executive in the Board Room as Well," 1 January 1984; "The Two Hats of Mayor Young," 9 April 1982; and "Latest Trip a Reflection of Young's Global Vision," 13 March 1983.

14. Art Harris, "Too Busy to Hate," *Esquire,* 103 (June 1985): 132.

5. Macon and Lowndes Counties

1. U.S. Commission on Civil Rights, "Fifteen Years Ago . . . Rural Alabama Revisited" (Washington: Clearinghouse Publication, 1983), 1–19. See also U.S. Bureau of the Census, *1980 Census of the Population: Alabama, General Social and Economic Characteristics,* PC80-1-C2.

2. Charles S. Bullock III, "The Election of Blacks in the South: Preconditions and Consequences," *American Journal of Political Science* 19 (November 1975): 738.

3. "Businesses Said to Have Barred New Plants in Largely Black Communities," *New York Times,* 15 February 1983. See also Reginald Stuart

and Laurie Baum, "Firm Rejects Georgia Areas with Large Black Populations," *Atlanta Journal & Constitution,* 20 February 1983.

4. Keith Schneider, "Bypassed," *Atlanta Weekly* in the *Atlanta Constitution,* 17 June 1984, 7ff.

5. Watters and Cleghorn, *Climbing Jacob's Ladder,* 298–99. See also Matthews and Prothro, *Negroes and the New Southern Politics,* 331.

6. Johnny Ford. Interview with Southern Oral History Project, University of North Carolina. 11 July 1974, 19.

7. Charles E. Fager, *Selma 1965* (Boston: Beacon Press, 1974 and 1985), 159.

8. Ibid., 205. See also Marshall Frady, *Southerners: A Journalist's Odyssey* (New York: New American Library, 1980), 138–56.

9. Claiborne Carson, *In Struggle: SNCC and the Black Awakening of the 1960s* (Cambridge: Harvard University Press, 1981), 165.

10. Ronald J. Green. Interview with author. Tuskegee, Alabama, 8 March 1985.

11. Neal Peirce, *The Deep South States of America* (New York: W.W. Norton, 1974), 281.

12. U.S. Commission on Civil Rights, "Rural Alabama Revisited," 70.

13. Andrew Kopkind, "Lowndes County, Alabama: The Great Fear Is Gone," *Ramparts* 13 (April 1975): 9.

6. Birmingham

1. Stephen Oates, *Let the Trumpet Sound: The Life of Martin Luther King, Jr.* (New York: Harper & Row, 1982), 210.

2. Virginia Van der Veer Hamilton, *Alabama: A History* (New York: W. W. Norton, 1977), 139.

3. Oates, *Let the Trumpet Sound,* 210.

4. Van der Veer Hamilton, *Alabama,* 141.

5. Testimony of Gordon Graham before the Senate Judiciary Committee, *Confirmation of William Bradford Reynolds to be the Associate Attorney General of the United States,* 99th Cong., 1st sess., 4, 5, and 18 June 1985, 548.

6. Van der Veer Hamilton, *Alabama,* 142.

7. Matthews and Prothro, *Negroes and the New Southern Politics,* 239. A full account of the Birmingham crusade is found in Howell Raines, *My Soul Is Rested: Movement Days in the Deep South Remembered* (New York: Putnam's Sons, 1977), 139–85.

8. Richard Arrington. Interview with Southern Oral History Project, University of North Carolina. 18 July 1974, 9.

9. Gordon Graham, *Confirmation of William Bradford Reynolds,* 546–49.

10. Ibid., 555.

11. Roger A. White. Interview with author. Birmingham, 11 February 1986.

12. "Jesse Jackson: Effort by Arrington Helped Mondale Win Black Districts," *Birmingham News,* 14 March 1984.

13. Michele McDonald, "Arrington Is City's 'Secret Weapon' at Capital," *Birmingham News,* 26 February 1984.

14. Dave White, "Mayor Gives Partner City Contract Worth as Much as $240,000," *Birmingham News,* 1 August 1985. See also Dave White, "Mayor Now Working with Ex-Consultant," *Birmingham News,* 26 July 1985. Dave White, "Parker Renting Space Without City Approval," *Birmingham News,* 25 July 1985.

7. Richmond

1. Henry Marsh. Interview with author. Richmond, 20 February 1985.

2. *Richmond Times-Dispatch,* 8 August 1978.

3. William Hefty. Telephone interview with author. Richmond, 13 February 1985.

4. A.J. Dickenson, "Myth and Manipulation: The Story of the Crusade for Voters in Richmond, Virginia," unpublished doctoral dissertation, Yale University, 1967, 42.

5. Gilbert Carter. Interview with author. Richmond, 15 March 1985.

6. Virginius Dabney, *Richmond: The Story of a City* (New York: Doubleday & Co., 1976), 70.

7. Michael B. Chesson, *Richmond After the War 1865–1890* (Richmond: Virginia State Library, 1981), 10.

8. Michael B. Chesson, "Richmond's Black Councilmen," in *Southern Black Leaders of the Reconstruction Period,* ed. Howard N. Rabinowitz (Urbana: University of Illinois Press, 1982), 191.

9. *Virginian-Pilot,* 7 January 1967.

10. John V. Moeser and Rutledge M. Dennis, *The Politics of Annexation: Oligarchic Power in a Southern City* (Cambridge: Schenkman Publishing Co., 1982), 12.

11. Ibid., 157.

12. Ibid., 114.

13. *Richmond Times-Dispatch,* 8 March 1977.

14. Shelley Rolfe, "A Place in Time," *Richmond Times-Dispatch,* 21 May 1980.

15. Elliott Cooper, "Marsh Fears New Hotel Is Peril to Project One," *Richmond Times-Dispatch,* 1 August 1981.

16. Jerry Turner, "West Urged to Be More Responsive," *Richmond Times-Dispatch,* 19 May 1984.

17. J. John Palen and Richard D. Morrison, "Representation of Blacks and Women in Positions with Policy Making Potential in the Greater Richmond Area, 1970–1980," a report of the Department of Sociology and Anthropology, Virginia Commonwealth University, Spring 1982, 15.

8. Sunflower County

1. James W. Loewen and Charles Sallis, eds., *Mississippi: Conflict and Change* (New York: Pantheon, 1974), 256.

2. Oates, *Let the Trumpet Sound,* 261.

3. James W. Silver, *Mississippi: The Closed Society* (New York: Harcourt, Brace & World, 1963), 151.

4. "Black Elected Officials in the United States," *Focus* 14 (September 1986): 5.

5. U.S. Bureau of the Census, *1980 Census of the Population: Mississippi, General Social and Economic Characteristics,* PC80-1-C26.

6. Loewen and Sallis, *Mississippi,* 152.

7. Silver, *The Closed Society,* 18.

8. Lawson, *Black Ballots,* 100.

9. E.R. Shipp, "The Races in Mississippi: Old Order and New," *New York Times,* 2 April 1985.

10. Silver, *The Closed Society,* 95. See also Raines, *My Soul Is Rested,* 247.

11. Watters and Cleghorn, *Climbing Jacob's Ladder,* 113. See also Silver, *The Closed Society,* 86.

12. Raines, *My Soul Is Rested,* 250.

13. Silver, *The Closed Society,* 41.

14. Frank R. Parker and Barbara Y. Phillips, "Voting in Mississippi: A Right Still Denied" (Washington: Lawyers' Committee for Civil Rights Under Law, 1981), 13.

9. Greene County

1. Ray Jenkins, "Majority Rule in the Black Belt: Greene County, Alabama," *New South* 24 (Fall 1969): 60–67. See also Lawson, *Pursuit of Power,* 160; and "Alabama: A Black Day in Eutaw," *Newsweek* 74 (11 August 1969): 24–25.

2. Tommy Stevenson, "To Meet Payroll Friday, Greene Official Stresses," *Tuscaloosa News,* 11 December 1984. See also Ed Clark, "Greene Employees Put on Part-time Status," *Birmingham Post-Herald,* 7 December 1984.

10. Harvey Gantt

1. Cole, *Blacks in Power,* 5.

2. James W. Clay, ed., "Atlas of Charlotte-Mecklenburg" (Charlotte: University of North Carolina, 1981), 2.

3. Charlotte Chamber of Commerce research reports.

4. Frank Barrows, "School Busing: Charlotte, N.C.," *Atlantic Monthly* 230 (November 1972): 19.

5. Frye Gaillard and Polly Paddock, "Charlotte's Busing Breakthrough," *The Progressive* 39 (October 1975): 37.

6. Text of speech by Harvey Gantt to the Mecklenburg Council on Adolescent Pregnancy, 7 February 1985.

7. George McMillan, "Integration with Dignity: The Inside Story of How South Carolina Kept the Peace," *Saturday Evening Post* 236 (16 March 1963): 15–21.

8. Ken Eudy, "Most Doubt Race Will Be a Factor in Charlotte Mayoral Contest," *Charlotte Observer,* 12 April 1983.

9. Bullock, "The Election of Blacks in the South," 737.

10. Karnig and Welch, *Black Representation*, 154.

11. Doug Wilder

1. Larry Sabato, "The 1985 Statewide Election in Virginia: History Quietly Writ Large," draft chapter to be published in 1987 edition of *Virginia Votes* (19 December 1985), 18.

2. Cavanagh and Stockton, "Black Elected Officials and Their Constituencies," 17.

3. Rabinowitz, ed., *Southern Black Leaders of the Reconstruction*, xx.

4. Joint Center for Political Studies and Gallop Poll of 902 blacks in August 1984 showed 57 percent of southern blacks listing themselves as "strong Democrats," compared with 49 percent of easterners, 52 percent of westerners and 57 percent of midwesterners. See also "The New York Times/CBS News Poll," *New York Times,* 6 November 1986 showed 93 percent of southern blacks supporting Democratic candidates in the 1986 elections, compared with 87 percent in the East and 84 percent in the Midwest. Figures were not available for the West.

BIBLIOGRAPHY

Interviews

Many of the individuals interviewed in researching this book are listed here. They are identified by name and position at the time of the interview. The location and date of the interview are included. Individuals contacted by telephone are designated with a (T).

Adams, Adell. Political action chairperson for the South Carolina NAACP. Columbia, South Carolina. 6/18/85. (T)

Amerson, Lucius D. Macon County sheriff. Alabama's first black sheriff. Tuskegee, Alabama. 3/4/85.

Anderson, Joseph. State representative from Edgefield County. Edgefield, South Carolina. 5/15/85. (T)

Anderson, Reuben. Justice of the Mississippi Supreme Court. First black graduate of the University of Mississippi Law School. Jackson, Mississippi. 7/19/85.

Andrews, Hunter B. Majority leader of the Virginia Senate. Hampton, Virginia. 9/30/85.

Armstrong, Louis E. City councilman in Jackson. Director of the Mississippi Legal Services Coalition. Jackson, Mississippi. 7/18/85.

Arrington, Marvin S. President of the Atlanta City Council. Atlanta, Georgia. 2/27/86.

Arrington, Rachel. Wife of Birmingham's mayor. Birmingham, Alabama. 2/11/86.

Arrington, Richard. Mayor of Birmingham. Birmingham, Alabama. 3/7/85; 2/25/86.

Augustine, Israel M. Former Louisiana appeals court judge. 1984 congressional candidate in he 2nd District. New Orleans, Louisiana. 3/21/86. (T)

Baird, Joe. Member of the board of supervisors, Sunflower County. Indianola, Mississippi. 7/15/85.

Baker, Don. Co-chairman of Harvey Gantt's mayoral campaign in 1985. Charlotte, North Carolina. 10/21/85.

Baker, Jim. Birmingham city attorney. Birmingham, Alabama. 3/5/86. (T)

Bargainer, Linda. Lowndes County tax collector. Hayneville, Alabama. 3/6/85.

Barlow, Alma. Executive director of the Richmond Tenants Association. Richmond, Virginia. 2/12/85.

Belk, John. Former mayor of Charlotte. Chairman of the board of Belk Stores. Charlotte, North Carolina. 10/22/85.

Bell, William. President of the Birmingham City Council. Birmingham, Alabama. 2/1/86.

Benham, Robert. Georgia Court of Appeals Judge. Atlanta, Georgia. 6/19/85. (T)

Berryhill, Dave. Former Charlotte councilman. 1985 GOP candidate against Harvey Gantt. Charlotte, North Carolina. 10/20/85.

Bishop, Edward. Alderman in Corinth. Corinth, Mississippi. 7/26/86. (T)

Bowie, Harry. Episcopal priest working in community development in McComb. McComb, Mississippi. 6/24/85. (T)

Brady, Jim. Louisiana Democratic state chairman. Alexandria, Louisiana. 11/19/85. (T)

Branch, William McKinley. Probate judge of Greene County. Forkland and Eutaw, Alabama. 3/6/85; 2/13/86.

Bright, Willie. Chairman of the county council in Edgefield County. Johnston, South Carolina. 5/6/85.

Brylski, Cheron. Press aide to Mayor Ernest Morial. New Orleans, Louisiana. 3/19/85. (T)

Burkhalter, David A. City manager of Charlotte, 1971–81. Charlotte, North Carolina. 10/22/85.

Burriss, Roland W. Comptroller of Illinois. Vice-chairman of the Democratic National Committee. Richmond, Virginia. 1/11/86.

Calhoun, Credell. State representative from Hinds County. Former field organizer for the Mississippi Democratic Party. Jackson, Mississippi. 6/18/85. (T)

Campbell, William C. Atlanta city councilman. Atlanta, Georgia. 2/28/86.

Carroll, Don. Former Charlotte councilman. Co-chairman of Harvey Gantt's 1985 campaign. Charlotte, North Carolina. 10/21/85.

Carson, Rufus. Mayor of Franklin. Montgomery, Alabama. 7/26/86. (T)

Carter, Gilbert. EEOC officer for Richmond. Richmond, Virginia. 3/15/85.

Cavanagh, Thomas. Research associate at the Joint Center for Political Studies. Washington, D.C. 1/23/85.

Chambliss, Alvin. Attorney with the North Mississippi Rural Legal Services. Oxford, Mississippi. 8/30/85. (T)

Chance, John. Chairman of the Sunflower County Democratic Committee. Indianola, Mississippi. 7/17/85.

Clark, Robert G. Mississippi state representative. Congressional candidate in the 2nd District, 1982 and 1984. Ebenezer, Mississippi. 7/16/85.

Clyburn, James E. South Carolina human affairs commissioner. Candidate for secretary of state in 1978. Columbia, South Carolina. 11/19/85. (T)

Coleman, Lemon. Councilman in Pineville. Pineville, Louisiana. 7/25/86. (T)

Collins, Betty Fine. Birmingham city councilwoman. Birmingham, Alabama. 2/11/86.

Cooks, Stoney. Campaign manager and former aide to Mayor Andrew Young. Atlanta, Georgia. 2/26/86.

Corder, James W., Jr. Chairman of the Sunflower County board of supervisors. Indianola, Mississippi. 7/15/85.

Cross, Elmo. Virginia state senator. Hanover, Virginia. 9/18/85.

Cross, Frieda. Co-owner of the "Lowndes Signal." Fort Deposit, Alabama. 3/5/85.

Cummins, William. Member of the board of supervisors, Sunflower County. Indianola, Mississippi. 7/15/85.

Daniel, David. Alabama Cooperative Extension Service county agent for Lowndes County. Hayneville, Alabama. 3/6/85.

Davis, Howard Q., Jr. GOP chairman in Sunflower County. Indianola, Mississippi. 7/17/85.

DeBolt, Edward. Republican campaign consultant. Arlington, Virginia. 9/25/85; 11/12/85. (T)

Derfner, Armand. Attorney handling voting rights litigation. Washington, D.C. 1/23/85.

Donahoe, Edgar N. Member of the board of supervisors, Sunflower County. Indianola, Mississippi. 7/15/85.

Eaves, A. Reginald. County commissioner in Fulton County. Former commissioner of the Atlanta Department of Public Safety. Atlanta, Georgia. 2/26/86.

Ellis, John. City councilman in Fort Deposit. President of the Fort Deposit Bank. Fort Deposit, Alabama. 4/23/85.

Ely, Sam J., Jr. Circuit clerk for Sunflower County. Indianola, Mississippi. 7/15/85.

Etheredge, Jamie. Director of the Alabama Industrial Development Office. Montgomery, Alabama. 4/23/85. (T)

Evans, J. Randall. Director of the Richmond Renaissance project. Richmond, Virginia. 1/31/85.

Evers, Charles. Mayor of Fayette. Mississippi congressional candidate, 1968; gubernatorial candidate, 1971 and 1983; senatorial candidate, 1975. Fayette, Mississippi. 11/18/85. (T)

Floyd, D.B., Jr. Superintendent of schools in Indianola. Indianola, Mississippi. 7/17/85.

Ford, Johnny. Mayor of Tuskegee. Tuskegee, Alabama. 3/4/85.

Fowler, Don. Past chairman of the South Carolina Democratic Party. Member of the Democratic National Committee. Columbia, South Carolina. 11/19/85. (T)

Franklin, David M. Campaign manager for Maynard Jackson. Atlanta, Georgia. 2/25/86.

Fratesi, Phillip. Mayor of Indianola. Indianola, Mississippi. 7/15/85.

Frye, Henry E. Associate justice of the Supreme Court of North Carolina. Raleigh, North Carolina. 6/25/85. (T)

Gantt, Harvey. Mayor of Charlotte. Charlotte, North Carolina. 10/21/85.

Gillis, Richard S., Jr. Mayor of Ashland. Hanover, Virginia. 9/18/85.

Goldman, Paul. Campaign manager for Doug Wilder. Richmond, Virginia. 7/3/85; 10/29/85; 11/6/85; 11/7/85.

Graham, Gordon. Birmingham personnel director. Birmingham, Alabama. 2/6/86.

Gray, Jerome. Field director of the Alabama Democratic Conference. Montgomery, Alabama. 2/15/85; 6/22/85. (T)

Green, Ronald J. Chairman and chief administrative officer for Macon County commissioners. Tuskegee, Alabama. 3/8/85.

Greene, Benjamin. Chairman of the Jefferson County Citizens Coalition. Administrative assistant to the mayor. Birmingham, Alabama. 2/12/86.

Greene, Elizabeth. Electoral board member and clerk. Edgefield County, South Carolina. 5/9/85.

Hancock, Paul F. Head of litigation in the voting section of the Civil Rights Division of the U.S. Justice Department. Washington, D.C. 8/27/85.

Hargett, Herbert. Superintendent of Schools in Sunflower County. Indianola, Mississippi. 7/15/85.

Harper, Jack E., Jr. Chancery Clerk in Sunflower County. Indianola, Mississippi. 7/15/85.

Haynes, Euralee. Superintendent of Schools in Lowndes County. Hayneville, Alabama. 3/5/85.

Hefty, William. Richmond city attorney. Richmond, Virginia. 2/13/85. (T)

Henderson, Arnold. Chairman of the Richmond Planning Commission. Richmond, Virginia. 2/13/85. (T)

Henderson, Clayton. Mississippi state representative. Tunica, Mississippi. 7/14/85.

Herring, David S. Birmingham city councilman. Former council president. Jefferson County Democratic Party chairman. Birmingham, Alabama. 2/11/86.

Hill, Oliver. Longtime civil rights lawyer. Former Richmond city councilman. Richmond, Virginia. 2/6/85.

Holt, Curtis. Voting Rights Act plaintiff. Richmond, Virginia. 2/14/85.

Hudson, Mark. Former candidate for Tunica County Board of Supervisors. Tunica, Mississippi. 7/14/85.

Hulett, John. Lowndes County sheriff. Hayneville, Alabama. 3/5/85.

Hutton, Christopher. Hampton commonwealth's attorney. Hampton, Virginia. 9/30/85.

Jackson, Jesse L., Jr. President of the National Rainbow Coalition. Chicago, Illinois. 12/14/85.

Jackson, Nathaniel. President of the Edgefield County NAACP. Johnston, South Carolina. 5/9/85.

Johnson, Kenny. Interim director of the Southern Regional Council. Atlanta, Georgia. 11/18/85. (T)

Jones, Gerald W. Chief of the voting section in the Civil Rights Division of the U.S. Justice Department. Washington, D.C. 8/27/85.

Jones, Sabra. Director of information for Housing Opportunities Made Equal. Richmond, Virginia. 2/5/85.

Jones, Miles. Former Richmond school board chairman. Past president of the Baptist Ministers Conference in Richmond. Richmond, Virginia. 2/21/85. (T)

Jordan, David L. President of the Greenwood Voters League. Greenwood city alderman. Greenwood, Mississippi. 7/16/85.

Kahn, Bobby. Executive director of the Georgia Democratic Party. Campaign manager for Judge Robert Benham. Atlanta, Georgia. 11/20/85. (T)

Katopodis, John. Former city councilman in Birmingham. Birmingham, Alabama. Mayoral candidate in 1983. 2/6/86. (T)

Kemp, G. S. Former Richmond councilman. Richmond, Virginia. 2/12/85.

Kendall, Randolph, Jr. Executive director of the Richmond Urban League. Richmond, Virginia. 2/14/85.

Kennard, John. Tax assessor of Greene County. Eutaw, Alabama. 3/7/85; 2/13/86.

King, Johnny. President of the C & K Manufacturing Co. Tuskegee, Alabama. 3/8/85

Kirksey, Henry. Mississippi state senator. Jackson, Mississippi. 7/2/85.

Knox, Eddie. Former mayor of Charlotte. Charlotte, North Carolina. 10/22/85.

Koczman, John V. Superintendent of Schools in Macon County. Tuskegee, Alabama. 3/4/85.

LaMonte, Edward. Executive secretary to Birmingham's mayor. Birmingham, Alabama. 2/10/86.

Lee, Howard. Former mayor of Chapel Hill. Chapel Hill, North Carolina. 11/18/85 (T)

Lee, Jimmy C. Chairman of the board of Buffalo Rock Bottling Co. Birmingham, Alabama. 2/12/86.

Leidinger, William. Richmond city councilman. Former Richmond city manager. Richmond, Virginia. 1/30/85.

Lewis, John. Atlanta city councilman. Richmond, Virginia and Selma, Alabama. 1/15/85; 3/3/85.

Lomax, Michael L. Chairman of the board of commissioners in Fulton County. Atlanta, Georgia. 2/28/86.

Loudermilk, Charles. Co-chairman of Mayor Andrew Young's 1981 campaign. Atlanta, Georgia. 2/25/86.

Lowery, Joseph E. President of the Southern Christian Leadership Conference. Atlanta, Georgia. 2/28/86.

Lucas, F. Charles. Johnston Town Council member. Johnston, South Carolina. 5/7/85.

McBride, William E., Jr. County councilman in Edgefield County. North Augusta, South Carolina. 5/8/85.

McCain, John and Emma. Parents of Tom McCain. Edgefield County, South Carolina. 5/8/85.

McCain, Thomas C. Edgefield County administrator. Edgefield County, South Carolina. 5/6/85; 5/8/85.

McCarty, Deborah O. Atlanta city councilwoman. Atlanta, Georgia. 2/24/86.

McComas, James. Richmond economic development director. Richmond, Virginia. 2/8/85.

McDaniel, Claudette Black. Richmond city councilwoman. Richmond, Virginia. 2/5/85.

McDonald, Laughton. Director of the American Civil Liberties Union's southern regional office. Atlanta, Georgia. 4/22/85. (T)

McKenzie, Don. Democratic Party activist. Montross, Virginia. 9/18/85.

McLemore, Leslie B. Chairman of the Hinds County Democratic executive committee. Dean of the graduate school and chairman of the Political Science Department at Jackson State University. Jackson, Mississippi. 7/18/85.

McNair, Chris. Mississippi state representative. Birmingham, Alabama. 2/14/86.

McTeer, Victor. Voting rights lawyer. Greenville, Mississippi. 9/2/85. (T)

McWilliams, Tommy M. County attorney for Sunflower County. Indianola, Mississippi. 7/17/85.

Malone, Wallace D., Jr. Chairman of the board of SouthTrust Corp. Birmingham, Alabama. 2/12/86.

Marsh, Henry L., III. Former Richmond mayor. Richmond city councilman. Richmond, Virginia. 2/20/85; 2/21/85; 2/22/85.

Means, Elbert Lee. Lowndes County tax assessor. Hayneville, Alabama. 3/6/85.

Meggers, Linda. Director of the reapportionment services unit for the Georgia legislature. Atlanta, Georgia. 8/30/85. (T)

Merhige, Robert R. U.S. District Court judge for the eastern district of Virginia. Richmond, Virginia. 2/8/85.

Miglionico, Nina. Former Birmingham city councilwoman. Birmingham, Alabama. 2/14/86.

Miller, Dave J. Purchasing director for Atlanta. Former manager of airport planning and development. Atlanta, Georgia. 4/25/86. (T)

Mims, B. Lovick, III. Edgefield County council member. Edgefield, South Carolina. 5/6/85.

Mims, Nancy. Director of the Edgefield County courtesy center. Edgefield, South Carolina. 5/9/85.

Moore, Calvin A. Circuit clerk and former sheriff in Holmes County. Lexington, Mississippi. 7/16/85.

Myrick, Sue. City councilwoman in Charlotte. Charlotte, North Carolina. 10/22/85.

Newton, Don A. Executive vice-president of the Birmingham Chamber of Commerce. Birmingham, Alabama. 2/10/86.

Noel, Everette. Chairman of the board of trustees of the Edgefield County School District. Johnston, South Carolina. 5/7/85.

Norman, Ralph R., Jr. Mayor of Fort Deposit. Fort Deposit, Alabama. 3/5/85.

Offenburger, Tom. Press secretary to Mayor Andrew Young. Atlanta, Georgia. 5/9/86. (T)

Oslin, Dallas. Senior planner in the Richmond planning department. Richmond, Virginia. 2/18/85.

Paris, Wendell. Sumter County school board member. Eutaw, Alabama. 3/6/85.

Parker, Frank. Director of the voting rights project of the Lawyers Committee for Civil Rights Under Law. Washington, D.C. 1/24/85; 8/27/85.

Parker, J.A. President of the Alabama Exchange Bank. Tuskegee, Alabama. 3/4/85.

Parker, Raymond "Billy". Edgefield County sheriff. Edgefield, South Carolina. 5/7/85.

Patterson, Randall G. Executive assistant in the secretary of state's office. Former director of the Mississippi Democratic Party. Jackson, Mississippi. 7/19/85.

Patterson, Steve. Chairman of the Mississippi Democratic Party. Jackson, Mississippi. 11/14/85. (T)

Peterson, Dennis. Campaign manager for John Chichester. Richmond, Virginia. 9/25/85; 11/21/85.

Rainsford, Bettis C. President of the Rainsford Development Corp. and publisher of the *Citizen News*. Edgefield, South Carolina. 5/8/85; 5/9/85.

Randall, James B., III. President of the Indianola branch of the Planters Bank. Indianola, Mississippi. 7/17/85.

Randle, Carver A. Lawyer and civil rights activist in Sunflower County. Indianola, Mississippi. 7/15/85.

Robinson, Amelia Boynton. Leader in 1965 Selma marches. Selma, Alabama. 3/3/85.

Robinson, James D. Vice-mayor and alderman in Indianola, Mississippi. 7/15/85.

Sanders, Hank. Alabama state senator. Washington, D.C. 9/26/85.

Scott, Robert C. Virginia state senator. Newport News, Virginia. 9/30/85.

Scott, S. Buford. Chairman of the board of Scott & Stringfellow. Richmond, Virginia. 2/1/85.

Seaborn, Eli. Superintendent-elect of schools in Lowndes County. Hayneville, Alabama. 3/5/85.

Shell, John. Vice-president of Virginia development for Faison Associates. Richmond, Virginia. 2/22/85. (T)

Shores, Arthur D. First black member of the Birmingham City Council. Birmingham, Alabama. 2/11/86.

Shropshire, Jay. Clerk of the Virginia Senate. Richmond, Virginia. 11/13/85.

Slabach, Fred. Executive director of the Mississippi Democratic Party. Jackson, Mississippi. 7/19/85.

Slaughter-Harvey, Constance. Assistant secretary of state for Public Lands and Elections. Jackson, Mississippi. 7/19/85.

Smitherman, Joe. Mayor of Selma. Selma, Alabama. 3/3/85.

Snyder, V. Reitzel. President of Synco Inc. Charlotte, North Carolina. 10/21/85.

Spear, Mary Alice. Hampton Democratic chairman. Hampton, Virginia. 9/30/85.

Spurlock, Willie, Jr. Attorney handling voting rights litigation. Greenville, Mississippi. 7/15/85.

Squier, Robert. Democratic campaign consultant. Washington, D.C. 11/22/85. (T)

Stoddart, George. Press secretary to Gov. Charles Robb. Richmond, Virginia. 11/21/85

Strong, Rodney. Acting director of the Office of Contract Compliance for the city of Atlanta. Atlanta, Georgia. 2/26/85.

Sweat, Dan E., Jr. President of Central Atlanta Progress Inc. Atlanta, Georgia. 2/26/86.

Thomas, James L. Alabama state representative. Selma, Alabama. 3/3/85.

Thomas, Mable. Georgia state representative. Washington, D.C. 9/26/85.

Thompson, Bennie G. Hinds County supervisor. Democratic national committeeman for Mississippi. Bolton, Mississippi. 7/18/85.

Thompson, Geraldine. Executive director of the Voter Education Project. Atlanta, Georgia. 2/26/85.

Trosch, Minette. Mayor pro-tempore of the Charlotte City Council. Charlotte, North Carolina. 10/22/85.

Turner, Albert. Longtime civil rights activist in the Alabama Black Belt. Washington, D.C. 9/26/85.

Valentine, Henry L. Former Richmond vice-mayor. Richmond, Virginia. 2/6/85.

Vivian, C. T. Director of the Anti-Klan Network. Selma, Alabama. 3/3/85.

Wake, Carolyn C. Richmond city councilwoman. Richmond, Virginia. 2/7/85.

Walls, Johnnie E., Jr. Attorney in civil rights cases. Chairman of the Washington County Democratic executive committee. Greenville, Mississippi. 7/14/85.

Watkins, Hays T. Chairman of the board and chief executive officer of the CSX Corporation. Richmond, Virginia. 3/25/85.

Watt, Mel. North Carolina state senator. Charlotte, North Carolina. 10/21/85.

West, Roy C. Mayor of Richmond. Richmond, Virginia. 2/16/85.

White, Lewis. Administrative assistant to the mayor of Birmingham. Birmingham, Alabama. 2/6/86.

White, Roger A. Contract compliance officer for Birmingham. Birmingham, Alabama. 2/11/86.

Wilder, L. Douglas. Virginia state senator. Elected lieutenant governor in November 1985. Richmond, Virginia. 1/29/85; 5/14/85; 7/3/85; 1/7/86.

Williams, Hosea. Atlanta city councilman. Former Georgia state legislator. Atlanta, Georgia. 2/27/86.

Williams, Linda. Senior research associate at the Joint Center for Political Studies. Washington, D.C. 11/20/85. (T)

Williams, Sara. County council member in Edgefield County. Johnston, South Carolina. 5/6/85.

Willie, Louis J. Executive vice-president of the Booker T. Washington Insurance Co. Vice-president of Citizens Federal Savings Bank. Birmingham, Alabama. 2/12/86.

Willis, Kent. Executive director of Housing Opportunities Made Equal. Richmond, Virginia. 2/5/85.

Wilson, Bernice. Associate county agent for the Alabama Cooperative Extension Service. Tuskegee, Alabama. 3/4/85.

Wilson, Jerry. Director of the voting project of the Southern Regional Council. Atlanta, Georgia. 6/6/86. (T)

Wilson, Taylor. Commissioner of Revenue. Hampton, Virginia. 9/30/85.

Woodruff, O.P. Probate judge and former commissioner in Lowndes County. Hayneville, Alabama. 3/5/85.

Woolfolk, Odessa. Director of the Center for Urban Affairs, University of Alabama at Birmingham. Birmingham, Alabama. 2/12/86.

Worrell, Bill. Editor of the "Richmond Afro-American." Richmond, Virginia. 1/31/85.

Books

Allen, Ivan, Jr., and Hemphill, Paul. *Mayor: Notes on the Sixties.* New York: Simon and Schuster, 1971.

Banfield, Edward C. *Big City Politics.* New York: Random House, 1965.

Barone, Michael, and Ujifusa, Grant. *The Almanac of American Politics, 1984.* Washington: National Journal, 1983.

Bartley, Neuman V. *The Creation of Modern Georgia.* Athens: The University of Georgia Press, 1983.

Bass, Jack, and DeVries, Walter. *The Transformation of Southern Politics.* New York: Basic Books, 1976.

Buni, Andrew. *The Negro in Virginia Politics, 1902–1965.* Charlottesville: The University of Virginia Press, 1967.

Carson, Clayborne. *In Struggle: SNCC and the Black Awakening of the 1960s.* Cambridge: Harvard University Press, 1981.

Chesson, Michael B. *Richmond After the War 1865–1890.* Richmond: Virginia State Library, 1981.

Cole, Leonard A. *Blacks in Power: A Comparative Study of Black and White Elected Officials.* Princeton: Princeton University Press, 1976.

Dabncy, Virginius. *Richmond: The Story of a City.* New York: Doubleday & Co., 1976.

Davidson, Chandler. *Biracial Politics: Conflict and Coalition in the Metropolitan South.* Baton Rouge: Louisiana State University Press, 1972.

Davidson, Chandler, ed. *Minority Vote Dilution.* Washington D.C.: Howard University Press, 1984.

Evers, Charles. *Evers.* New York: World Publishing Co., 1971.

Fager, Charles E. *Selma 1965.* Boston: Beacon Press, 1974.

Frady, Marshall. *Southerners: A Journalist's Odyssey.* New York: New American Library, 1980.

Garrow, David J. *Protest at Selma: Martin Luther King Jr. and the Voting Rights Act of 1965.* New Haven: Yale University Press, 1978.

Hamilton, Virginia Van der Veer. *Alabama: A History.* New York: W.W. Norton, 1977.

Havard, William, ed. *The Changing Politics of the South.* Baton Rouge: Louisiana State University Press, 1972.

Joint Center for Political Studies. *Black Elected Officials, A National Roster, 1984.* New York: UNIPUB, 1984.

Karnig, Albert K., and Welch, Susan. *Black Representation and Urban Policy.* Chicago: The University of Chicago Press, 1980.

Key, V. O., Jr. *Southern Politics.* New York: Random House, 1949.

King, Martin Luther, Jr. *Where Do We Go From Here? Chaos or Community.* Boston: Beacon Press, 1967.

Kluger, Richard. *Simple Justice.* New York: Vintage Books, 1975.

Lander, Ernest M., Jr., and Calhoun, Richard J., eds. *Two Decades of Change: The South Since the Supreme Court Desegregation Decision.* Columbia: University of South Carolina Press, 1975.

Lawson, Steven F. *Black Ballots, Voting Rights in the South, 1944–1969.* New York: Columbia University Press, 1976.

Lawson, Steven F. *In Pursuit of Power: Southern Blacks and Electoral Politics, 1965–1982.* New York: Columbia University Press, 1985.

Loewen, James W., and Sallis, Charles, eds. *Mississippi: Conflict and Change.* New York: Pantheon Books, 1974.

Lord, Walter. *The Past That Would Not Die.* New York: Harper & Row, 1965.

Matthews, Donald R., and Prothro, James W. *Negroes and the New Southern Politics.* New York: Harcourt, Brace & World, 1966.

Moeser, John V., and Dennis, Rutledge M. *The Politics of Annexation: Oligarchic Power in a Southern City.* Cambridge: Schenkman Publishing Co., 1982.

Moody, Anne. *Coming of Age in Mississippi.* New York: Dial Press, 1968.

Morris, Milton D. *The Politics of Black America.* New York: Harper & Row, 1975.

Myrdal, Gunnar. *An American Dilemma: The Negro Problem and Modern Democracy.* New York: Harper and Bros., 1944.

Namorato, Michael V., ed. *Have We Overcome? Race Relations Since Brown.* Jackson: University of Mississippi Press, 1979.

Oates, Stephen B. *Let the Trumpet Sound: The Life of Martin Luther King Jr.* New York: Harper & Row, 1982.

Peirce, Neal R., *The Deep South States of America.* New York: W.W. Norton, 1974.

Pinkney, Alphonso. *The Myth of Black Progress.* Cambridge: Cambridge University Press, 1984.

Preston, Michael B.; Henderson, Lenneal J., Jr.; and Puryear, Paul, eds. *The New Black Politics.* New York: Longman Inc., 1982.

Rabinowitz, Howard N., ed. *Southern Black Leaders of the Reconstruction Period.* Urbana: University of Illinois Press, 1982.

Raines, Howell. *My Soul Is Rested: Movement Days in the Deep South Remembered.* New York: Putnam's Sons, 1977.

Rozier, John. *Black Boss: Political Revolution in a Georgia County.* Athens: The University of Georgia Press, 1982.

Sibley, Celestine. *Peachtree Street, USA.* New York: Doubleday & Co., 1963.

Silver, James W. *Mississippi: The Closed Society.* New York: Harcourt, Brace & World, 1963.

Sowell, Thomas. *Civil Rights: Rhetoric or Reality?* New York: Morrow and Co., 1984.

Stone, Chuck. *Black Political Power in America.* Indianapolis: Bobbs-Merrill Co., 1968.

Tindall, George Brown. *The Disruption of the Solid South.* Athens: University of Georgia Press, 1972.

Watters, Pat, and Cleghorn, Reese. *Climbing Jacob's Ladder: The Arrival of Negroes in Southern Politics.* New York: Harcourt, Brace & World, 1967.

Webb, Sheyann, and Nelson, Rachel West. *Selma, Lord, Selma.*
University: University of Alabama Press, 1980.

White, Marjorie L. *The Birmingham District: An Industrial History
and Guide.* Birmingham: Birmingham Historical Society, 1981.

Articles, Documents, and Miscellaneous Materials

"Alabama: A Black Day in Eutaw." *Newsweek,* August 11, 1969,
24–25.

Alabama Department of Examiners of Public Accounts. Audits.
Office of Judge of Probate, Bullock County, October
1983–September 1984. Office of Judge of Probate, Lowndes County,
October 1981–September 1984. Office of the Judge of Probate,
Greene County, October 1981–September 1983.

Alabama Department of Industrial Relations. "Alabama—
Occupational Profiles of State, SDA's, MSA's, GUTA Regions and
Counties." November 1985.

"Annual Report on Black Business." *Black Enterprise,* June 1985.

Arrington, Richard. Southern Oral History Project, University of
North Carolina. July 18, 1974, interview.

Atlanta Community Relations Commission. "Blacks and Women on
Corporation Boards in Atlanta." January 1979.

Barrows, Frank. "School Busing: Charlotte, N.C." *The Atlantic
Monthly,* November 1972, 17ff.

Bass, Jack. "Atlanta's Mayoral Mishmash." *The New Republic,*
September 23, 1981, 18–21.

Birmingham City Personnel Department. "Affirmative Action Report
on Fulltime Employment by Race and Sex." Period ending
December 31, 1985.

Birmingham City. "1985 Minority Business Enterprise Report."
January 28, 1986.

Black, Merle. "Racial Composition of Congressional Districts and
Support for Federal Voting Rights in the American South." *Social
Science Quarterly,* December 1978, 435–50.

Bode, Ken. "Crying Wurf." *The New Republic,* July 2, 1977, 14–17.

Bullock, Charles S., III. "Congressional Voting and the Mobilization
of a Black Electorate in the South." *Journal of Politics,* August
1981, 662–82.

_____. "The Election of Blacks in the South: Preconditions and Consequences." *American Journal of Political Science,* November 1975, 727–39.

Bullock, Charles S., III, and MacManus, Susan A. "Policy Responsiveness to the Black Electorate: Programmatic Versus Symbolic Representation." *American Politics Quarterly,* July 1981, 357–68.

Campbell, Bruce. "Patterns of Change in the Partisan Loyalties of Native Southerners." *Journal of Politics,* August 1977, 730–61.

Campbell, David. "The Lowndes County Freedom Organization: An Appraisal." *New South,* Winter 1972, 37–42.

Cavanagh, Thomas E., ed. "The JCPS Congressional District Fact Book." Washington: Joint Center for Political Studies, 1984.

_____. "Election '84: The Impact of the Black Electorate." Washington: Joint Center for Political Studies, 1984.

_____, ed. "Race and Political Strategy: A JCPS Roundtable." Washington: Joint Center for Political Studies, 1983.

Cavanagh, Thomas E., and Foster, Lorn S. "Jesse Jackson's Campaign: The Primaries and the Caucuses." Washington: Joint Center for Political Studies, 1983.

Cavanagh, Thomas E., and Stockton, Denise. "Black Elected Officials and Their Constituencies." Washington: Joint Center for Political Studies, 1983.

Clark, Robert. Southern Oral History Project, University of North Carolina. March 28, 1974, interview.

Clay, James W., ed. "Atlas of Charlotte-Mecklenburg." UNCC Monograph Series in Geography, No. 3. Charlotte: University of North Carolina at Charlotte, 1981.

Cohen, Jeffrey E.; Cotter, Patrick R.; and Coulter, Philip B. "The Changing Structure of Southern Political Participation: Matthews and Prothro 20 Years Later." *Social Science Quarterly,* September 1983, 536–49.

Community Relations Commission. City of Atlanta. Annual Reports for 1968–73.

_____. "City of Atlanta, Minority Hiring and Promotion, Update '72." August 16, 1972.

————. "Minority Hiring and Promotion Practices, City of Atlanta."
July 31, 1970.

————. "Report on the Grievences of Black Firemen to the Board of
Fire Masters, City of Atlanta." December 29, 1969.

Corry, John. "A Visit to Lowndes County, Alabama." *New South,*
Winter 1972, 28–36.

Cox, Jane Reed, and Turner, Abigail. "The Voting Rights Act in
Alabama: A Current Legal Assessment." Legal Services
Corporation of Alabama, June 1981.

Dickinson, A. J. "Myth and Manipulation: The Story of the Crusade
for Voters in Richmond Virginia." Unpublished doctoral
dissertation, Yale University, 1967.

Dowe, Kelly. "Birmingham's Mayor Richard Arrington." *Down
Home,* August 1983, 8–15.

Felder, Henry H. "The Changing Patterns of Black Family Income,
1960–82." Washington: Joint Center for Political Studies, 1984.

Ford, Johnny. Southern Oral History Project, University of North
Carolina. July 11, 1974, interview.

Gaillard, Frye, and Paddock, Polly. "Charlotte's Busing
Breakthrough." *The Progressive,* October 1975, 36–37.

Goolrick, Chester; Lieberman, Paul; and Willis, Ken. "Voting: A
Right Still Denied." *Atlanta Constitution,* December 7–11, 1980.

Graves, Earl. "Why Black Mayors Are More Than Symbolic
Figures." *Black Enterprise,* January 1982, 7.

Hamer, Andrew M., ed. "Urban Atlanta: Redefining the Role of the
City." Research Monograph No. 84. Atlanta: Georgia State
University, 1980.

Harris, Art. "Too Busy to Hate." *Esquire,* June 1985, 129ff.

Hearings before the Subcommittee on the Constitution of the
Committee on the Judiciary, United States Senate, 97th Congress,
2nd Session, on Bills to amend the Voting Rights Act of 1965.
January 27–March 1, 1982.

Hearings before the Subcommittee on Civil and Constitutional Rights
of the Committee on the Judiciary, House of Representatives, 97th
Congress, 1st Session, on the Extension of the Voting Rights Act.
May 6–July 13, 1981.

Ifill, Gwen, and Maraniss, David. "In Atlanta, Struggling with Success." *Washington Post,* January 20, 1986.

Jackson, Maynard. "The State of the City: 1974. A Message by Mayor Maynard Jackson to the City Council and the People of Atlanta, Georgia." January 6, 1975.

———. "The State of the City." January 3, 1977.

Jaret, Charles. "Is Atlanta a 'Black Mecca?': Black Migration and Living Conditions in the Urban South." A paper presented at the 1985 annual meeting of the Southern Sociological Society in Charlotte, North Carolina. April 10–13, 1985.

Jenkins, Ray. "Majority Rule in the Black Belt: Greene County, Alabama." *New South,* Fall 1969, 60–67.

Journal of the Richmond City Council. March 1977–October 1979; July 1982–January 1983.

"Judge Branch of Greene County." *Ebony,* August 1971, 82–85.

Klein, Joe. "The Emancipation of Bolton, Mississippi." *Esquire,* December 1985, 258–62.

Kopkind, Andrew. "Lowndes County, Alabama: The Great Fear Is Gone." *Ramparts,* April 1975, 8ff.

Lee, Howard. Southern Oral History Project, University of North Carolina. December 13, 1973, interview.

Lewis, John. Southern Oral History Project, University of North Carolina. November 20, 1973, interview.

Lieberman, Paul, and Goolrick, Chester. "Blacks Pin Seven Years of Hopes on Voting Law." *The Atlanta Constitution,* January 24, 1981.

MacPherson, Myra. "Douglas Wilder: Winning the Waiting Game." *Washington Post,* February 2, 1986.

Marable, Manning. "Tuskegee and the Politics of Illusion in the New South." *Black Scholar,* May 1977, 13–24.

McDonald, Laughlin. "Voting Rights in the South: Ten Years of Litigation Challenging Continuing Discrimination Against Minorities." New York: American Civil Liberties Union, 1982.

McManus Associates Inc. "Economic Growth Strategy for the Birmingham MSA." Management and research consultant's report, prepared for the Birmingham Chamber of Commerce, April 24, 1985.

McMillan, George. "Integration with Dignity: The Inside Story of How South Carolina Kept the Peace." *Saturday Evening Post,* March 16, 1963, 15–21.

Mississippi Research and Development Center. "Handbook of Selected Data for Mississippi." Jackson: Mississippi Research and Development Center, 1983.

Morial, Ernest. Southern Oral History Project, University of North Carolina. January 9, 1974, interview.

Mundt, Robert J., and Heilig, Peggy. "District Representation: Demands and Effects in the Urban South." *Journal of Politics,* November 1982, 1035–48.

O'Hare, William P. "Blacks on the Move: A Decade of Demographic Change." Washington: Joint Center for Political Studies, 1982.

Palen, J. John, and Morrison, Richard D. "Representation of Blacks and Women in Positions with Policy Making Potential in the Greater Richmond Area, 1970–80." Richmond: Virginia Commonwealth University, Spring 1982.

Parker, Frank. "The Mississippi Congressional Redistricting Case: A Study in Minority Vote Dilution." A paper prepared for the Symposium on Voting Rights sponsored by the Howard University Law Journal, January 19, 1985.

Parker, Frank R., and Phillips, Barbara Y. "Voting in Mississippi: A Right Still Denied." Washington: Lawyers' Committee for Civil Rights Under Law, 1981.

Porter, David D., and Porter, Rosalyn Gist. "The Changing Profile of Charlotte." *Black Enterprise,* June 1983, 178ff.

Preston, Michael B. "Black Elected Officials and Public Policy: Symbolic or Substantive Representation?" *Policy Studies Journal,* Winter 1978, 196–201.

Range, Peter Ross. "Making It in Atlanta: Capital of Black Is Bountiful." *New York Times Magazine,* April 7, 1974, 28ff.

City of Richmond. Annual Reports. 1968–84.

Sabato, Larry. "The 1985 Statewide Election in Virginia: History Quietly Writ Large." Draft chapter to be published in 1987 edition of *Virginia Votes.* December 19, 1985.

Schmidt, William E., and Shipp, E. R. "Race Relations: The Changing South." (A six-part series) *The New York Times,* February 27, 1985–May 6, 1985.

Shores, Arthur. Southern Oral History Project, University of North Carolina. July 17, 1974, interview.

Simpson, William. "The Birth of the Mississippi 'Loyalists Democrats' (1965–1968)." *Journal of Mississippi History,* February 1982, 27ff.

Southern Studies Institute. "Stayed On Freedom." *Southern Exposure,* Spring 1981.

Taeuber, Karl. "Racial Residential Segregation, 28 Cities, 1970–1980." A working paper of the Center for Demography and Ecology. University of Wisconsin-Madison, March 1983.

———. "Research Issues Concerning Trends in Residential Segregation." A working paper of the Center for Demography and Ecology. University of Wisconsin-Madison, November 1982.

Thompson, Kenneth H. "The Voting Rights Act and Black Electoral Participation." Washington: Joint Center for Political Studies, 1982.

Toner, Robin. "Arrington: An Outsider on the Inside." *Atlanta Constitution,* January 14, 1985.

U.S. Bureau of the Census. "Census of the Population, 1980. Alabama. General Social and Economic Characteristics." U.S. Department of Commerce, PC-80-1-C2.

———. Georgia. PC80-1-C12.

———. Louisiana. PC80-1-C20.

———. Mississippi. PC80-1-C26.

———. North Carolina. PC80-1-C35.

———. South Carolina. PC80-1-C42.

———. Virginia. PC80-1-C48.

U.S. Commission on Civil Rights. "A Citizen's Guide to Understanding the Voting Rights Act." Washington: Clearinghouse Publication, 1984.

———. "Fifteen Years Ago . . . Rural Alabama Revisited." Washington: Clearinghouse Publication, 1983.

———. "The Voting Rights Act: Unfilled Goals." Washington, 1981.

Viorst, Milton. "Black Mayor, White Power Structure." *New Republic,* June 7, 1975, 9–11.

Welch, Susan and Karnig, Albert K. "The Impact of Black Elected Officials on Urban Social Expenditures," *Policy Studies Journal,* Summer 1979, 707–14.

Wells, T. E. "They Began in Reform and Quickly Rolled into Controversy." *The Atlanta Constitution,* December 7, 8, and 9, 1981.

Wilder, Douglas. Southern Oral History Project, University of North Carolina. March 15, 1974, interview.

Williams, Linda. "New Black Politicians, Skillful and Pragmatic, Transcend Civil Rights." *Wall Street Journal,* January 9, 1986.

Wright, Gerald C. "Community Structure and Voting in the South." *Public Opinion Quarterly,* Summer 1976, 201–15.

Young, Andrew. "The State of the City, 1985." January 21, 1985.

_____. Southern Oral History Project, University of North Carolina. January 31, 1974, interview.

INDEX